KT-143-366

RAT PACK
Confidential

Shawn Levy is the author of *King of Comedy: The Life and Art of Jerry Lewis*. His writing has appeared in the *New York Times*, the *Los Angeles Times*, *Village Voice*, *Loaded*, *Movieline*, *Film Comment* and *Pulse!* He is a former senior editor of *American Film*.

Shawn Levy

RAT PACK

Confidential

Frank, Dean, Sammy, Peter, Joey & the Last Great Showbiz Party

FOURTH ESTATE • *London*

This paperback edition published in 1999
First published in Great Britain in 1998 by
Fourth Estate Limited
6 Salem Road
London W2 4BU

Copyright © Shawn Levy 1998

1 3 5 7 9 10 8 6 4 2

The right of Shawn Levy to be identified as the author
of this work has been asserted by him in accordance
with the Copyright, Designs and Patents Act 1988.

A catalogue record for this book is
available from the British Library.

ISBN 1-84115-001-0

All rights reserved. No part of this publication
may be reproduced, transmitted, or stored in a retrieval
system, in any form or by any means, without
permission in writing from Fourth Estate Limited.

Text design by Maria Carella
Plate section design by Bonni Leon-Berman

Typeset by Avon Dataset Ltd, Bidford on Avon B50 4JH
Printed in Great Britain by Clays Ltd, St Ives plc

For my mom, Mickie Levy,
who arranged for me to see Frank at the
500 Club when I was still in utero . . .

Sands

A PLACE IN THE SUN

FRANK SINATRA
DEAN MARTIN
SAMMY DAVIS JR.
PETER LAWFORD
JOEY BISHOP

part 1

This was Frank's baby.

Onstage, Dean, singing almost straight, then pissing away anything like real feeling with jokes.

In the wings, Sammy, Peter, Joey.

Out front, a mob scene: Marilyn, Little Caesar, Kirk, Shirl, Mr. Benny, that Swedish kid that Sammy was so crazy for, that senator and his tubby kid brother, a few broads without addresses, a few guys without real names . . .

Famous faces at ringside for the cameras, infamous ones in the shadows in the back, plus a hundred or so civilians as bait for the rest of the world—suckers with money to blow and dames to blow it with them until it ran out.

In the casino, every schmuck that couldn't pay or beg or muscle his way in was betting his rent money just to feel as big as the ones who could.

The joint was packed; the rest of town might as well have been dark.

And for what?

A movie, a party, a floating crap game, a day's work, a hustle, a joke: They'd make millions and all they had to do was show up, have a good time, pretend to give a damn, and, almost as an afterthought, sing.

Sometimes it seemed like Dean had the right idea: "You wanna hear the whole song, buy the record . . ."

But there *was* something in the music, wasn't there? With the right band and the right number, it was like flying—and like you could drag everybody up there with you.

So let Dean do jokes, and Sammy—Sammy would start numbers and they'd stomp all over them and he'd like it.

But when Frank sang, it would be straight. It could be New Year's Eve, the very stroke of midnight, the middle of Times Square, and he would stop time, stop their hearts beating, and remind them where the power was.

It was in his voice.

It was his.

When they finally had enough and dropped the curtain, they would wander out into the casino.

Some act'd be up there on the little stage in the lounge, and maybe they'd go over and screw around; Sammy liked that the best—more eyes on him, always more eyes.

What Dean and Frank liked was dealing. They had points in the joint, and who was gonna stop them from horsing around at a table: It was their money, right?

Dean actually knew what he was doing. He'd push aside a blackjack dealer and do a little fancy shuffling and start dealing around the layout: his rules.

"You got five? You hold. That's a winner.

"Nineteen? Hit. Twenty-six? Another winner."

He'd shovel out chips and make sure that everyone took care of the real dealer, who'd stand there looking nervous over at big Carl Cohen, the casino manager, who normally didn't go for clowning.

But Carl would be quiet. He'd lose a couple hundred during this monkey show, sure, but he'd get it all back and more:

There were crowds five or ten deep just waiting to get at the tables. Besides, Dean was like family; he'd worked sneak joints back in Ohio before the war with Carl's kid brother. The big guy could afford to be a little bit indulgent.

Which wasn't the case with Lewis Milestone, the poor director saddled with making a movie in the middle of it. Every morning he came to work in an amusement park that his boss owned and woke his boss up and tried to get him to jump through hoops for a few hours, and you had to look deep into his dark old eyes to see what he really thought about it.

This movie wasn't some work of art, this wasn't *All Quiet on the Western Front* with poetic butterflies and mud and a moral. This was a sure thing, a money machine, a way to bring the party to the people who could only read about it in the papers. Hell, the only reason they hired him in the first place was that Jack Warner insisted on a pro and Peter guaranteed that the old guy—who was making Lassie shows, for chrissakes—would do whatever they told him.

But, still, they didn't want to make a career out of it. So come the morning, they let Millie run them around in circles for a little bit, even if they hadn't gone to sleep yet on account of last night was, as they liked to say, a gasser.

Or at least everyone but Frank let him do it. Frank was the boss, after all, and picture or no picture, he was going to work when he felt like it. He used to say that he only had one take in him, like he was an artist about it. The truth was he only had one take he gave a shit about, and if they wanted that one in the movie, then they'd have to wait until he was ready to give it.

So Sammy, a Salty Dog or two down the hatch, would show up on the set at 9:00 or 10:00 in the morning, and Dean and Peter would show up at 9:00 or 10:00 in the morning, and

Joey—who was lucky to be here at all, let's face it—would be there at 7:00 or whenever they said so, showered and alert.

But Frank: 4:30 in the afternoon, maybe 5:00; and twice, *twice,* before lunch; and most days not at all.

They worked on the picture twenty-five days in Vegas; Frank showed up nine.

Oh, it was his show, all right.

In the early evenings, between a few hours of the movie and going back out onstage, the steam room. Frank had it built— the first one on the Strip—and when he was in town it was off limits to anyone else. They'd drink in there and make phone calls and give each other the needle: the only time they could all be together and alone.

Some other people were allowed in: the ultimate VIP room. This Rickles would take these incredible liberties with Frank and Frank would kill himself. Sammy would take one humiliation after another— "You can't wear a white towel. Here's a brown towel for you!"—and act like he was killing himself. Actors from the movie. Business guys. Other guys who didn't say who they were. This was an *inner* inner circle. Men capable of all sorts of acts of power would sit like convent girls just for the pleasure of having been allowed inside. Compared to this, the show and the movie were, well, for *anyone.*

But not just anyone was welcome. This was a group that Frank handpicked, gliding through the world, sizing people up, then giving them the golden tap on the shoulder and bringing them in.

Talent, money, power: None of these was quite enough. You had to have something Frank had, or something that he wanted to have more of. You were a cool, leonine Italian, or a dazzling black ball of fire, or a British sophisticate with powerful relatives, or a Jewish wiseguy who could brush off the world with a shrug. You were an Irish millionaire senator or a psychotic Mafia lord. You were the acme, the original, one of a kind, and Frank wanted you up close to study. He gathered everyone around him and sat in the middle and saw little parts of himself, little things he could fix or steal—Dr. Frankenstein building a hip new kind of superman.

Frankenstein, though, or Nosferatu? Because, though everyone got rich, got famous, got laid, Frank got *more*. They made movies; Frank was the producer. They cut records; Frank owned the company. They played Vegas and Tahoe; it was Frank's hotel. Everyone did good work; Frank was Michelangelo.

They called him the Leader; they asked him to be their best man; they named their kids after him, their *daughters*, even. And when it all spun out of control, when the precious, delicate balance came undone, when the merry-go-round stopped with a jerk, everyone got thrown on their ass—or worse—except Frank, who stood there in the middle, unfazed.

Divorce, drugs, bankruptcy, death, irrelevancy: Every single one of them took a major hit.

Frank didn't get so much as a scratch.

But that would all be later. That would be after the golden time, when, for a while, no matter what they did, it would sell. No matter how many broads, no matter how much booze, no matter who they got mad at or cozied up to, it had reached a point where Frank could simply do no wrong.

The press knew the story. They didn't *write* it, but they *knew* it. They didn't rat him out because they needed him more than he needed them, and except for a few he'd chosen as whipping boys, they lined up to do whatever he wanted them to do.

He was drinking with this one or that one or fucking this one or that one—who was gonna talk?

And anyone he wanted around him, the same thing: You hiding from the G? You don't need to hide around Frank. You got a wife back home who reads the gossip page? Frank'll see that you're not in it. You running for president? Frank'll throw a little juice your way and make sure everything looks on the up-and-up.

Up close, the whole thing was not to be believed. You wanna talk about rebellion? Those rock 'n' roll punks had no idea what a *real* rebel did in private. They couldn't begin to understand the power and the appetites and how little you had to care. *La Dolce Vita* nothing: This bunch made Nero look like a Cub Scout.

But outside, from far away, it didn't look like ego or license or indulgence. It looked like a big, beautiful party in the desert, with laughs and music and cars and clothes and incredible women, and no one ever ran out of money, and no one ever got tired, and no one had to answer to anyone, and no one ever grew old, and you would just die unless you could be there—even if the closest you ever got was a movie theater or a record player.

Wherever they went, they drew a crowd. And not just yokels, but Friars and sex symbols and made men and the president himself. They made Vegas Vegas, Miami Miami, and Palm Springs Palm Springs. And they made and broke people like they were pieces of toast.

For a while, everything took a backseat. For a while, the whole world was like a gyroscope, spinning so fast that it looked like it was standing still, with Frank and his cronies smack-dab in the middle of it, smiling at you, making you think you could do anything.

The world wasn't big enough for them to bother with so they made it bigger and took it over.

And instead of resenting it, people loved it.

And there was never anything like it before or since.

Between 1957, when his hero Humphrey Bogart died, and 1963, when his friend Jack Kennedy died, Frank Sinatra was the biggest star in all of showbiz.

There was Elvis, of course, and John Wayne and Danny Thomas and Ray Charles and Marlon Brando and Bob Hope and Pat Boone and Tony Curtis and Frankie Avalon and Jerry Lewis and a whole lot of other people who were Kings of Pop, or certain quadrants of it, at the time.

But nobody was so sheerly supreme as Frank as an icon, artist, or draw, none held his mighty sway over the mass imagination, and none was so ascendant for so long.

With his stunning LPs for Capitol Records—*Songs for Swingin' Lovers, In the Wee Small Hours, Come Fly with Me, Only the Lonely,* a good dozen more—he was releasing classics at the rate of several a year and moving big numbers in the record stores.

With a string of commercial hit movies—and good ones, frequently, like *The Man with the Golden Arm, The Joker is Wild, High Society,* and the Oscar-winning *From Here to Eternity*—he ranked among the era's top-grossing movie stars.

He had regular specials on television (though rarely very good, they always drew well); he was the top act in nightclubs from Miami to Chicago to Las Vegas; he performed with ceremonious duty at charity events, Academy Award telecasts —all the orthodox showbiz sacraments.

Arguably no single entertainer had ever held the top spot in so many media for so long—Bing Crosby, *maybe,* back in radio days.

No, Frank was *It*.

And It in ways that nobody ever had been.

Because as big a deal to the popular American mind as Frank's considerable musical and cinematic lives was his private life.

Flitting from gorgeous bedmate to gorgeous bedmate, rubbing elbows with tough guys, throwing punches, pounding back whiskey, romancing in a cigarette's glow, he was the envy of every American male who had left off worshiping Mickey Mantle and Ted Williams for more grown-up pursuits: the rakish kid brother-in-law they'd all secretly give their left arms to trade places with.

There was nothing, it seemed to the average working stiff, that Frank didn't have.

But Frankie—and who could have guessed it?—didn't like to be by himself: He got antsy. He liked to have entourages of like-minded he-men around him, guys to drink and schmooze and play cards and go to the fights and hit the bars with: chums.

He wanted an accumulation of bosom fellows around him, and he thought it would be wonderful if they could work together. He began to play with his buddies in nightclubs, to make films with them, to pop in on their TV shows and invite them onto his.

He started smallish—a picture with one or two here, a spontaneous walk-on there—but then his horizons expanded. Various threads in his personal and professional lives began to merge in ways that no one would ever have predicted: his affectations toward politics and the Mafia, for instance, his ownership of film and record companies and shares in casinos, his friends and debtors and vassals.

At the end of 1959, he concocted an intoxicating brew of money, power, talent, romance, gall, a nexus of showbiz and muscle, politics and glamour, a brilliant netherworld spinning at 33⅓ with himself stock-still at the center, conducting it all with his mind.

They alit in Las Vegas for a month to make a movie and play a historic nightclub gig that they called the Summit; they hit Miami, the Utah desert, Palm Springs, Chicago, Atlantic City, Beverly Hills, Hollywood back lots, illegal gambling dens, saloons, yachts, private jets, the White House itself.

It was what a good portion of America was about for a few remarkable years.

It was sauce and vinegar and eau de cologne and sour mash whiskey and gin and smoke and perfume and silk and neon and skinny lapels and tail fins and rockets to the sky.

It was swinging and sighing and being a sharpie, it was cutting a figure and digging a scene.

It was Frank and Sammy Davis Jr. and Dean Martin and Peter Lawford for a while and Joey Bishop when they asked him and Jack Kennedy and Sam Giancana and tables full of cronies and who knew how many broads.

It was the ultimate spasm of traditional showbiz—both the *last* and the *most* of its kind.

It was the high point of their lives and a midlife crisis.

It was the acme of the American Century and a venal, rancid, ugly sham.

It was the Rat Pack.

It was beautiful.

part 2

Slacksey o'brien

Grow up with immigrant parents and a last name that no one can pronounce right, with an ear mangled by a midwife's forceps and no meat on your slight bones, with no brothers or sisters, and a mother always on the go, and a queer little dream that you can win the whole world over with a song; grow up with all this, and then win wealth and fame and acclaim and power—the whole world and more—and you'll likely find no embarrassment in living as if your every action was the stuff of legend.

Throughout his life, Frank would be boosted in his perception that his progress through the world was of great import, and if he ever lapsed into doubt, there would always be someone around to reassure him: a wife, a dame, a publicist, a thumbbreaker, a daughter, a fan, even, though not quite so reliably, the press. Frank could count on being spiffed-up, spoiled, spirited out of jams; he expected it of life. And it was an expectation born not in the flush of his success but in the earliest days of his youth: Of all the hangers-on, sycophants, yes-men, and boosters, his mother was first and foremost.

There was undeniable steel in Natalie Garavante, the little pug-faced Genoese firebrand known to everyone in Guinea Town, Hoboken, as Dolly. She prodded the men around her to let her through doors that she herself would've battered down in a world that cut women an even break. She had a stunningly foul mouth: "Her favorite expression was 'son of a bitch bastard,' " recalled a mayor of Hoboken who knew her in his youth; a mob lawyer who met her in the 1960s compared her way with profanity favorably to Jimmy Hoffa's. She made the slow-moving Italian men around her jump at her command, and she carried enough clout to get political bosses and city officials to do the same. She was a shit-stirrer and a hollerer; she worked hard and she took no prisoners; she spoke simpatico with the people in the streets and defied the men of power. If she'd've been born a boy, she might've been an Italo-American Huey Long.

But she was a woman and it was the 1910s—and an Italian neighborhood at that—and so she had to find a husband, and she settled on a handsome, illiterate kid from the neighborhood, a guy who couldn't hold a steady job but cut a dashing figure in the boxing ring. Dolly's brothers were boxers, which was probably how she came to meet Marty O'Brien, a stout, quiet little guy with tattoos on his arms. Maybe she first took him for Irish, which would've appealed to her social-climbing instincts; soon enough, she learned he wasn't an O'Brien but a Sinatra, but that didn't make him any less attractive. He might've been an unfinished project, but Dolly was sure she could make something of him. Despite her parents' fears of a layabout Sicilian for a son-in-law, they eloped and married in a civil ceremony. A year and a half later, she bore their first and only child.

Later on, he would try to depict himself as some kind of Dead End Kid turned good, but the truth was that Frank was always plushly seen to. In a neighborhood where the men worked menial jobs and the women raised broods of five, eight, ten brats, only-child Frank had two working parents and a surfeit of candy, toys, bikes, clothes. The homes in which he grew up were the finest to which Italians in Hoboken could aspire. A lot of the Sinatras' neighbors on the tony streets on which they lived didn't even know they *were* Italian: Marty ran a popular speakeasy under his boxing name, and Dolly routinely introduced herself as Mrs. O'Brien; when Frank's buddies wanted to tease him about his Little Lord Fauntleroy wardrobe—he had his own charge account at Geismer's department store—they dubbed him Slacksey O'Brien. They were a family on the rise; a local newspaper society page reported on a New Year's Eve party Dolly threw after they bought a grand home at the height of the Depression.

By then, Frank had revealed himself as a perfect mix of his parents' temperaments. Hotheaded and ambitious on the one hand, he liked to loaf and schmooze and was an indifferent student on the other. For all that he inherited from his parents, he was, typically, embarrassed by them as well. Marty was no world-beater, everybody knew that, and he seemed pronouncedly meek even among his friends and colleagues; Dolly was outrageous, flamboyant, earthy, loud, an unignorable commotion whose affectations and ambitions grated on as many people as they inspired. Worse yet, she was the neighborhood abortionist, known to all the Italian girls as the person to turn to when they were in trouble; Frank's ears would turn red whenever he heard people talk about his mother the "rabbit catcher." Like everyone else, he was attracted to Dolly's exuberance, but like Marty and the other men in the family, he feared her. "She was a pisser," he'd say later, "but she scared the shit outta me. Never knew what she'd hate that I'd do."

As if to erase the shame Dolly put him through—the dudish threads, the mortifying secret work, the rowdy spectacle she made of herself on nights out with the girls—Frank seemed, at first, to take after Marty. He dropped out of school; he couldn't keep even a menial job; and he took up a fancy even less promising than Marty's boxing: Smitten with Bing Crosby, he wanted to be a singer.

At the sight of her boy sporting a yachting cap and crooning in a mirror, Dolly was, as her parents had been by Marty, disgusted, but the idea of denying her boy something that he wanted was worse. She bought him a spiffy electric P.A. system and convinced acquaintances to let him sing in their saloons and restaurants; eventually, she used her clout to get him a job chauffeuring a rising local trio, the Three Flashes, who were preparing to make a few movie shorts for Major Bowes, the era's great promoter of amateur showbiz talent; with his mom's backing, Frank quickly rose from driver to jester to full-fledged singer in the group.

The older guys in the act, which Bowes redubbed the Hoboken Four, didn't care much for the mama's boy in the midst, even less so when Frank's singing improved and his solos became a centerpiece of the show. During a several-month nationwide tour as part of one of Bowes's traveling road shows, they began picking on the skinny kid, beating him up when they felt he needed to be taken down a peg. Frank quit and returned to Hoboken—where Dolly had salted the press with news of his successes.

Three years of scattered, aimless work followed, then a steady job—singing waiter at the Rustic Cabin in Englewood Cliffs, a roadhouse which had a broadcast wire to New York's powerful WNEW radio station. In June 1939, bandleader Harry James heard Frank on the radio and drove out to see whose voice that was. Shazam: Frank was in. James signed him, they hit the road and cut some records, and Frank got a little bit of notice. In December, Tommy Dorsey auditioned him and he left James with a handclasp and best wishes.

This wasn't just the call of Lady Luck or the reward of sheer ambition. Somewhere sometime in there, a miracle bloomed. Frank's voice went from pleasant to stunning: a beautiful, tender instrument possessed of uncanny rhythmic sense and breath control, one of the great talents of the century, a gift no more explicable than those of Joyce and Picasso, recognizable as such even in its juvenile state. Everyone who heard him for the first time was staggered.

As a member of the Dorsey orchestra, Frank became famous: hit records, magazine covers, appearances in movies, flattering press. Like he'd learned from Dolly, he milked it, aggressively courting the press, disc jockeys, anyone he thought could boost his career. He spent more than he earned on his wardrobe alone (he was so finicky about his personal cleanliness that his bandmates with Dorsey nicknamed him Lady Macbeth). Within three years, he was convinced that Dorsey was holding him back from a career that would rival Crosby's, and he left—after months of bitter, petty infighting, a lucrative settlement, and a grudging goodbye.

Suddenly, everything: Frank signed to play the Paramount Theater in Times Square as an "extra added attraction" with the popular Benny Goodman orchestra; when Goodman introduced Frank, the response from the packed theater was so volcanic that he asked his band, "What the fuck was that?" Within a few months, the whole world would know. Spontaneously, Frank had become the beloved of a generation of wild-eyed fans—young girls, mostly—who made him a teen idol decades before anyone ever thought to manufacture such a thing.

Boosted by the devilishly clever press agent George Evans, Frank became bigger than Crosby or Vallee or Caruso—the biggest thing ever in showbiz, in fact. There was a core of critics and musicians among the cognoscenti who admired his artistry (James Agee spoke fondly of his "weird, fleeting resemblances to Lincoln"), but the wellspring was the kids— the bobby-soxers, as they were named for an affectation of footwear. *Sinatratics* they called themselves, forming cultish cells in devotion to their new god: the Slaves of Sinatra, the Sighing Society of Sinatra Swooners, the Flatbush Girls Who Would Lay Down Their Lives for Frank Sinatra, the Frank Sinatra Fan and Mahjong Club.

These daughters of flappers were quick to connect the longing in Frank's voice with their own longings, his quavery presence with the absent boys who were off fighting the Hun and the Nip (Frank was 4-F: punctured eardrum). Odd as it may have seemed to everyone in the business, the wiseass runt with the heavenly voice was some kind of sex symbol. (And he'd always be one: For a half-century, Frank was one of the ways America made love, quite often the most popular; he was able to get away with anything because he hit people in their most personal spots.)

By the late fifties, by Rat Pack time, when his audience had grown up, Frank could be as sexy as he felt, but in the first blush of his fame, he had, like all teen idols, to be officially Off Limits. Conveniently, he had a cozy domestic life to play up: He'd been married to a girl-next-door type since 1939; by 1944, they had two kids, one named after each of them: Little Nancy and Frankie Jr.

For George Evans—and for Frank's many important employers: Columbia Records, CBS radio, MGM, Lucky Strike—this was a perfect setup: a talented, massively popular young guy with a solid family and a wholesome aspect. But Frank seemed hell-bent on screwing it up. There was that entourage —big, unlikely guys, boxing writers, gamblers, songwriters buttering him up—and there were women and there was this habit of snapping back at the press and there was all the politics: Bad enough he was 4-F; did he have to sing "Ol' Man River" and break bread with Eleanor Roosevelt? Evans spent the better part of the forties covering Frank's ass, cozying up to some columnists and scratching and clawing at others while his client carried on however he pleased, simply assuming that somebody else would sweep it up.

He rose to insane heights. In 1939, he was waiting tables at the Rustic Cabin for $15 a week; by the end of the war, he was a bigger star in more media than anyone in the world and had grossed an estimated $11 million. By sheer earnings standards, he was probably the biggest star ever, anywhere; it almost didn't matter that he was an artistic genius with more pure vocal talent than virtually anyone who'd ever been recorded.

Still and all, he was a creature of the popular culture and, as such, subject to the public's whimsies. As the forties closed, talk leaked into the press about ties to communism and mobsters, there were ugly spats with writers, photographers, waiters, carhops, fans. His once-promising film career had sputtered—*The Kissing Bandit*, anyone?—and, after Frank made a wisecrack about one of Louis B. Mayer's mistresses, MGM gave him his release. On the radio, he was bumped down from *Your Hit Parade* to a fifteen-minute, B-level show; on TV, CBS just plain dumped him.

He had trouble with his voice—he opened his mouth once at the Copa and couldn't make a sound come out—and he seemed, further, to have lost his aesthetic way, letting Columbia's new A&R man, Mitch Miller, talk him into making horseshit records with arrangements scaled wrong for his voice and dog barks thrown in as comic relief. The pathetic fall seemed poetically complete in 1952 when he returned to the Paramount Theater in support of a film of his own (the forgettable *Meet Danny Wilson*) and couldn't even fill the balcony, much less stop traffic in Times Square.

Frank had gone from "extra added attraction" to King of the Universe in a couple of years; then, in about the same time span, he couldn't get a job—and not a few people in the business were glad of it. With his ambition, quick temper, and iconoclasm, he'd done a lot of pissing off in his decade on the scene. His reputation was poison: When Capitol Records president Alan Livingston told his staff that he'd signed Sinatra at terms very favorable to the company, they groaned as one.

Presaging all of this calamity, turning the bobby-soxers against him and making him look like some pathetic pussy-whipped Milquetoast, was his wanton affair with Ava Gardner. Frank had never been faithful to Nancy in even a loose sense of the word, but, like many showbiz wives, she seemed willing to put up with peccadilloes even with such hot numbers as Marilyn Maxwell and Lana Turner. But this thing with Ava was more passionate and public than any of his other dalliances; it might have begun as a meaningless Hollywood fling, but they carried on all over the country throughout 1949, and Frank's cardboard marriage finally became untenable. In the spring of 1950, he left the pretty Italian girl and the three cute kids that were his P.R. chastity belt. George Evans, enervated and skinny to begin with, bald from defending him, up and died one night after arguing with a columnist about Frank and Ava; he was forty-eight, and his heart had given out.

The affair and subsequent marriage were absurdly tempestuous and about as private as a presidential campaign; Ava was a lioness and Frank was her plaything. She was as promiscuous, lustful, hard-drinking, and profane as he was, and she had the hooks into him but good. She busted his balls mercilessly, running off with bullfighters and making him look like an ass in front of the world. He threatened suicide several times and took two stabs at it—once in Lake Tahoe with pills, once in New York with a razor. His disgrace and comeuppance were complete: Not only was he a has-been as a singer, an actor, and a performer, he was a flop as a cocksman. He was a joke: last year's punch line.

When he finally managed to crawl out of his hole, then, it was all the more resoundingly triumphant. He achieved it in part through a movie role—Maggio, the pip-squeak private who died horribly at the hands of a bullying sergeant in *From Here to Eternity*. Throughout the latter half of 1952, Frank campaigned actively with Columbia Pictures president Harry Cohn to get the part, and Cohn's relationship with the Chicago Outfit's West Coast point man, Johnny Rosselli, assured Frank at least a hearing. He got the job, he did really good in it, he got the Oscar, poof: He was all better. Once considered an overweening interloper in Hollywood, he was suddenly in the spring of '54 a resilient, dues-paying member of the acting club. He had done the good thing; he had died for his fame and resurrected himself. He made more movies and he had hit after hit; he was even good in some of them.

At the same time, he took a new turn musically. No longer was he the reed-thin, warbling young crooner with a voice like a viola and a closet full of floppy bow ties. Now working for Capitol Records, he was more propulsive and dynamic, his voice richer and deeper—a cello. He was wearing fedoras and stylish suits; he was singing up-tempo about swinging and in dramatic, elegiac tempi about loss.

As in the movies, he seemed to have earned the right to his station; what's more, as a singer, he expanded the very art form. He cut whole albums of songs built on the same musical ideas—saloon songs, swing numbers, waltzes—and even lyrical ideas: flying, dancing, the moon. Through the decade, he made the greatest pop records in history—one after another, sometimes as many as four a year.

Come 1959, he could look back twenty years and see a punk kid with nothing but ambition to his credit, he could look back a decade and see a big star dumped by the world, or he could look into the mirror and see the most influential and talented popular entertainer of the century.

Now what?

*

Frank was to become such a colossus of American popular culture that it would've been crazy in his heyday to think of him as needy. But his heroic Last Honest Man posture always had as a counterpart a little boy's thirst for camaraderie and love. "I don't think Frank's an adult emotionally," his friend Humphrey Bogart sniffed. Shirley MacLaine was more clinical, calling Sinatra "a perpetual performing child who wants to please the mother audience."

Never mind all the gruff stuff offstage: The evidence of what was in his heart was in his art. Here was a man who lived amid an entourage that could expand, if he wished it to, to infinity, a man who had virtually every woman he ever desired, a man for whom no material comfort was unattainable; yet his music was at its richest and most intense when he sang piteously about loneliness. His familiar swinging cockiness would be overwhelmed by a gray, anguished fog hovering over a profound, hollow core—the achy soul of the Tender Tough. "I'll Be Seeing You," "These Foolish Things," "Guess I'll Hang My Tears out to Dry," "In the Wee Small Hours," "Angel Eyes," "What's New?," "One for My Baby"—a world of crushed dreams, blasted hopes, distant, impossible romance. People called it suicide music and couldn't understand why he slowed down every show to perform it—sometimes exclusively. But loneliness was the most vibrant color in his musical palette, and it obviously came from someplace very deep inside of him.

Indeed, he was born to it. He was, of course, an only child—try to name another Italo-American only child of his generation!—and grew up with a yearning for the companionship that his friends, neighbors, and cousins all enjoyed in their homes. The cash and clothing that his mother lavished on him were his first means of acquiring a society: He handed down suits to kids whose friendship he courted; he bought burgers and candy and comic books, cultivating early on a habit of "gifting"—treating the house to drinks or meals or clothes or women or more. The assets Dolly spotted him as a teenager— his wardrobe, his car, his sheet music arrangements, his portable sound system—they were a way for him to get a leg up in show business, true, but they were also a means of being part of a bigger group.

Which is what made it so perfect that Sinatra came into his own as a performer during the big band era, when a singer was by necessity a piece of a large, vibrant whole. The Harry James and Tommy Dorsey bands were like big clubs of chums for him—and he didn't have to buy his way in, either. He gorged himself on the grand bonhomie that the bands instantly provided him—the card games, hazing, drinking, dreaming, and bonding that he and his fellow musicians engaged in during endless bus rides. He was like a congenital junkie who became addicted with his very first hit. As soon as he'd begun life in that dazzling musical fraternity, he wanted to live no other way.

Witness his recollection of the day on which he left James for Dorsey: January 1940, Buffalo; the James band was headed to Hartford; Frank would briefly visit New York, then join Dorsey in Rockford, Illinois; it was the single big break of his career, and he'd yearned for it and schemed to make it so; still, he struggled through the separation from his bandmates of a mere six months: "The bus pulled out with the rest of the boys at about half-past midnight. I'd said good-bye to them all, and it was snowing, I remember. There was nobody around and I stood alone with my suitcase in the snow and watched the taillights disappear. Then the tears started and I tried to run after the bus." (This was, keep in mind, a married man with a child on the way.)

Of course, the Dorsey band was to offer Frank the same sort of companionship he enjoyed with James. Moreover,

Dorsey himself would come to serve as a hero and model for his young singer; Frank dressed and spoke like him, he studied his famous breathing technique, he even took up his hobby of model railroading. Still, even with the prospect of a new gang of buddies assured him, he arrived in Illinois with the beginnings of his own coterie, a safeguard against ever finding himself staring longingly at the receding taillights of a bus again: Nick Sevano, a Hoboken haberdasher who dressed him, did his errands, and even lived with him and his family when they weren't on the road, and Hank Sanicola, accompanist, business manager, and, as his girth suggested, sometime thumbbreaker.

Two years later, when the allure of profits and aesthetic freedom drove Sinatra to seek his release from the Dorsey band, he was, once again, bereft of bandmates, so he gathered to his bony bosom a band, of sorts, of his own. He expanded his entourage to include such semiregulars as Mannie Sachs, a Columbia Records executive; Ben Barton, his music publisher and business partner; composer Jimmy Van Heusen; lyricist Sammy Cahn; bruisers Tami Mauriello and Al Silvani; and Jimmy Taratino, a boxing writer whose mob ties eventually formed a costly web for the singer. And he gave them all, guilelessly, a name: the Varsity.

En masse, the Varsity hit all the swell spots—nightclubs, saloons, showbiz eateries, and, especially, the Friday night fights at Madison Square Garden, where they mingled with mobsters, Times Square sharpies, and other supernumeraries of the fight game. Grown men actually vied to be admitted to their numbers, but that privilege was rarely granted, and the resultant loyalty of its members was embarrassingly high: When Mauriello was inducted into the service and sent overseas to fight, he gave Frank his golden ID bracelet, which the singer wore with puppy-dog pride.

After the war, the Varsity evolved, with some members

resuming their lives without Frank (not always peaceably or voluntarily) and others accompanying him out West, where he had joined the extended family of MGM studios. There was a softball team—Sinatra's Swooners, with uniforms and cheerleaders (and Ava Gardner as, ahem, honorary bat girl); there were card games, pub crawls, the works.

But then the spiral that demolished his career began: Divorced, his voice uncertain, his name connected with reds, hoods, and a dozen drunken little fistfights, without a record company, film contract, or agent to call his own, he suddenly didn't seem like a Sun King anymore. A few steadfast partisans held on; the larger crowd vaporized.

It was a subtle thing: People didn't so much snub Frank as stop courting him. He couldn't get tables in the same restaurants, or not the same tables, anyway. He couldn't round up a poker game or gang of drunks to obliterate a night with him. Early one morning at the dawn of the fifties, Sammy was walking through Times Square, overjoyed with just having been allowed to break the color barrier long enough to schmooze with the big stars at Lindy's. He passed the Capitol Theater—the place where Frank had once hired him and his dad and uncle when they were still unknown—and lo, there Frank was, walking along with a wounded air.

"Not a soul was paying attention to him," Sammy recalled later. "This was the man who only a few years ago had tied up traffic all over Times Square. Thousands of people had been stepping all over each other trying to get a look at him. Now the same man was walking down the same street and nobody gave a damn."

For Sammy, to whom the clubbiness and fame of showbiz were brass rings worth one's very soul, it was a stunning sight. "I couldn't take my eyes off him, walking the streets alone, an ordinary Joe who'd been a giant. He was fighting to make it back again but he was doing that by himself, too. The 'friends' were gone with all the presents and the money he'd given them. Nobody was helping him."

There were others who sensed Sinatra's pain and tried to help. L.A. gangster Mickey Cohen, an admirer of the singer's ("If you call Frank's hole card," he said approvingly, "he's gonna answer"), tried to rally his spirits by hosting a testimonial dinner for him at the Beverly Hills Hotel. Instead, the sparsely attended event simply underscored Sinatra's dilemma. As Cohen recalled in his hilarious autobiography, "A lot of people that were invited to that Sinatra testimonial, that should have attended but didn't, would bust their nuts in *this* day to attend a Sinatra testimonial. A lot of them would now kiss Frank's ass after he made the comeback, but they didn't show up when he really needed them. I don't know the names of a lot of them bastards in that ilk of life, but I remember the people that I had running the affair at the time telling me, Jesus, this and that dirty son of a bitch should have been here."

At the time, Frank wasn't really keeping up with all the snubs—he was far too bewildered by life with Ava and the prospect of resuscitating his career. But he was still Dolly's boy, and he had to have noticed the slights. And if he'd ever shown himself to be curt and exclusive *before* bottoming out and being left behind, when he recovered he became more demanding than ever of the loyalty of those he allowed around him. Only the surest would be abided.

Such a one was Humphrey Bogart, the movie god whose blessing upon Frank was one of the lifelines that kept him hopeful that he might someday emerge from the straits in which fate had left him foundering.

In all Hollywood, nobody had a flintier or more enviable reputation than Bogart. An Upper West Side sissy boy who went from playing juvenile walk-ons to psychotic killers, paranoid adventurers, and cynics with soft hearts, he danced just within the boundaries of the game. His drinking, womanizing, and bellicosity never quite made the front pages, his bad-mouthing of bosses never quite stooped to insubordination, and his liberal political beliefs and headstrong independence never quite severed him from the basis of his wealth, fame, and popularity. The one potential faux pas of his life—his affair with starlet Lauren Bacall—was easily cast by studio flacks and gossip mavens as a great May–December romance, especially after the couple wed and started a family.

For a large part of the movie colony, Bogie was a cult hero—a Knight of the True Way. He did his work best by being something that no one else could be: himself. Off-camera, he drank away afternoons in restaurants, went out of his way to upset prigs at parties, cruised the Pacific on his sailboat, and made, with his young wife, a home that offered haven to those very select few in his business who, like him, weren't fooled for a minute by their own press.

Nothing, but nothing, rattled Bogart more than the sight of Hollywood kissing its own behind, especially over unproven new talent, and *especially* unproven male talent that was rooted in alleged sex appeal. So in 1945, when the jug-eared boy singer who made the bobby-soxers wet their pants showed up in town to great foofaraw, Bogart was ready to dismiss him out of hand. They ran into one another for the first time at the Players, the Sunset Boulevard restaurant, bar, and theater owned by Preston Sturges.

"They tell me you have a voice that makes girls faint," said Bogart, an expert needler. "Make me faint."

Sinatra stood right up to him: "I'm taking the week off."

Bogart liked the response, liked the kid. And Frank, of course, saw in Bogart all the things he always wanted to be: aloof, profound, world-weary, slightly drunk, slightly sentimental, romantic, tender, tough, loyal, and proud. (He could take his hero worship too far. Once, when a date of Frank's declared, in Bogart's presence, "You sound like Bogie sometimes," the actor laughed and said, "Don't remind him, sweetheart, the poor bastard's trying to kick it!") He tried to cajole producers into casting him in *Knock on Any Door* as a tough street kid opposite Bogart's impassioned lawyer; such was Sinatra's stock as an actor that the role went to John Derek.

Nevertheless, the two men got into the habit of spending time together whenever the occasion arose, which, given Frank's hectic schedule of filmmaking, recording, and touring, wasn't often. In 1949, though, Frank moved his family from Toluca Lake to Holmby Hills, just blocks from Bogart's house. This new proximity allowed the two stars more frequent contact; soon after moving into the neighborhood, Sinatra organized a guys-only baby shower for Bogart when Lauren Bacall was pregnant with their first child.

The relationship got a little strange. After Frank had left Nancy and the kids, he was still welcome in their house; he would frequently crash on his estranged wife's couch after nights of bingeing with Bogart, shuttling between the two homes as if, in his mind, they constituted one. "He's always here," Bogart told a reporter. "I think we're parent substitutes for him, or something." Bacall empathized with Frank's need for companionship, but Bogart warned her against getting wrapped up in it. "He chose to live the way he's living—alone," he admonished his wife. "It's too bad if he's lonely, but that's his choice. We have our own road to travel, never forget that—we can't live his life."

In fact, Bogart was one of the few people who were willing to tell Frank exactly what they thought of some of the things he did. There was the time he hosted Sinatra, David Niven, and Richard Burton for a night of drinking on his beloved yacht, *Santana*. Frank was at a career ebb, and he passed part of the night on deck, serenading yachters on the other boats moored nearby; Bogie grew so irate with Sinatra's preening performance, recalled Burton, that he and Frank "nearly came to blows."

There was the time when Frank, riding high on the early reviews for *From Here to Eternity*, visited his hero in search of approval. "I saw your picture," said Bogie. "What did you think?" Frank asked. Bogart simply shook his head no.

And there was Bogart's famous line about Frank's thin-skinned egoism: "Sinatra's idea of paradise is a place where there are plenty of women and no newspapermen. He doesn't know it, but he'd be better off if it were the other way around."

Still, there was a bond between the two: father-son, mentor-acolyte, king-pretender—somehow the dynamic was agreeable to them both. They both reviled the traditional cant and decorum of Hollywood protocol, they both had deep political concerns for the everyman, and they both loved to needle people, especially the thin-skinned twits their lives as famous performers gave them so many chances to meet. Frank was always welcome in the Bogart home; the Bogarts, in turn, accepted his hospitality when he would want to scoop up a gang of pals and run off for a weekend in the Springs or Vegas.

In June 1955, for instance, he gathered a dozen or so chums, rented a train, and took off to catch Noel Coward's opening at the Desert Inn (yes, *that* Noel Coward and *that* Desert Inn; Vegas was always great with novelties). During that particular spree, legend has it, the group had gotten so deep into its cups that Bacall was startled by their debauched appearance when she caught a gander of them ringside in a casino showroom. She looked around at all the famous flesh—Frank; Bogart; Judy Garland; David Niven; restaurateur Mike Romanoff; literary agent Swifty Lazar and his date, Martha Hyer; Jimmy

Van Heusen and his date, Angie Dickinson; a few well-oiled others.

"You look like a goddamn rat pack," she muttered.

It broke them up. A few nights later, back in Romanoff's joint in Beverly Hills, she walked in and declared, "I see the rat pack's all here." Again, a big hit, but this time the joke picked up momentum of its own: They founded an institution—the Holmby Hills Rat Pack. They drew up a coat of arms—a rat gnawing on a human hand—and coined a motto: "Never rat on a rat." And they assigned themselves ranks and responsibilities: Frank (and you can just see him standing there excitedly conducting the whole sophomoric enterprise) was named Pack Master; Bacall, Den Mother; Garland, Vice President; Sid Luft (Garland's husband and manager), Cage Master; Lazar (so full of pep they gave him two jobs), Treasurer and Recording Secretary; and humorist Nathaniel Benchley, Historian.

Bogart was named Rat in Charge of Public Relations, and the next day he spoke about the whole silly business with movieland reporter Joe Hyams. "News must be pretty tight when you start to cover parties at Romanoff's," Bogart responded when asked about the Rat Pack, but, assured that the story would be treated with such overblown pomp that it would obviously be seen as a goof, he acceded to an interview. The Rat Pack, he declared, was formed for "the relief of boredom and the perpetuation of independence. We admire ourselves and don't care for anyone else." They'd briefly considered adding some absent friends to the roster, he said, but the requirements were often too high: When Claudette Colbert, for instance, whom they all liked, was nominated, Bacall insisted that she not be admitted because she was "a nice person but not a rat." Hyams dutifully jotted it all down, agreed once again when Bogart insisted that "it was all a joke," and reported it the next day in the *New York Herald Tribune*.

Hyams's scoop was true enough: There was indeed a group, centered around Bogart, that hung out together to the exclusion of the remainder of Hollywood, which, though they were part of it, they had no qualms about mocking. "You had to be a noncomformist," said Bacall, "and you had to stay up late and drink and laugh a lot and not care what anybody said about you or thought about you" (one last criterion: "You had to be a little musical"). But the idea of an organization and a creed and all that, that was strictly a lark, another of Bogart's beloved practical jokes taken to an absurd height.

Nevertheless, the publicity incited a reaction that revealed that Bogart's attitude wasn't necessarily laughed off by the world at large. Hollywood was an extremely cliquish society, and Bogart's clique had always taken the perverse ethical stand that the local social mores—and the cliques it spawned —were bullshit. The notion of such a disdainful group legitimizing itself into an honorable cult, even in jest, struck some in the movie colony as an affront.

The poor schmucks didn't get the joke: There was no such thing as the Rat Pack, not *really*. The principals might all get together at Romanoff's or Bogart's house and carry on like a drunken fraternity, but that's all they really were: There were no dues or meetings or minutes or rules; there were just nights together in a company town of which they were all valued—and jaded—assets. If they wanted to pretend they were wild rebels, fine; they still all showed up on movie sets and in recording studios bright and early the next morning with their material prepared and their bodies and voices ready to perform. The whole Rat Pack thing was like bowling or square dancing or watching TV—the things they would've done together if they'd been squarejohns living between the coasts and not movieland royalty.

*

The subtle caste system out of which the Rat Pack arose became somewhat more manifest in 1956 when Bogart was diagnosed as having incurable throat cancer. A parade of friends, colleagues, and acquaintances spent the ensuing year paying fealty to this man who neither wanted nor acknowledged their sympathetic indulgence. "Haven't you people got anything better to do than come over here and bother me?" Bogie would admonish his guests. "How am I supposed to get any rest with the likes of you coming every day?" It was the sandpaper wit they'd come to expect from him, and they cherished it.

Despite his crusty bravery, though, the last year of Bogart's life was a horror of weight loss, discomfort, incapacity, depression. Bacall, still in her early thirties and an established star in her own right, bore it as well as she could, but she needed occasional escape from the traumatic scene unfolding in her home. Bogart insisted that she continue to go out on the town, and he was grateful whenever she took him up on the offer, most frequently escorted by Sinatra.

Frank had determined to remain steadfast during his idol's illness, visiting regularly even though he was mortified by Bogart's condition. "It wasn't easy for him," Bacall remembered. "I don't think he could bear to see Bogie that way or bear to face the possibility of his death. Yet he cheered Bogie up when he was with him—made him laugh—kept the ring-a-ding act in high gear."

More than that, it has been suggested, he filled the loneliness in Mrs. Bogart's life with more than just suppers at Romanoff's. Intimates of the group whispered about a budding love affair between Sinatra and Bacall—"It was no secret to any of us," said one—and they pointed to a Rat Pack trip to Las Vegas for Bacall's birthday which Bogart skipped, preferring to take his young son, Stephen, to sea on the *Santana*.

Bacall was aware of the dynamic, admitting that Bogart

"was somewhat jealous of Frank. Partly because he knew I loved being with him, partly because he thought Frank was in love with me, and partly because our physical life together, which had always ranked high, had less than flourished with his illness."

When the end finally came, Frank, a fixture in the Bogart household, was nowhere to be found. Bogart died on January 14, 1957, when Frank was in New York working a club date at the Copacabana. He canceled three days' worth of shows (Sammy, who was starring on Broadway in *Mr. Wonderful*, and Jerry Lewis, who was in the midst of a successful solo run at the Palace, subbed for him), but he didn't return to California for the funeral, holing up instead in his Manhattan hotel.

Even if he didn't have any reason to feel guilty, he couldn't have been too comfortable back on Maplewood Drive. Bogart's house had become a kind of shrine to his final days: His favorite chair, his clothes, his photos, his very aura hung about the place unaltered. Bacall couldn't bring herself to change a thing, even though she, too, found it difficult to live amid it all. Frank—always indulgent of widows—gave her and her children the run of his Palm Springs estate for as long as they needed it.

By the end of 1957, the time had arrived when he could offer her more. His Mexican divorce from Ava Gardner, a mere legal technicality in their shattered relationship, had coincidentally come through that June. Frank and Bacall began seeing one another socially, with all observers assuming they were intimate. When Frank entertained at his homes in Coldwater Canyon or Palm Springs, Bacall was hostess, and she was his date for the Las Vegas premiere of *Pal Joey* and the L.A. premiere of *The Joker Is Wild*. It made perfect sense: the Pack Master and the Den Mother, a golden couple come together after their storied marriages had ended, respectively, in passionate disaster and heart-wrenching tragedy.

Despite the fairy-tale appearance of the romance, though, they had to endure one another's considerable faults. Bacall got into the habit of checking up on him whenever he was with other women—taking a phone call from her while his latest conquest listened along in his hotel room, he made a big show of his impatience, answering, "Yes, Captain. Yes, General. Yes, Boss." In exchange, she was subject to Frank's moodiness. His swings between indulgent companionability and icy remove rattled her, especially, as she noted later, since she had previously "been married to a grown-up."

But her will was no match for his; like many of Sinatra's women, she was eager to do anything to please him. She even went so far as to give up her home on Maplewood Drive, in part because of the painful memories the place harbored for her, in part because, as she later told her son, "I don't think Frank was comfortable in that house. The ghost of your father was always there and I knew that Frank would feel better if I moved."

Her sacrifices and persistence paid off: In March 1958, after another of his sullen absences, he popped back onto the scene and proposed marriage. She accepted, agreeing to his desire to keep their intentions private for a while. Frank went off to a club date at the Fontainebleau; Bacall stayed in L.A. and kept denying rumors whenever reporters—even buddies like Joe Hyams and Richard Gehman—got snoopy. But she couldn't keep from blabbing to gossipy little Swifty Lazar, who spilled the beans to Louella Parsons, who made national headlines with it, which drove Frank into a fit.

"Why did you do it?" Frank harangued Bacall from Miami. "I haven't been able to leave my room for days—the press are everywhere. We'll have to lay low for a while, not see each other for a while."

Chastened, even in her innocence, Bacall did as she was

told—and Frank never tried to contact her again. "He behaved like a complete shit," she later said. "He was too cowardly to tell the truth—that it was just too much for him, that he found he couldn't handle it."

But there might have been a bigger truth: Maybe Frank had realized that he didn't have to marry Bogie's widow to become the actor's true heir and King of the Rat Pack. Maybe he realized that he could simply up and start a brand-new Rat Pack of his own.

105 percent

By at least one account, it was Dean's idea: The story goes that he had just rescued his career with his eye-opening work on *The Young Lions,* and he was sharking for a new project. In the summer of '58, he and his wife attended the premiere of *Kings Go Forth,* Frank's latest picture, and he walked over to Frank like he was pissed about something.

"You bum!"

Frank played along: "What've I done now?"

"You're hunting for a man for your next picture who smokes, drinks, and can talk real southern. You're looking at him."

"Well, whattaya know . . ."

Cute. And there might even be some truth to it, but the likely scenario is somewhat less colorful. For starters, if it had happened, it would've marked the first time in his life that Dean Martin went out of his way to further his career; indeed, one of the reasons for the dissolution of Martin and Lewis was that Jerry's overweening ambition struck Dean as degrading. More than that, the story assumes that Frank, who was forever throwing his chums roles in his movies (he once slated his squeeze Gloria Vanderbilt for a role in the western *Johnny Concho,* an inspiration lost to cinematic history when their love affair hit the rocks), hadn't already considered Dean for a role that he was practically born to play. In fact, it ignores altogether just how close Dean and Frank, a couple of olives off the same tree, had recently become.

For their first couple decades in the business, they hadn't palled around much, even though they'd been crossing paths since the war. Dean's big ticket to New York came when he followed Frank into the Riobamba nightclub; they shared a record label; they had appeared together on TV a few times; but they were no more a two-act than, say, Perry Como and Vic Damone.

Recently, though, that had begun to change. A couple of years earlier, Dean took in a Judy Garland show in Long Beach in Frank's company (Sammy and Bogey were also there), and they all popped onstage with the star for an impromptu number. After that, Frank appeared on a couple of Dean's NBC specials—on one, they sang a duet of "Jailhouse Rock"!—and Dean returned the favor when Frank began his catastrophic series on ABC.

Frank had grown to feel something fraternal for Dean. He would always be the first mate, a brother.

But it hadn't always been that way.

"The dago's lousy, but the little jew is great": thus Frank on Martin and Lewis, circa 1948, when the new singing-comedy act was tearing the roof off Frank Costello's Copacabana and quickly becoming the hottest thing in showbiz.

In a sense, it was an entirely apt critique. Martin and Lewis, one of the greatest two-man acts in history, was really Jerry Lewis's vehicle. Dean, the tall, handsome, crooning straight man, was more or less along for the ride. And when the ride ended, when Martin and Lewis devolved into an ugly spitting contest and finally broke apart, "the little jew" went on to solo success, just as everyone predicted, while "the dago" initially floundered.

It wasn't that Dean didn't have the chops. He had a charming voice in the Crosby mood—a stylish singer, if never a real artist. He cut a great figure in a tux, golf clothes, even overalls: real movie star looks. And he was funny, with a gift for whimsical one-liners and a canny, low-key delivery that were completely wasted in the years he spent alongside the spotlight-hogging Jerry.

But he seemingly didn't have the drive to go it alone. He was ten years older than Jerry and struggling under an absurd burden of debt when the two teamed up and launched their rocket to the moon. For all his gifts, he'd never, as a solo, gone anywhere useful. And for all the success that he eventually enjoyed, it seemed like the only reason he'd ever gotten anywhere at all in the world was that he'd been somehow blessed to thrive in it. He didn't have to work, he didn't have to sweat, he didn't have to think; he just had to show up and get paid—his whole life long.

Consider: Dean never wanted to get his hands dirty, so he learned how to deal cards and how to sing, and he made a living at it; he was too sanguine to chase women, so they threw themselves at him; he didn't have the fire in the belly to make himself a showbiz star, so he met a couple of wildly ambitious guys—Jerry and Frank—who dragged him along.

It was even luck that Dean was born in America—his father's bad luck, that is, to have been born in Abruzzi, a wind-scored plain south of Rome, dotted with cave-riddled mountains. Abruzzi spit forth disconsolate young men and women and exiled them to the New World, where they choked slums and factories. Steubenville, Ohio, where Dean's people turned up, was filled with steelworks that swallowed up Italian and Greek immigrants like so much coke.

After seeing the infernal wreckage of his older brothers,

who'd emigrated before him, Gaetano Crocetti, Dean's father, decided that selling his soul to a foundry wasn't for him. He chose instead one of the few respectable blue-collar jobs open to a young Italian immigrant, apprenticing himself to a barber. With his name anglicized (he became Guy Crocetti, pronouncing his last name *Crowsetti*) and his future assured, he was able to woo and wed Angela Barra, an orphan girl from the neighborhood with a bit of barbed wire in her makeup. They were kids when they married, but by June 1917, just three years later, Guy had his own barbershop, the couple had a one-year-old boy, and Angela produced another son. Born prematurely, he wasn't christened until the fall: Dino.

The Crocetti boys were raised among a healthy tribe of relatives and neighbors. They had a comfortable home, plush Christmases, plenty to eat; there were no riches, exactly, but nor were there rags. Guy was naturally easygoing—a good barber. He sat genially among the other men, sipping wine, eating tangerines and nuts, schmoozing away the twilight in the Abruzzese piazza that they simulated in their hearts and minds.

But Angela had grown up under more brutal circumstances than her husband—her mother had been committed to the Ohio Institution for the Feeble Minded—and she didn't see the world as so accommodating a place. She spoiled her sons like any good Italian mother, true, but she also tried to prepare them for the world by instilling her toughness in them, teaching that they mustn't be weak or free with their feelings, that they should make their way in the world like men.

Dino learned such lessons well. Like his dad, he refused to submit to a future in the foundries, but he wasn't soft enough for barbering. His mother's strength had given him the confidence to seek other opportunities—of which Steubenville was deliriously full. In fact, the town, known throughout the region as Little Chicago, was wide open: pool halls, strip joints, cigar shops fronting for gambling parlors; only a sucker, it seemed, could grow up amid it and not try to cash in.

By his early teens, Dino was running with a shady gang from around the neighborhood and showing up in school with his pockets full of silver dollars. At sixteen, he slipped out of school altogether and for good. He was tall and athletic, with dark, wavy hair and a bold Roman nose. He tried to turn his good looks, lithe body, and quick hands into a profit as a welterweight boxer—Kid Crochet. He flopped. So he turned to odd jobs, including a brief, terrifying stint in a steel mill— a vision of hell as a place where you spent eternity if you lacked the moxie to avoid it. He finally broke through into the sort of racket to which he aspired: dealing poker and blackjack in a local gambling den.

He took to fancy clothes and easy women. He and his pals ran around nights drinking, gambling, carousing. Guy and Angela disapproved, but their boy breezed along in merry indifference: Good times like these, who worried about the future?

Yet even though he was always one of the boys, there was something in Dino that set him apart: He sang—a fanciful affectation, perhaps, but one acceptable to Italian boys of his age, partly out of the respect accorded opera singers in their culture, and partly because of the novelty of the radio and the phonograph, which was making stars of crooners. It was the only thing that Dean applied himself to that didn't have the spoor of sin about it; he even took vocal lessons from the mayor's wife. And he performed in clubs and taverns and at parties whenever there was an open mike and a band willing to back him.

His pals encouraged him; his bosses liked it. Soon enough, he took work as a singing dealer at a sneak joint outside of Cleveland. He was approached by Ernie McKay, a band-leader from Columbus who offered to take him on. Before long, another eye was caught: Cleveland bandleader Sammy Watkins hired him away in the spring of 1940 to come to the shores of Lake Erie and play to a ritzier clientele.

That winter, performing under the newly minted stage name Dean Martin, he met a fresh-faced college dropout named Elizabeth MacDonald. Two years later, they married. Nine months after that, Dean was a father looking for a way to make more money.

A local MCA agent called: Frank Sinatra had canceled a date at the Riobamba in New York, and the club's owners were willing to give this new Italian boy singer from Cleveland a shot. Dean wanted to go, but he had to pay a steep price: For freedom from his contract, he gave Watkins 10 percent of his income for the next seven years; the agent took another 10 percent. In September 1943, at $150 a week, he debuted in Manhattan, the world's biggest candy store for a guy with his kind of sweet tooth.

The obvious pleasures aside, New York didn't prove easy. Money didn't come fast enough, and when it did, it disappeared even quicker. Hands reached into his pockets. An old Steubenville acquaintance turned up wanting to serve as his manager, offering $200 ready cash in exchange for a 20 percent piece of his earnings. Dean was in debt everywhere; he took the deal. He was courted by a Times Square agent who offered another cash payment for 35 percent of his earnings; he took it. Comedian Lou Costello offered Dean more money for another 20 percent; he took it.

Dean got his patrons to broker a nose job, turning the schnozzola he'd inherited into something more aquiline. He signed up for a nonsponsored radio show whose musical director took an interest in his future. Dean milked the guy for yet another cash payment in exchange for 10 percent of himself, making a grand total of 105 percent; for every dollar he earned, had he been up front with all his partners, he would've been out a nickel—but, of course, he never bothered to pay anybody.

In August 1944, he was booked into the Glass Hat nightclub, just another gig that only changed his life forever. Down the bill and serving as emcee was a skinny, acned kid pantomimist from New Jersey named Jerry Lewis: destiny with an overbite.

Like everyone else, Jerry adored Dean, and he grabbed every opportunity he could to pal around with him at gigs, at restaurants, at after-hours schmoozes. He even began edging into Dean's act. In the winter of 1945, when Dean was topping the bill at the Havana-Madrid club and Jerry was emcee, Jerry kibitzed from offstage as Dean sang. Dean didn't care much about what he was doing anyhow, so he played along, getting an appreciative rise out of the crowd.

The following summer, Jerry was playing the 500 Club in Atlantic City, a joint with ties to the Camden mob, and he found himself on the verge of being fired. He called New York in a panic, found out that Dean was available, and told the guys who ran the club that Dean was a great singer and that the two of them did "funny shit" together. Management bit, Dean got hired, and one of the brightest Roman candles ever to hit showbiz was lit.

Within a year, Martin and Lewis were the biggest act in nightclubs; two years later, they were the biggest act in the world: TV, movies, radio—they overran every single medium available to them. They made sixteen hit films, had the nation's number one TV show, and were one of the top-drawing live acts in the business, creating a sensation that recalled nothing so much as Sinatra's bobby-sox heyday; they even tied up traffic in Times Square.

The act was a farce, equal parts nightclub slickness and burlesque puerility. Dean would stand soberly (the drunkie routine didn't start till *after* Jerry) and try to put over a tune— "Oh, Marie," say, or "Torna a Sorriento"; Jerry would cavort wildly, trying to horn in on the act or take control of it for himself—a realer bit of shtick than anyone in the audience knew.

Of course, Dean could actually sing as well as play straight, combining the best of George Burns and Desi Arnaz with sex appeal neither of them had. But the point of Martin and Lewis was no more straight vocals than it was dramatics. Jerry would squeal and wheedle and practically run out and kiss the audience's ass to gain its love, and Dean would stand in dumbfounded awe of the spectacle, a substitute for the viewer, bemusedly, indulgently watching as his little buddy made a travesty of the accepted forms of showbiz. If Dean occasionally dove in and capered as well, that made it even more fun; for the most part, though, he hung back and let Jerry make a merry schmuck of himself.

This was the Dean Martin that the world came to love—the suave geniality covering up the calculating hedonism, the easy affability that belied the inner selfishness, the game sport whose willingness to go along with his wacky partner onstage was utterly at odds with the taciturn midwestern reserve that marked him when the arc lights dimmed. For four decades, he would project as much dignity and self-assurance as he ever did sauce or testosterone or jaundice.

The public loved him and it loved his partner and it loved the two of them together. Even when he divorced Betty and married Jeannie Biegger, a gorgeous-blonde beauty queen from Miami, he couldn't tarnish the golden glow of Martin and Lewis.

It took the two of them to do that.

By 1954, they weren't such good pals anymore. Jerry was styling himself a creator of artful comic narratives in a variety of media. He sought publicity and creative control—something, ultimately, other than partnership—and he couldn't stand to sit beside his pool for more than a few hours without setting himself to some sort of project.

Dean didn't want to be worked to death when they were doing so well; he mocked Jerry's aspirations as "Chaplin shit" and was less and less concerned with keeping a happy public face on their relationship. After a few well-publicized snubbings, Jerry grew haughty enough to shove Dean, and Dean shoved back—harder, and with no little relish. It got ugly, and by July 1956, on the Copacabana stage that was their first great showcase, they played their last gig together.

Everyone in show business knew that Jerry would do great, but most predicted a dire future for Dean. And when he debuted as a single, it was disastrous. His first picture, *Ten Thousand Bedrooms,* was numbered for years among the great movie turkeys of all time. Cynics were predicting he'd be out of the business altogether within months.

Like Frank, though, he was rescued by fate in the form of a new singing persona and a World War II movie. Actually, Dean didn't so much change his voice as what he did with it. Always languid, he became frankly indifferent; without Jerry around to interrupt his singing, he began to act the drunk and interrupt himself. It suited him; audiences loved it.

Another break: In 1957, his agents got him cast in a key role in the screen version of Irwin Shaw's best-selling novel, *The Young Lions.* Playing a roguish Broadway singer miscast as a G.I., Dean held his own against Montgomery Clift and Marlon Brando and was suddenly a hot commodity once again.

He might have drifted into anything, but he never really got the chance to go it purely alone; probably he didn't want it; he might have even been scared. Within two years of splitting with Jerry, he found himself teamed, unofficially but semipermanently, with Frank, starting with a trip to some sleepy town in the Midwest.

*

Of course, Frank knew that Dean would be a perfect choice for the role of Bama Dillert, a honey-drippin' card shark in the upcoming film *Some Came Running*. A gambler, roué, souse, and cynic with a southern accent just like the one Dean sported as a bit of shtick, he was capable of being played right by no other actor in the world. If it took till mid-'58 for Frank to offer Dean the role, the likely reason is that he was waiting to see how *The Young Lions* turned out.

It turned out fine; the role was Dean's.

Like Frank's career-saver, *From Here to Eternity*, *Some Came Running* was based on a big fat book by James Jones (even at twelve hundred pages, it had been cut in half by editors at Scribner's). Frank was cast as Dave Hirsch, an ex-G.I. with a literary bent who drunkenly wanders back to his small Indiana hometown, where he does battle with his respectable older brother, falls for a priggish schoolmarm, and is in turn fallen for by a big-city floozy who has floated into town in his wake. MGM production head Sol Siegel had bought the book for $200,000 before it was published, then assigned it to in-house auteur Vincente Minnelli, who'd almost entirely abandoned the gaiety of his classic musicals for broody, atmospheric melodrama. The $2-million production (not counting Frank's $400,000 guarantee against a piece of the gross) would be shot throughout the late summer and fall of 1958, with eighteen working days scheduled for location in Madison, Indiana, population 10,500, a wee bit of Americana just across the Ohio River from Kentucky, where mob-run casinos such as the plush Beverly Hills Club flourished.

Dean signed on to play Bama, an itinerant gambler who befriends Hirsch, and the cast was rounded out with Arthur Kennedy as the banker, Martha Hyer as the prig, and Shirley MacLaine as the floozy ("the pig," as Bama calls her), Ginny Moorhead. MacLaine knew Dean from having worked with him and Jerry on *Artists and Models*, her second film, three years earlier; she'd met Frank soon after on the set of *Around the World in 80 Days*—his one-shot in that dull parade of cameos came when she popped into a Barbary Coast saloon where he was playing the piano.

MacLaine was a kid when she showed up in Madison—just twenty-four, with a two-year-old daughter and a husband who spent most of his time on business in Tokyo. She'd worked in Hollywood for three years, but nothing in her green, bubbly life prepared her for the world in which Frank and Dean lived. For two weeks in Indiana, she got a glimpse of the strange, intoxicating lives to which powerful men entitled themselves.

For starters, each of them made an abortive visit to her hotel room, trotting over for a quickie from the house they'd rented next door. Rebuffed but nevertheless taken with her spunk, they adopted her as a mascot—the only woman who'd be allowed to enter their confidence without sexual payment in return. They dragged her along when they went on trips to gambling joints near Cincinnati; she was allowed to sit with them while they gussied themselves up for an evening's leisure. "Their white shirts were crisp and new," she recalled, "the ties well chosen, the suits expensive and impeccably tailored. . . . Their shoes were uncommonly polished and I was certain their socks didn't smell. Underneath it all, I sense their underwear was as white and fresh as soft, newly fallen snow."

There was nothing so pristine, though, about some of the people they hosted on the set. Frank didn't get to the Midwest too often, and his presence there occasioned visits from the region's hoods—Sam Giancana, top man of the Chicago Outfit, among them. If the sterilized grace of Frank and Dean descending a hotel staircase in fedoras hadn't convinced MacLaine that they were privy to things she'd never even imagined, then a few days around Giancana did the trick. He cheated her in meaningless games of gin and pulled a real .38

out of his jacket when she menaced him with a water pistol. "I knew he was a hood of some kind," MacLaine recalled, "but at that point it was all so theatrically dangerous and amusing to me."

Less amusing was the behavior of her costars around Madison and on the set. MacLaine had been bred with southern manners and was a fresh enough actress to still defer to her directors. Frank and Dean didn't particularly care whom they offended. They were, naturally, besieged by local gawkers throughout their stay, and they treated them with beastly crudeness. Riding the film company bus to and from work, Frank would sit by the window and disparage the fans who lined up outside for a glimpse of celebrity flesh; smiling and waving, he'd mutter deprecations under his breath: "Hello there, hillbilly!" "Drop dead, jerk!" "Hey, where'd you get that big fat behind?" Seized by hunger early one morning, he woke a hotel manager demanding a meal; the frazzled man arrived with food and beer, only to find himself in a shouting match with Frank that devolved into a fistfight—which Dean complained blocked his view of an old movie on TV.

On the set, Frank was just as bearish, walking around between takes grousing repeatedly, "Let's blow this joint." Many evenings, he'd go to such lengths to amuse himself in the small town that he was in no shape—or mood—to work the next morning. "His eyes would be like two urine spots in the snow," said one crew member, "and when I saw his hangover look I would keep walking."

Minnelli, of course, didn't have that luxury. A notorious perfectionist, he continually rankled the cast with requests for additional takes of scenes that Frank felt had already been filmed satisfactorily. Dean and Frank began to mock Minnelli's fussiness, his pursed lips, his aesthetic ambitions.

Not long into the production, with the town dressed up for the film's climactic carnival scene, Minnelli was taking, Frank thought, an inordinate amount of time setting up a shot. The director circled around the camera several times, sizing up various angles; he closed his eyes and fell into deep concentration; around him, extras made merry with the free rides and snacks, and his principal actors stood waiting for direction. MacLaine could feel Frank tightening up. Finally, Minnelli came to a solution to whatever was troubling him. He turned to his crew: "Move the Ferris wheel!"

That did it. Frank left the set, left the town, left the whole state. They found him at home in L.A., adamant that he would put up with not one whit more of artsy-fartsy bullshit. Sol Siegel, the budget ticking away, made Minnelli promise to compromise the purity of his vision for the sake of getting the damn film made.

They finally did it—only 10 percent over budget. When the picture finally came out, to so-so reviews and big box office, MacLaine got her first Academy Award nomination (Minnelli, ironically, swept the Oscars with his other film of the year, *Gigi*), and Frank walked away with at least a half million.

But Dean might've made out best of all: Not only did he prove that *The Young Lions* was no fluke, that he really could pull off a dramatic part, but he had a new best-friendship, sealed in booze, broads, gambling, and Italian food. *Some Came Running* premiered in January 1959; that same month, Frank served as conductor for Dean's album *Sleep Warm*, and the two of them screwed around together for the first time on the stage at the Sands. It was almost like the Martin and Lewis days all over again.

If Frank and Dean shared a natural kinship, it was also a curious one. Their talents were so disparate: Frank manly and passionate and artistic; Dean flippant and lazy, and, well, a little fruity.

Take Bama: Amid all this hot-blooded James Jones hooey, with Frank boozing and writing and chasing tail and being chased by it, there's Dean listlessly bridging a deck of cards in his hands, talking in a hokey cornpone accent, fussing about his wardrobe, tsking at the world and the way Frank's character reacts to it. Sure he gets a couple of broads as the thing unfolds, but they're nonentities compared to the full-blooded chicks Frank's involved with; even though Bama's girls are made to seem promiscuous, you don't imagine that he actually screws them—and certainly not that he does any of the hard work if he does.

Same with *Sleep Warm*. Dean always did queerer material than Frank in the studio: novelty records, Italian-language numbers, country-western songs. Dean's approach was always practically a lampoon, but it was a lampoon of masculinity and the troubadour pretensions of performers like Frank as much as it was of showbiz and the fact that he was actually getting paid so much to do something so easy.

Listen to the effeminate little spin he gives his sibilants on numbers like "All I Do Is Dream of You" and "Sleepytime Gal." Jerry liked to do all that nance shit onstage—the critics gave him hell for it—but Dean put it to another use: He wasn't parodying a gay man, he was parodying a *straight* man. He sounded at least as contemptuous of his beloved as solicitous.

It was a con: Sicilian Frank strove and suffered and made art; Abruzzese Dean chuckled a little bit to himself and did what he had to do to keep the whole shuck-and-jive afloat. If Frank wanted to conduct, produce movies, and host big events, he just had to tell Dean when and where and he'd be there—so long as he wasn't expected to bring anything with him or stick around after to clean up.

He had had Jerry already. If Frank wanted him as a brother, fine, but it would be on Dean's terms.

Sonny boy

For someone who would take orders, Frank could always count on Sammy.

Sammy Davis Jr. was the kind of guy about whom God seemed not to have been able to make up his mind. On the face of things, by his own reckoning, he had more strikes against him than you could count—he was short, maimed, ugly, black, Jewish, gaudy, uneducated. But he could do *anything:* song, dance, pantomime, impressions, jokes, and even, in a manner of speaking, drama. He overcame so much that his merely being there among them was an epochal triumph: He was the Jackie Robinson of showbiz.

And yet when he saw himself in a mirror he was disgusted: "I gotta get *bigger,*" he'd implore himself. "I gotta get *better.*"

He was so used to being excluded that he was willing to kill himself with work to be let in. He'd suffer all manner of indignities: Frank's clumsy racial jokes; years of Jim Crow treatment in theaters, hotels, and restaurants; the nigger-baiting of high-rolling southerners in Vegas casinos; a patently bogus marriage to a black dancer intended to quiet journalists about his taste for white girls; the explicit disdain of mobsters and other bosses. But he kept at it, convinced that sheer will and talent would stop the world saying no.

Who was he trying to impress? His mother, a showgirl, was a cipher in his life, a ghost whose approval he never seems to have missed; his father, a small-time song-and-dance man, he eclipsed when still a boy. All the know-it-alls, naysayers, and bigots who'd ever discouraged him he'd silenced with sheer talent, guts, and drive. The gods themselves nodded with pleasure upon him: "This kid's the greatest entertainer," declared Groucho Marx at Hollywood's Jewish mecca of leisure, the Hillcrest Country Club, one afternoon, "and this goes for you, too, Jolson" (to which Jolie merely responded with a smile). He was not only the first black man through the door but one of the all-time greats, regardless of origin.

Yet he felt hollow: All the money and fame and sex and sycophants in the world still couldn't squelch the nagging inner sense that he was a *nothing*—and that if he could only rouse a little more out of himself, he could finally be a *something*. He sang that he was "133 pounds of confidence," that he was "Gonna Build a Mountain," that he had "a lot of livin' to do," and he sounded like he meant it. But each garish boast gave off a vibe of whistling past a graveyard; in his heart of hearts, he could never vanquish the sense that all the work he'd done to get so far could be snuffed out by a mere wave of Fate's lordly white hand.

Sammy was the baby of the Rat Pack, born four days before Frank's tenth birthday, and that banal fact—more than race, size, taste, line of work, personal habits, common friends, political leanings, money, sex, or power—was the single governing factor in their relationship. Frank was always the big brother allowing the kid, Sammy, to hang out with the older guys; Sammy was always the precocious little brat tugging feverishly at his idol's sleeve. Neither had actual siblings, but they filled those roles for each other: Frank needed to be the patron as much as Sammy needed to be patronized. Everything about their mutual solicitude, affection, and trust, every aspect of their difference and of their symbiosis, lay in germ form in the simple age difference between them.

Uniquely among his peers in Frank's circle, Sammy was a showbiz brat. His mom, Puerto Rican-born Elvera "Baby" Sanchez, was so committed to her career as a chorus girl that she worked until two weeks before her child arrived; as soon as she was able to return to the stage, she left the kid with relatives in Brooklyn and hit the road along with Sammy Sr., who was the lead male dancer in Will Mastin's vaudeville act.

After that, there was barely a whiff of Elvera in her son's life. She and Big Sam split for good not long after their son was born, which might have made Sammy's story another "deprived baby beats the world to win his mama's love" yarn but for the fact that Big Sam and Mastin, with the approval of Sammy's extremely protective grandma, Rosa Davis, took the boy on the road with them from the time he was three and provided him with as big and loving a family as most children ever have. Chorus girls, singers, comics, and musicians were his society; dressing rooms, boarding-houses, and buses his playgrounds. He never attended so much as a day of kindergarten in his life—Big Sam and Mastin hid him from child welfare authorities by gluing whiskers on him and billing him as a midget—but he was steeped in a showbiz curriculum virtually from birth.

In later years, Sammy looked back on his tender introduction to showbiz as an idyll, but it was a terrifically difficult era. The Chitlin Circuit, as the route of black vaudeville and burlesque houses was known, never paid what the white theaters did; moreover, Sammy broke in when all forms of live entertainment were taking a hit from talking movies, radio, and recorded music. Scuttling back and forth between sporadic, low-paying jobs, Big Sam and Mastin frequently went without food so that their little protégé might not go hungry—and even then his supper might consist of a mustard sandwich and a glass of water. With grim regularity, they all returned to Harlem to sit waiting for new offers of work, which became even less steady with the advent of the Depression.

This was hell for Mastin, by all accounts a decent, intelligent, gifted man who'd risen to a position of respect within the narrow world of black showbiz. Although he never crossed over to broad white appeal, Mastin was a success, able to keep dozens of people on the road with him throughout the twenties. When he had to dissolve his traveling show to a two-man act featuring just himself and Big Sam, he surely felt as though he'd shrunk in the world; trouper that he was, though, he never let on, least of all to Sammy, that there was anything small about the small time.

And Sammy would've noticed if he had, because he was watching. He spent his early years studying acts from the wings, then imitating what he'd seen for the backstage entertainment of his makeshift family. He was a natural, and Mastin and Big Sam quickly realized it would give the show a lift if they put the little ham onstage. They slathered him in blackface and sat him in a prima donna's lap while she sang "Sonny Boy," the Al Jolson hit; mugging and mimicking during her sober reading of the song, Sammy brought down the house.

In time, he would master little comic bits, dance steps, vocal impressions, and songs of his own, and his skills grew along with his exposure. From special billing—"Will Mastin's Gang featuring Little Sammy"—he became a full-fledged part of the act, the Will Mastin Trio, with all three sharing equally in the profits. They were flash dancers: Cat-quick and athletic, they could do time steps together or improvise wild solos, all energy, all arms, legs, and deferential smiles; for six or eight minutes a night, they could wring an audience limp with their sheer gutty bravado.

It was as a member of the trio that Sammy found himself in Detroit in the dog days of 1941, a substitute opening act for the Tommy Dorsey band. As he wandered backstage marveling at the size of Dorsey's operation, Sammy was offered a handshake by a skinny white guy in his twenties: "Hiya. My name's Frank. I sing with Dorsey."

"That might sound like nothing much," Sammy recalled later, "but the average top vocalist in those days wouldn't give the time of day to a Negro supporting act." And Frank did more: For the next few nights, until the regular opening act returned, he would sit with Sammy in his dressing room shooting the breeze, talking about the show life. The kid couldn't believe his luck.

But if meeting Sinatra was a glimpse of a raceless Eden, the next few years were a crushing racist hell. Sammy was drafted into an army that was a cesspool of bigotry. He felt it the moment he arrived in Cheyenne, Wyoming, for basic training.

"Excuse me, buddy," he asked a white private he came across while trying to find his way around. "Can you tell me where 202 is?"

"Two buildings down. And I'm not your buddy, you black bastard!"

It was a slap in the face, but it was only the beginning. For two years, Sammy was denigrated, demeaned, and, truly, tortured. He was segregated by a corporal who created a no-man's-land between his bed and those of white soldiers. His expensive chronograph watch (a going-away gift from Mastin and Big Sam) was ground into useless pieces under a bigot's boot. He was nearly tricked into drinking a bottle of urine offered to him as a conciliatory beer; his tormentors reacted to his refusal to imbibe it by pouring it on him. He was lured to an out-of-the-way building and held against his will while

"Coon" and "I'm a Nigger" were inscribed on his face and chest with white paint.

And there were the beatings. "I had been drafted into the army to fight," he remembered, "and I did." He was goaded frequently into using his fists as a means of settling the score with the pigs who abused him, breaking his nose twice, scoring his knuckles with cuts.

Only when he was asked by an officer to take part in a show for the troops could he lift his spirit above the dreadful situation. At first, he didn't want to expose himself on a stage and entertain the very people who'd been mistreating him, but he couldn't resist the temptation to perform. George M. Cohan Jr. was also stationed in Cheyenne and convinced Sammy to help him create a touring production that would visit a number of military installations. Sammy threw himself into the work with a kind of violence, seeking release, vindication, and even revenge by being the best song-and-dance man anyone had ever seen.

"My talent was the weapon," he recalled, "the power, the way for me to fight." For the last eight months of his service time, the show was continually on the road, far from his most virulent antagonists. It kept him sane, maybe even alive.

But when he got out, his eyes having been opened to his situation as a black man with grand aspirations in America, he found himself increasingly crushed by the gap between his ambitions and his opportunities. He was befriended by Mickey Rooney, who, though still one of the hottest stars in Hollywood, was unable to get him movie work. He winced at the ebonic clichés employed by performers on the Chitlin Circuit. In reaction, he adopted a stage manner so patently artificial that he sounded, in his own words, like "a colored Laurence Olivier." Even the tone-deaf Jerry Lewis was to encourage him to forgo his "with your kind permission we would now like to indulge" routine, but Sammy only did so after, typically, listening for several self-lacerating hours to tape recordings of his own inflated persiflage. And he reacted with despair and self-loathing whenever he was confronted with the insidious—and frequently overt—limits placed upon him in the Jim Crow era.

Nowhere were these barriers more painfully imposed than in Las Vegas, where the Will Mastin Trio debuted in 1944. Vegas was still a cowboy town, "the Mississippi of the West," as blacks unfortunate enough to live there called it. The black population, whose members swelled the ranks of janitors, porters, and maids at the emerging hotel-casinos on the Los Angeles Highway (which had yet to be christened the Strip), was restricted to living, eating, shopping, and gambling in a downtrodden district known as Westside—a Tobacco Road of unpaved streets bereft of even wooden sidewalks, lined by shacks that lacked fire service, telephones, and, in many cases, electricity and indoor plumbing.

Sammy ought to have been used to segregation. The trio arrived in Vegas not long after a stint in Spokane, where they were forced, for lack of a black rooming house, to sleep in their dressing room. But Vegas galled him more than anything he'd experienced before, in part because of the appalling contrast between the glamour of the Last Frontier hotel and the shack in which he was forced to spend all of his offstage time, and in part because the gaiety and glitz of the casino—which he wasn't allowed to walk through or even *see*—had an almost visceral allure for him.

As in the past, the only time he ever felt lifted out of himself and his miserable situation was onstage—"for 20 minutes, twice a night, our skin had no color." As in the past, he fought off his frustrations and the indignities of racism with ferocious performances—"I was vibrating with energy and I couldn't wait to get on the stage. I worked with the strength of 10 men." But never, as he dreamed might happen, did a casino manager or owner grow so enamored of his performance that he broke the color line by offering him a drink and a chance to try his luck at the tables.

And so it went. He forced himself higher and higher in the ranks of showbiz, garnering accolades, cutting records, standing out a bit more from Big Sam and Mastin with each performance, getting paid a little better with each gig. At the same time, he was hustled by cops to the backs of movie theaters, snubbed at the doors of the Copacabana and Lindy's, barred even from men's rooms in some of the theaters he packed with paying customers. If he grew to hate himself in some twisted fashion, he could hardly be blamed.

But repeatedly he found in his corner that skinny guy he'd met in Detroit. When Sammy was in the army, Frank had become a monster star, and when he was discharged and caught up with Mastin and Big Sam in Los Angeles, he made his way over to NBC studios in Hollywood, resplendent in his dress uniform, to watch Sinatra perform his weekly stint on *Your Hit Parade*. After the show, he waited out back with the bobby-soxers and autograph hounds and sheepishly offered Sinatra a piece of paper to sign.

"Didn't you work with your old man and another guy?" Frank asked, and he invited him to the next few shows, letting Sammy drink in rehearsals and backstage ambiance until another gig dragged the Mastin Trio back onto the road.

Two years later, Frank insisted that Sidney Piermont, manager of New York's Capitol Theater, book the Mastins as his opening act at $1,250 a week—a sum that staggered Mastin and Big Sam. Sinatra never told Sammy that he was behind the act's being hired—Piermont had wanted the Nicholas Brothers and then gagged at the price Sinatra wanted to pay Mastin—but in every other respect he treated Sammy like a peer throughout the engagement. They parted bosom pals: "Remember," Frank told Sammy as he left for his next booking—and this was his most profound gesture of friendship—"if anybody hits you, let me know."

But in the early fifties, no one, it seemed, wanted to hit Sammy. He was the quickest-rising star in nightclubs and theaters, particularly among the New York and L.A. cognoscenti. In 1951, the Will Mastin Trio opened at Ciro's, the hot Sunset Strip nightclub. The room was packed with Hollywood royalty, and Sammy and Company couldn't do enough. Dancing, singing, little comic bits, everything was a hit, nothing more so than Sammy's impersonations of such white stars as Jimmy Cagney, Cary Grant, and Humphrey Bogart. The same good fortune followed at an engagement at the Copacabana, the dream club of Sammy's youth, some months later. He was on the map to stay.

There was nevertheless a feeling of vertigo to it all. Although all the right people came to his shows, although he was welcome in the homes of Hollywood's crown royalty, he sensed a distance between himself and the fellow to whom all this good fortune fell, an inner gap separating the real man from the personality he'd become. He became famous for his tight pants, his extravagant spending, his largesse, his energy. But he'd also become infamous, in the tabloid press, as a consort—often only rumored—of white actresses, and the black press could be cutting in their comments about his seeming disregard for his race.

He was calculating and savvy enough to know that all publicity was good publicity—he was thrilled that his name made for hot ink—but he was wounded by the unfairness at the root of it. His race excluded him from a number of opportunities, so he created his own success; his success lifted him out of his race and made him a star simply because of his sheer talent; yet his talent could never entirely erase his race and, in fact, made him more visible as a black man and thus more open to injustice and prejudice. He walked a perilous line between one self, the black man who could be snubbed at the doors of exclusive New York nightclubs, and another self, the showbiz whirligig whom everybody wanted a piece of. He couldn't avoid being "Sammy Davis Jr.," even when "Sammy Davis Jr." was the butt of jokes, gossip, and irrational hate.

Success, money, career offers, work—all this kept the doubts at bay for some of the time, but he was still profoundly susceptible to anxiety about his hold on his life. He would read reviews and compare them to previous notices from the same critics; he would call up clubs he was playing and ask, his voice disguised, if it was still possible to get a table for that evening's performance, collapsing in secret gratitude at the news that his shows were sold out. He was such a lost, addled soul that he began seeking answers in, of all places, Judaism, the religion of so many of the showbiz uncles who'd taken him so readily under their wings. He knew he could never escape who he was, but he kept searching for ways to somehow, maybe, evolve out of it.

Little by little, barriers fell as to the sheer force of his talent. In 1954, the Mastin Trio was invited not only to play the Frontier but to stay there, to eat, gamble, and socialize among the white customers and make a whopping $7,500 a week besides. Sammy would have to commute back and forth to L.A., where he was doing some record work, but it was a dream gig and they leapt at it. You simply couldn't do any better than that.

Which was why it was so tragic, the car crash. Driving his Cadillac convertible to Los Angeles late on the night of November 19, 1954, listening to his own hit record "Hey There" on the radio, Sammy crossed into oncoming traffic in order to avoid a car that was making a U-turn right there in front of him on the highway. In the ensuing collision, his head hit the steering wheel. A stylized cone of chrome sticking out of the center of it like a battering ram put out his left eye.

His thoughts upon seeing his own mangled face in a piece of broken mirror as rescuers came to fetch him? "They're going to hate me again."

He was rushed to a hospital near Palm Springs, and Hollywood rushed to his side. Tony Curtis and Janet Leigh waited on him as he was in surgery; Frank visited constantly, as did a steady parade of showbiz lights; Jeff Chandler took the stage in his stead in Las Vegas—and nobody complained.

And when he came back, at Ciro's, dancing and singing and gagging with maybe even more energy than before, not to mention a rakish eye patch, the world clapped its hands raw and cried with affection for him. The accident turned out to be the thing that put him over the top; he could do it all, even beat death. It was like Frank dying on-screen in *From Here to Eternity:* It made him forever more.

An entire Broadway show, *Mr. Wonderful,* was built around him. There was a rags-to-riches story to it, and Chita Rivera and Jack Carter had parts, but the point of it was Sammy's nightclub-style performance in the second act, a partially scripted, partially free-form extravaganza of the sort that Al Jolson used to deliver when he was still in the legitimate theater. Mastin and Big Sam were on the stage with him, but it was Sammy's name on the marquee. He did benefits, TV spots, radio appearances; he partied every night in restaurants and clubs and later in his hotel suite; he became a notorious tomcat on the prowl.

Soon enough, he was so big that the movies came calling. He played Sportin' Life in Otto Preminger's *Porgy and Bess,* and, in a great legends-of-Hollywood yarn, stunned producer Samuel Goldwyn into silence by declaring that he refused to work on Yom Kippur. "Directors I can fight," Goldwyn lamented. "Fires on the set I can fight. Writers, even actors I can fight. But a Jewish colored fellow? This I can't fight!"

A Jewish colored fellow: a whirling dervish: an up-and-coming superstar: just as he'd always dreamed.

America's guest

Poor Peter.

Try this for a curse: You have looks, breeding, savoir faire, but no real talent other than the ability to deploy your mien to ingratiate yourself to the world; nevertheless, fate rewards you with sex, money, fame, station; you spend a decade or two floating atop a gigantic bubble; you can do no wrong; then it all goes slowly sour; a few missteps, two or three vicious body blows, innumerable little jabs and lacerations, and one day you wake up in your own shit, bankrupt, dazed, strung-out, a laughing-stock, alone—Whatever Happened To *You?*

You wouldn't wish it on a dog, but it's all true. Fortune granted Peter Lawford more for less than anyone ever dared hope, then reneged with such perverse violence that even his most envious enemies took pity on him.

And it all started with such promise. Indeed, in a queer way, Peter Lawford was a sparkling gem in the crown of English glory. Scion of two distinguished military lines, he toured the world as a young boy, conquered Hollywood as a teen, and grafted himself onto America's royal family as an adult. Handsome, poised, and, in a fashion, deft, he was a perfect figure, to American eyes, of British sophistication. You look at Peter Lawford in 1959, and you're looking at quite possibly the most fortunate man who'd ever lived.

Which makes a nice twist on this most full-of-twists life. Because on the face of things, there wasn't a chance in hell that the maimed bastard son of Lieutenant General Sir Sydney Lawford and May Somerville Bunny would ever get *anywhere*, under any circumstances. A one-in-a-million combination of traits, gifts, habits, predilections, biases, and flaws made and broke Peter—a curse that only May Lawford could have concocted.

Lady Lawford, as she insisted on being addressed with technical correctness but technical presumption as well, was more than just some daft embodiment of Victorian eccentricities and perversions—though she never failed to display such traits in excess. She was a genuinely disturbed woman whose contradictions, pretensions, and megalomania consumed her and those around her—chief of all, of course, her only child.

That May Lawford ever even *had* a child should be reckoned something of a miracle. In her own words (captured frighteningly in her illiterate memoir, *Bitch!*), she was repulsed by "that horrible, messy, unsanitary thing that all husbands expect from their wives." Her own mother, although an otherwise worldly woman, and her father, a physician in the Royal Army, never told her the facts of life, and her first husband, another military surgeon, Harry Cooper, so respected his teenage fiancée's chastity that he never importuned upon her for so much as a kiss before they wed.

Their wedding night devolved, as might be expected, into a horror show of fright, tears, frustration, anger, Harry finally inducing May with biblical verses about spousal obedience. From this merry start, the marriage went downhill, with sex as the chief sticking point. May grudgingly submitted once a month, and then only lay passively. Cooper endured six months of celibacy until he was posted to India; May didn't join him. Alone in London, secure in the cloak of marriage, May passed her time in amateur theatricals and a bustling social life. (Where she had mortal aversions to actual physical intimacy, she had none whatever to open flirting.) Cooper received strange reports of May's behavior and assumed the worst. One night, two and a half years after the wedding, the rejection, rumors, guilt, and grief overwhelmed him: He blew his brains out in his office with a pistol.

Strangely disassociating herself from this ghastly event, May met and was courted by another military surgeon, Ernest Aylen, and married him within two years of Cooper's death. Once again, the fruits promised by May's quite modern behavior proved illusory when her wedding night arrived. Aylen, however, was made of tougher stuff than Cooper; his marriage became a kind of swap meet, with sex a form of currency. Once a month, May would allow herself to be "mauled," but only when rewarded prior to the act with jewelry. "I felt like a tart," she confessed, "a French tart!"

She didn't act the part well: In his priapic despair, Aylen lashed out at her, "I'd rather be in bed with a dead policeman!" Claiming his wife's two favorite bits of pillow talk were "Don't!" and "Hurry up!," the wretched doctor cried, "It's a good thing you don't have to make your living off of sex; you'd starve to death."

After nearly two poisonous decades and many separations, the two agreed at last to live apart. As before, separation from her husband afforded May the opportunity to find another. This time she set her sights higher than the army hospital, however. She became acquainted with her husband's commanding officer, Sydney Lawford, a dashing hero of the war himself mired in an unhappy union.

He was a hell of a catch. "Swanky Syd," as fellow soldiers

branded him in recognition of his sartorial dash, had been knighted for his legendary valor in the fight against the kaiser. His men adored him; women were invariably taken with his combination of physical charm and high rank.

May, though still married to a junior officer in his charge, became a favorite of the general's, and she reciprocated the attention, if, as usual, a bit grudgingly. When, two years into her separation, she found herself a guest at his sister's country estate, she allowed him to escort her to her bedroom after dinner; he followed her inside; "Oh, no, not this again," she thought to herself, but this fish was too big not to reel in over such a qualm. She granted the general her meager favors, and, at age thirty-eight, conceived their only child with their very first intimate act.

When May's pregnancy became apparent, she importuned upon Aylen to do the noble thing; although the baby wasn't his, he agreed to stay married to her until it was born, granting it the generous gift of his name. The general, too, convinced his spouse to play along for decorum's sake. But when the baby, christened Peter, was born in September 1923, there was no saving either marriage: Divorce petitions, filed within days of the birth's being registered, were granted within a year; one week after that, May and the general were wed.

It may have seemed a coup on paper, but May's lot was decidedly mixed. The scandal surrounding Peter's birth drove the Lawfords from the country; they were to live in France, India, the South Pacific, Hawaii, Florida, and California for the rest of their days, maintaining, frequently enough, a sufficiently high standard of living to seem gay globe-trotters, but, in reality, terrified to return home to the hisses of English scandalmongers.

The general, like Cooper and Aylen before him, expected sexual compliance from his wife, but May hit upon an ingenious ruse to keep him at bay, responding to his overtures by "slipping to the kitchen and getting uncooked meat which I rubbed against my nightdress. I was *always* having my period!" Time was on her side: The general was fifty-nine when they married and soon lost his interest in his wife's body. "I never," May boasted, "had sex with him after Peter was three."

Ah, yes, of course, Peter, the device by which May had landed the general but a horrid encumbrance nevertheless. May said she'd nearly taken her first husband's way out during childbirth, putting a revolver in her mouth in response to the pains of labor. Delivered of her child, she suffered the indignities of his infancy: "I can't stand babies," she groused. "They run at both ends; they smell of sour milk and urine."

Peter was, whenever possible, fobbed off on nurses and servants. And, of course, being a child of May's, he was raised with a combination of notions both indulgent and bizarre. "Peter wasn't brought up, he was dragged up," said a sympathetic cousin—and the phrase was keenly apt. Like other Englishwomen of her era, May dressed her boy as a girl, but she persisted in the habit, at least in private, until Peter was nearly in his teens. She allowed him to sleep in his parents' bed until he'd nearly hit puberty and instilled in him a fanatical discipline for cleanliness (a fussiness also shared by Frank Sinatra): He bathed and gargled at least twice every day. And May had ideas about diet, too. Peter was allowed only a strict regimen of fruits, vegetables, whole-wheat bread, and, rarely, meat, with sweets of any sort taboo.

Peter was never formally schooled and spoke only broken English for much of his childhood (French was, in a way, his native tongue); he was probably some sort of dyslexic, but he had to diagnose his problem—and treat it—on his own. Tutelage in nonscholastic matters, unfortunately, was provided him by others: At nine, he became a target of pedophiles, both male and female—a horror that lasted through his teens.

May knew nothing of Peter's tortures, concerning herself instead with cultivating his desire to playact and perform. A perfect Little Lord Fauntleroy, Peter charmed crowned royals, ships' captains, film directors, and journalists alike with his impeccable manners and precocity. At eight, he played a part in *Poor Old Bill,* an English kiddie film. He acquitted himself so well that he surely would've received more offers of work had not the general put his foot down—"My son a common jester with cap and bells, dancing and prancing in front of people!"—and hied the family off on an extended sojourn to India and the South Pacific.

It would be seven years before Peter had another chance to act, and then only because of a freak accident that maimed and nearly crippled him. Returning to his parents' French Riviera home after a game of tennis, he shattered a window-pane and sliced his right arm straight through to the bone. The first doctor to examine the arm declared it unsalvageable. Counseled to amputate, May responded with aplomb—"Fuck off, doctor!"—and found a physician willing to stitch Peter's muscles back together. The arm was saved. To combat the lingering pain and stiffness, however, the Lawfords were advised to relocate Peter to a dry climate—Los Angeles, say. Although the arm would never fully heal (in its natural state of relaxation, Peter's right hand was clawlike), it gave him, perversely, his ticket to success.

He found bit parts right away, but it would take five more years of on-again, off-again work before Peter was granted a full contract by MGM. But when the deal was done, it was as near as a twenty-year-old could imagine to a golden ticket from God Almighty.

May and the general thrived as well, becoming staples of the British expatriate community in Los Angeles and earning a reputation as grand old eccentrics among the Hollywood crowd: Frank once asked May about her son, and she responded in what she thought was perfect Hollywoodese —"Peter? That schmuck!"—bringing him to his knees with laughter.

Aside from affording May a society in which she could act the grande dame, Hollywood gave Peter the opportunity to chase every famous skirt in the world: Lana Turner, Rita Hayworth, Anne Baxter, Judy Garland, June Allyson, Ava Gardner . . . you name her. His appetites weren't necessarily orthodox: He had chances, for instance, to bed both Elizabeth Taylor and Marilyn Monroe, but refused the former because she had what he considered "fat thighs" and the latter because her living room was dotted with chihuahua poop when he rendezvoused with her. But he was always being floated in the gossip pages as some pretty young thing's fiancé, and he was swain enough to travel with sexual gear—towels, blankets, mouthwash, changes of clothes—in his car.

Despite this impressive record of cocksmanship, though, he was constantly plagued by rumors of homosexuality. He was chummy with Van Johnson and Keenan Wynn, and scuttlebutt put all three of them in bed together with Wynn's wife, Evie (who, in fact, married Johnson within hours of getting a divorce from Wynn). Later on, stories circulated about trysts with other young actors, of loitering in notorious public men's rooms, of all-boy parties in Hawaii, of Peter's being "the screaming faggot of State Beach." Most insidiously, May Lawford responded to her son's growing apart from her by walking into Louis B. Mayer's office and telling the prudish studio chief that Peter was a homosexual, a charge that Peter was forced to refute by soliciting the explicit testimony of Lana Turner; the canard drove a permanent wedge between him and his mother.

At MGM, Peter was little more than an English pretty boy,

but he had the good fortune of appearing on the scene just as Freddie Bartholomew's career was in decline. He played light romantic roles well, didn't shame himself out of the business when he essayed a bit of song and dance, could play gravely enough for small roles in serious drama: a good all-round B-movie lead, or nice support for an A production. He'd never make them forget Olivier, but he was a reliable asset for a studio at something like its height.

Despite his lack of professional distinction, Peter was a highly sought-after invitee, an especially glittering extra in the diadem of Hollywood nightlife; he became known as "America's guest," as much for his habit of showing up at every noteworthy party as for his reluctance to pick up a dinner tab.

There was, however, another social group with which Peter mingled and to whom he showed an especially generous and loyal side of his nature. Having been introduced to surfing as a young boy in Hawaii, Peter had a genuine love for beach life, and he spent all the time he could at the shore, catching waves, playing volleyball, and steeping himself in the lingo and rituals of beach bums—a cultish society whose vocabulary and attitudes would later be borrowed, in a fashion, by the Rat Pack. May hated the ne'er-do-well manner of this crowd—which, of course, attracted her son to it even more. Moreover, Peter relished mixing his surfing and acting cronies, watching the cultures clash with sophomoric delight.

As he neared his thirties and seemed stuck on a treadmill of light comedy and dull drama at MGM, as his genteel parasitism grew wearying, two life-altering events befell him. At eighty-seven, General Lawford died contentedly in his garden, so deeply rattling Peter that he initially refused to return from Hawaii and endure the funeral. Nine months later, he found himself engaged once again, seriously this time, to Patricia Kennedy, the strong-willed sixth child of

Irish-American Croesus and political dynast Joseph P. Kennedy.

Pat Kennedy was not a soft, obliging Hollywood gal. She was not as pretty as Peter's other fiancées, nor as sensual, but she was sharp-witted and independent and spunky. She didn't just throw open her legs for him because he was a handsome movie star who talked nice; she challenged his opinions and stood up for her own beliefs in a fashion that must've reminded Peter at least a little bit of May. Peter and Pat drew toward one another with surprising ease, not slaving over one another but respectful of their mutual independence. They were in their thirties and set in their ways; their relationship seemed as much one of siblings as of lovers.

Everyone knew what Pat saw in Peter, but many observers, especially Pat's very jaded father, Joe Kennedy, saw something suspicious in Peter's commitment to the relationship: Pat, though smart and vivacious, was no beauty, so Peter's affection tended to give off a mercenary vibe, at least at first blush; moreover, Joe was appalled at Peter's baroque Hollywood manner—the actor wore red socks to their first meeting—which seemed to lend credibility to the gossip he'd heard about Peter's catamitic proclivities.

To satisfy himself as to the first matter, he had Peter agree to a prenuptial pact that protected Pat's fortune (at the crucial moment, though, he forgave Peter from signing it, satisfied at his willingness to do so). As for the other, he importuned upon J. Edgar Hoover to open his infamous store of Official and Confidential files, which revealed that Peter was a well-known patron of Hollywood prostitutes. Rather than blanch at this evidence of Peter's moral character, lascivious Old Joe, who approved of hearty sexuality, even in potential sons-in-law, was delighted. The courtship climaxed in a lavish April 1954 wedding. Peter Lawford had graduated from waning pretty-boy actor to American royal—a hot number all of a sudden.

Frank, for one, took notice.

Through the dusty haze kicked up by his killing schedule, Frank had begun to set his sights on something higher than mere success as a singer, actor, or even mogul.

He had always seen himself as a representative man, a "little guy" whose ascent in the world was a vindication of his parents' immigration to America and his own combative resiliency in overcoming ethnic prejudice, loneliness, and, if you could call it that, economic privation. It wasn't enough for a guy like that to simply be busy at his job—Sammy, say, was at least as active. No, he had to have an impact on the world.

So in 1958, when it looked like this handsome young senator from Massachusetts, Jack Kennedy, would make a bid for the presidency, Frank decided to become part of it the way he did everything else he was passionate about: both hands, feetfirst, no looking back.

It was a sign of his own success. Into his forties, he had come to see himself as a man of station and discernment, a world-beater worthy of helping shape the future. But it was also a kind of inheritance: He had learned about politics by watching his mother work the ward system in Hoboken. Dolly Sinatra had the barest formal education and should've been kept from achieving any kind of power as a woman, an immigrant, as a midwife and abortionist. But she had spunk: She married a Sicilian against her Genoese parents' will; she dressed up like a man to watch her husband box in men-only joints; she exploited her fair features to pass herself off as Irish; she drank; and she talked like a stevedore, cursing vividly even when, in her dotage, attended constantly by a nun.

Such spirit distinguished her from other Italian mothers of her generation, but not so dramatically as did her political activities. In a corrupt little town run by an ironclad political machine, she won over the kingmakers by consistently turning out the vote and becoming the person to whom her neighbors came for jobs, food, and the sort of generic wheel-greasing and ass-saving they associated with Men of Respect. Dolly, of course, could never hold office, but she had the ears of men who could forgive crimes, erase debts, grant sinecures, and make life bearable or hellish as they chose. With her assistance, scores of Hoboken's Italians made their way toward the better life they'd come to America to enjoy.

Dolly didn't achieve her station simply by virtue of gumption. She worked hard at her glad-handing and ward-heeling, and she was even willing to broker her only child for political advantage; as his godfather, she chose none of his five uncles or other male relatives but Frank Garrick, an Irish newspaperman whose uncle was a police captain. The choice proved strangely fateful. In a mix-up that marked the child forever, the priest at the baptism named the boy Francis— for Garrick, whom he somehow came to believe was the father—instead of Martin, the name Dolly and Marty had chosen. Dolly, still recuperating from the delivery, wasn't at the ceremony to protest, while Marty stood there in characteristically mute impotence, saying nothing as his patrimony was diluted.

For all that she fussed over her boy, for all the clothes and spending cash and good words put in with people who could get him jobs and, later, gigs, Dolly nevertheless found it more exigent to leave him to the care of others and pursue her political work. Frank was fobbed off on relatives and neighbors. Politics, in effect, was the sibling from whose charms he could never divert his mother's eye; naturally, it came to seem to him an extension of family life, a way of linking up with his absent mother and creating a community around himself.

Plus it had perks. Dolly got Marty a well-paying job in the city fire department despite his inability to pass a written test, and she eventually got him promoted to captain—though few of his colleagues reckoned him worthy of the honor. Comfort and largesse flowed from political power, Frank could see, and when he was old enough to court it he did.

Frank's political instincts weren't entirely mercenary. He genuinely felt compassion for the underdog and championed civil rights as soon as he had a platform from which to be heard. In 1945, virtually the moment his career as a solo artist granted him a public profile, he spoke out against prejudice at a high school in Gary, Indiana, where black students had recently been admitted to a hostile reception from whites.

He also godfathered a curious little film project, *The House I Live In*, a ten-minute docudrama in which he preached a lesson in ethnic harmony to a mixed-race gang of street kids. "Look, fellas, religion makes no difference except to a Nazi or somebody as stupid," he explained. "My dad came from Italy, but I'm an American. Should I hate your father 'cause he came from Ireland or France or Russia? Wouldn't that make me a first-class fathead?" Then he launched into the title song, a syrupy ode to American equality, and ended by admonishing his audience of converted Schweitzers, "Don't let 'em make suckers out of you." (The film won Special Academy Awards for its creators, including Sinatra, director Mervyn LeRoy, and screenwriter Albert Maltz, a future member of the famous Hollywood Ten group of blacklisted authors.)

And Frank practiced what he preached. He was among the earliest and most visible proponents of civil rights in all of show business. He worked and traveled with black musicians, always insisting that they get treatment equal to that afforded him in restaurants and hotels, and he did what he could to give a boost to such acts as the Will Mastin Trio.

Frank's political liberalism even led him to a deliberate reprise of the accident that gave him his own name. His only son was always known as Frank Jr., but the kid was actually named Franklin Wayne Emmanuel Sinatra in tribute to, among others, his father's hero Franklin Roosevelt.

And he didn't merely communicate his convictions in symbols. On the night in 1944 that FDR beat Thomas Dewey, Frank, in New York for a series of concerts at the Waldorf-Astoria, celebrated with a bar crawl in the company of Orson Welles. The two decided to cap their gambols by razzing right-wing columnist Westbrook Pegler, also resident at the hotel. They rowdily pounded the door to Pegler's suite to no satisfactory response, then returned, discouraged, to their debauch.

Four years later, Frank won $25,000 on a bet that Harry Truman would be reelected. In 1952, Frank campaigned for Adlai Stevenson, and then again in 1956, when he sang the national anthem at the opening session of the Democratic National Convention in Chicago and stuck around to get a close-up look at the action. (He caused some of his own as well. After he sang "The Star-Spangled Banner," Frank was on his way offstage when he was grabbed by Speaker of the House Sam Rayburn, who asked him if he'd also be performing "The Yellow Rose of Texas." "Get your hands off the suit, creep," Sinatra replied.)

It was there that his eye was first caught by Jack Kennedy, then a dazzling, photogenic young senator with a pretty wife and a baby on the way. After Stevenson had secured the presidential nomination, he'd thrown the vice-presidential slot to the convention without naming a candidate of his preference; Kennedy, against his father's wishes, sought the spot and was locked in battle for it with Tennessee's Mafia-baiting senator, Estes Kefauver. Frank hung close to the

Kennedys as the convention progressed, impressed with the amount of money and degree of organization the family applied to the campaign. When Kefauver won the nomination, the Kennedys were briefly stunned.

Then Frank noticed Bobby, the senator's younger brother and campaign manager, telling folks around him, "OK, that's it. Now we go to work for the next one." The stubborn will in those words was invitingly familiar, an echo of Dolly's gumption. Frank determined to keep tabs on Jack Kennedy.

He just needed an in.

And what do you know: At a dinner party at Gary and Rocky Cooper's house in the summer of '58, there was Peter.

Frank had seen Lawford among his in-laws at the Democratic convention two years earlier; he was working, incongruously, with Bobby, trying to gain support from the Nevada delegation, which was run by Peter's sometime Desert Inn boss, Wilbur Clark.

At the time, even though they'd been chummy at MGM in the forties, Frank was carrying a grudge against Peter—a misunderstanding about a woman. In late '53, after she and Frank had split, Ava Gardner had a drink with Peter at an L.A. nightspot. When Louella Parsons reported the little tête-à-tête, Frank went bonkers, calling Peter at two in the morning and shouting at him, "Do you want your legs broken, you fucking asshole? Well, you're going to get them broken if I ever hear you're out with Ava again. So help me, I'll kill you."

Peter was terrified: "Frank's a violent guy and he's good friends with too many guys who'd rather kill you than say hello." He asked a friend to intervene, and when Frank realized that it really was just an innocent drink, he cooled off. But he didn't bother with Peter until he'd become a Kennedy, and even then grudgingly. Pat Kennedy, presuming with some reason to install herself as a society queen in Hollywood, had tried for years to have Frank attend some or other event; he had always brusquely refused her.

But as her brother's star rose, and as Frank's interest in politics merged subtly with his naked ambition, Peter's near-trespass didn't seem so awful. So it came to pass that on that fateful night at the Coopers', with Peter working late at the studio on his *Thin Man* TV series, Pat found herself rapt in conversation with Frank, who had gone out of his way to break the ice with her. Dolly Sinatra's boy, ever aware of who held the power, knew that she could provide quite a high level of access to what was clearly a growing political concern.

When Peter arrived at the party—bandaged after an injury on the set—he was amazed to discover his wife and Frank amiably chatting. He quietly took a seat at the table, not knowing what sort of greeting to expect. Frank looked at him, then looked back at Pat and said, "You know, I don't speak to your old man." The two of them laughed, and Peter did, too, a beat later, when he realized he'd been forgiven.

Within a few months, a suddenly intimate relationship formed between Peter and Frank. When Pat had a daughter that November, the child was christened Victoria Francis— the first name in recognition of her Uncle Jack's reelection to the Senate that day, the second in recognition of Frank.

The following year, vacationing together in Rome, Frank actually apologized to Peter for the way he'd blown up over Ava: "Charlie, I'm sorry. I was dead wrong." It was the rarest of moments: another smile of fate upon Peter Lawford.

He and Frank became fast pals, frat brothers with nicknames, booze, broads, matching cars. He got work: the Pacific theater war movie *Never So Few,* his first picture in six years, came his way strictly because Frank insisted on it—and at a price that made MGM choke, also at Frank's insistence. The two became partners in a Beverly Hills restaurant, Puccini, and served spaghetti and chops to the stars; Frank was so glad to have Peter on board that he put up both halves of the seed money.

And Frank had his avenue to Jack Kennedy. Peter admitted that he and his wife "were very attractive to Frank because of Jack." Sure enough, once he was connected, Frank leapfrogged over the guy he came to call "the brother-in-Lawford" and ingratiated himself with both Jack and Old Joe.

Indeed, though his cavorting with Jack was famous, Frank may have been closer to the father, the primary source of money and power in the family and the one most familiar with the courtship of disreputable outsiders, whether they were mobsters, corrupt politicians, larcenous power brokers, or temperamental pop stars. Joe had, it was said, prevailed on Sam Giancana to help erase public records of Jack's annulled 1947 marriage to a Florida socialite; he called upon the Chicago don again in the late fifties to smooth things between himself and Frank Costello when Kennedy's reluctance to recognize his obligations to the New York mobster almost resulted in a contract on his life; later, during the 1960 presidential campaign, he was seen dining at a New York restaurant with a select group of top mobsters from around the country. Jack may have had all the buzz, but Joe was, in Frank's eyes, the real man of the world in the family.

If Jack didn't inherit his father's intimacy with the ways of men of dark power, he had plenty of Joe's lustful wantonness. In this, Frank made a perfectly agreeable playmate, especially when it came to the young senator's favorite diversions—women and gossip. The two began partying together soon after Frank reconciled with Peter—"I was Frank's pimp and Frank was Jack's," Lawford ruefully recalled. "It sounds terrible now, but then it was really a lot of fun."

Whenever Jack came to the West Coast for fund-raising or other official duties, he made sure to hook up with Frank, more often than not with Peter in tow. They didn't hide their budding friendship from the press: "Let's just say that the Kennedys are interested in the lively arts," Peter told a reporter, "and that Sinatra is the liveliest art of all."

In November 1959, Jack extended a trip to Los Angeles by spending two nights at Frank's Palm Springs estate. Frank got a huge belly laugh out of him by introducing him to his black valet, George Jacobs, and suggesting that the senator ask the mere servant about civil rights. "I didn't like niggers and I told him so," Jacobs remembered. "They make too much noise, I said. The Mexicans smell and I can't stand them either. Kennedy fell in the pool he laughed so hard."

Fun over, Jack had to return East, even though he would've just loved the next night, when Frank, joined by Joey Bishop, Tony Curtis, Sammy Cahn, Jimmy Durante, Judy Garland, and about a thousand others toasted Dean at the Friars Club. But he made a mental note to catch up with them the next time they'd all be together: the following winter in Las Vegas when they'd be making a movie.

It was one last bit of patrimony thrown Peter by his new best friend. Frank had taken a literary property off his hands: *Ocean's Eleven*, a movie about a group of World War II vets who hold up Las Vegas.

I was told to come here

Never So Few, Peter's comeback picture, was shaping up into quite a party, maybe even bigger than *Some Came Running*. After rescuing Peter from TV, Frank used his weight to get Sammy a $75,000 part. (The producers had balked, "Frank, there were no Negroes in the Burma theater." And Frank shot them down: "There are now.")

To Sammy, it only seemed proper: With his talent, youth, versatility, vitality, and powerful friends, he was on the verge of being the biggest star of his time.

Then he stumbled. Speaking to a radio interviewer in Chicago, he trashed Frank, just trashed him: "I love Frank and he was the kindest man in the world to me when I lost my eye in an auto accident and wanted to kill myself. But there are many things he does that there are no excuses for. Talent is not an excuse for bad manners—I don't care if you are the most talented person in the world. It does not give you the right to step on people and treat them rotten. This is what he does occasionally." (As a coup de grâce, asked who the number one singer in the country was, Sammy replied that it was he. "Bigger than Frank?" "Yeah.")

It didn't take long for him to regret his words. "That was it for Sammy," Peter remembered. "Frank called him 'a dirty nigger bastard' and wrote him out of *Never So Few*." The part went to Steve McQueen—one of his first important roles. Sammy, who was nearing $300,000 of debt, certainly regretted losing the work, but he was far more concerned with the way Frank had written him off.

"You wanna talk destroyed?" said Lawford's manager, Milt Ebbins. "Sammy Davis cried from morning to night. He came to see us when Peter was at the Copacabana, appearing with Jimmy Durante. He said, 'I can't get Frank on the phone. Can't you guys do something?' Peter told him, 'I talked to Frank but he won't budge.'"

Sammy was banished from Frank's very presence. "For the next two months Sammy was on his knees begging for Frank's forgiveness," Lawford recalled, "but Frank wouldn't speak to him. Even when they were in Florida together and Frank was appearing at the Fontainebleau and Sammy was next door at the Eden Roc, Frank still refused to speak to him." (He wouldn't even be in the same building with him; he had Sammy banned from his shows and wouldn't go next door to watch him perform.)

But there must have been some sort of bond there, because Frank relented, even when he had nothing in particular to gain from it. "Frank let him grovel for a while," Peter said, "and then allowed him to apologize in public a couple of months later."

The reconciliation went as far as new offers of work. Frank was assembling the cast of *Ocean's Eleven*. He would let Sammy back in the fold in time to take a role in the movie, but one with a bit of a sting to it: For no obvious reason other than petty spite, Sammy was cast as a singing, dancing garbageman.

Sammy was nevertheless overwhelmed to be asked aboard because *Ocean's Eleven* had begun to take shape as something more than just a movie. Frank decided that he would film it at his place, the Sands, and fill it with chums—everybody from

Dean and Sammy and Peter to vibraphonist Red Norvo and actor buddies like Henry Silva and Richard Conte.

As a bonus, there'd be a freewheeling live show in the Copa Room each night featuring the actors. For that, Frank realized, he'd need a traffic cop, somebody who fit in with the A-list names but with the nightclub experience to get guys on and off the stage and who wouldn't embarrass himself in front of the movie camera.

He had just the guy in mind: Joey Bishop.

Frank called him "the Hub of the Big Wheel" and preferred him to almost every other stand-up comic. He addressed the world with a stiff-shouldered, side-of-the-mouth delivery that was as much jab as shrug, a deft emcee who knew how to keep the show moving and not draw attention from the stuff the people really came to see.

But nevertheless, to most observers it was the Big Mystery of the Rat Pack: What was Joey Bishop doing up there?

Frank, Dean, and Sammy were clearly peas from the same pod, and Peter was a guy who swung like them and provided entrée to the Kennedys.

Joey, however, had neither powerful relatives nor a reputation as a roué, and as performer he was plainly one-dimensional: He acted about as well as Sammy, sang about as well as Peter, danced about as well as Dean.

But he had an air about him—the world-weary little guy with the plucky, jaded attitude—that appealed to Frank, who indirectly sponsored his career from the early fifties on. Other comics would try to win an audience with dazzling wit or class clown antics. Joey went the other way, wearing a stage face that suggested he found the idea of entertaining the crowd slightly undignified. It was largely a matter of style—"My technique is to be *overheard* rather than heard," he liked to say—but there was temperament there as well.

"My cynicism is based upon myself," he told a reporter in a self-analytic moment. "I don't tell audiences to be cynical. I just bring them down to reality. I feel that when you try to cheer somebody up, you probably have a guilt complex. When a child sulks, eventually you ask him what's wrong because you probably feel you're the reason he's sulking."

He should've known. For a guy best known as a chum among chums, he could be taciturn, moody, aloof, exclusive. Even when he was among the honored guests at the Party of Parties, he kept to himself. "I was always a go-homer," he admitted. "When we were doing the Summit Meeting shows in Vegas, the other guys would stay up until all hours, but I went to bed. I may rub elbows, but I don't raise them."

In fact, he gave off an almost perverse aura, as if he resented his own success and the hand his *padrone*, Frank, had in it. "I met Frank in 1951," he said, "and, sure, he's helped me a lot. We've worked together many times, and I enjoy it, but we don't socialize afterwards." And he didn't care if he pissed him off. During the Summit, Frank was feuding with a Vegas club owner and declared the guy's joint officially off limits; Joey, the story went, went anyhow.

His independence was his trademark, his currency, and he gambled that Frank would read it not as insolence but rather a sign of maturity and maleness. It almost backfired. "I have always respected Frank's moods," Joey recalled. "I have never walked over to Frank when he's having dinner with someone and just sat down uninvited. Which, I think, was another reason why he chose to have me with him. Then it got to the point where he would say to me, 'What's the matter, Charlie? You're getting stuck up?'"

It was a fine line that he braved. Reporters who got close to him during the Rat Pack era seemed genuinely to like him, but few of them depicted him as, in the cliché of the showbiz puff piece, rough on the outside but sweet at heart. "You can pretend to be happy if you want to," he told one; "I'm a worrier by nature," he confessed to another. "No worrier is ever good-humored. I don't know if a worrier ever is happy."

Of all the moons in Frank's orbit, only Dean had anything like Joey's need for independence. They were the only ones who ever seemed willing to do without Frank's blessing—or even to outright defy him. Maybe it was because they had a few things in common. Unlike Sammy, Frank, and Peter, they'd grown up with siblings and stable homes, and their career successes came relatively late in their lives. Dean was thirty when he broke through with Jerry Lewis; Joey was nearly forty when the public and the business started taking real notice of him.

He'd had a few brushes with the big time, and their failure to materialize seemed to cauterize him against the world all the more: "Once, when I was sharing a bill with Frank at the Copacabana, the audience kept me going 28 minutes overtime almost every night," he told a reporter. "Frank kept telling me, 'You're solid now—you're on your way.' Know what happened? I didn't work for six weeks."

It was the kind of mixed success his career had accustomed him to. He'd been trying to make it big for more than twenty years when he was picked by Frank for the cast of *Ocean's Eleven*. Prior to that, he'd glimpsed the top frequently enough to develop a sardonic attitude about not ever having reached it. He was a plugger, and he knew it: "I'm a slow starter. There can never be a big, hitting thing with me . . . I don't have the type of personality that shatters you right off. I have to work at being funny. The work is hard. I'm hard sometimes." That way he had of dismissing things, deflating things—it came naturally to a guy who'd had to fight for everything and even then didn't quite get it.

He was born in the Bronx in 1918, the fifth and last child of Jacob Gottlieb, a machinist and bike repairman, and his wife, Anna. He was sickly—the littlest baby, he used to brag, ever born in Fordham Hospital (he told the story to an incredulous Buddy Hackett, who responded with a look of concern, "Did you live?"). At three months, the family moved to Philadelphia, where the slight baby grew into a slight child.

The Gottliebs never had much money, and the kids learned to tiptoe around Jacob, who was always irritable with the vagaries of his business. He could be nurturing, encouraging Joey and his older brother Morris in pursuing music (Jacob himself played the ocarina and sang Yiddish songs), but he could also terrify them—a kid could get spanked for the mere offense of coming home with a dime, a sum their father believed no child could earn honestly. Joey, who began his schooling as an apt, engaged student, once won a fifty-cent prize in a spelling bee; when he came home, he caught a beating from one of his brothers who, in imitation of Dad, was certain the money was stolen.

After that spelling bee, Joey did nothing to distinguish himself as a student other than quit altogether after two years of high school to work in the bike shop. It was a dispiriting experience—"What would anyone want with a bicycle during the Depression?" he asked a reporter years later—and being around Jacob all day was no picnic. Joey took on work in a luncheonette and then decided he'd move to New York to try and break into show business.

Show business? Okay, maybe he was funny around school and the shop, always ready with a cocky, cutting jibe, and he'd won a few amateur-night contests with his patter, his impressions, even a bit of tap dancing. But this wasn't exactly the sort of ambition Jacob had tried to instill in his sons—"It was a choice of either getting a steady job or getting killed," Joey remembered. He told his folks he'd stay with relatives in Manhattan and keep a day job; they gave him the green light. For a brief moment, it looked like he might pull it off—he worked in a hat factory by day and got a gig as an emcee in a Chinese restaurant on Broadway at night. But soon enough he was back with the smock and the spokes and the inner tubes in Philly, a flop.

He didn't give up the stage, though. With Sammy Reisman and Morris Spector, a pair of kids from the neighborhood, he formed a comic singing-dancing-spritzing act called, cleverly, Gottlieb, Reisman and Spector. They met a black kid who was willing to drive them around if they'd adopt his surname as their stage names: They became the Bishop Trio. They were scraping by on the burlesque circuit when Reisman got ill; Joey and Spector (now known as Rummy Bishop) took the act to Florida and got lucky—two years' work on and off at the Nut Club in Miami. When Spector was drafted in 1941, Joey opened as a single in El Dumpo, a Cleveland nightspot, at $100 a week.

He had married—the bride was Sylvia Ruzga, a shiksa from Oak Park, outside of Chicago, whom he'd met in Florida (her first words to him: "I don't think you're funny")—but they had no children by the time Joey's draft notice came. He would spend the better part of the next four years in the special service of the army, finally receiving an emergency discharge when Sylvia was hospitalized.

The couple spent a while in San Antonio, and Joey found a few gigs. He got noticed by a small-time bandleader, who recommended him to the William Morris Agency. A booking at the Greenwich Village Inn followed—one week blossomed into eleven—but New York once again proved a chimera. Running out of options, Joey and Sylvia went to her hometown, where he was recognized by musician Russ Carlyle, who invited him to do a little comic spritzing onstage during his act. The owners liked Joey's shtick and hired him on. He spent the next two years working in Chicago clubs like the Oriental, the Vine Gardens, and the Chez Paree, where he finally broke the $1,000-a-week barrier in 1949, billed, to his chagrin, as "The Frown Prince of Comedy."

In 1952, after jumping to New York, he was playing the Latin Quarter and he caught Sinatra's eye; as he had with Sammy, Frank encouraged the younger man's career. He saw that Joey got booked on the bill with him when he was playing around New York—the Riviera, the Copa, the Paramount— and sometimes on the road. Audiences who were initially cool to the comic, who viewed him as a necessary burden of being allowed to see Sinatra, became converts: He got a reputation as that tough little funny guy who opened for Frank. He always remembered his 1952 date opening for Frank at the Riviera: "my first job in a class club before an audience of the 'right' people."

But his following remained too select; the "right" people seemed to be the only ones who wanted to see him. Through most of the fifties, he was burdened with that most left-handed of praises: He was a comedian's comedian, the sort of indisputably talented performer who lacked the charisma to reach beyond an audience of aficionados.

His biggest successes had come in front of showbiz crowds. He played a star-studded benefit at which Danny Thomas killed for nearly an hour; backstage, the other comics huddled in fright—no one had the balls to go on next; Joey volunteered; he grabbed his overcoat, folded it over his arm, walked up to the mike, muttered, "Folks, what he said goes for me, too," and walked offstage to a roar. Some years later, he floored the audience at the Friars Roast of Dean; following a string of entertainers who'd declared how happy they were to be in attendance, he opened his bit by declaring, "I was *told* to come here."

Showbiz-as-bullshit jokes: Frank loved it.

(Joey could always get a laugh out of Frank. He was leaving the stage after opening for Frank at the Copa one night and Frank asked how the crowd was: "Great for me," Joey said, breaking him up. "I don't know how they'll be for you.")

Still, for all his good buzz, he never quite made it over the top, never quite became the star his friends assured him he'd be. His act was based on his feel for the common man, but he was maybe a little too much like the real thing. One night when he was playing on the bill with Frank at the Copa, manager Julie Podell stopped him at the entrance and told him to get in line with the other customers.

It was this sort of thing that probably encouraged him to give up nightclubs—and the lucrative contracts they'd been bringing him—and take to the movies and TV, where he could court a larger audience. He made three films in 1958, all service pictures: *Onionhead*, about the Coast Guard; *The Deep Six*, about the navy; and *The Naked and the Dead* ("I played both parts," went his stock line), the big-budget-flop adaptation of Norman Mailer's classic army novel. That same year, he became a regular on a quiz show, *Keep Talking*, and, more memorably, on *The Tonight Show*, where he was one of Jack Paar's semiregular sidekicks. He cut his hair into a tight buzz—no big deal, maybe, but he thought "it made the jokes seem funnier"—and he became known for a catchphrase: "son of a gun . . ."

The Paar show, the movies, a growing reputation as a funnyman: Frank, who'd always been happy to toss him a bone, was pleased. He needed an emcee, he needed an opening act, he needed almost a dozen chums who knew how not to trip over the cables on a movie set. Who was he gonna call, Corbett Monica?

Joey was in.

I'm not going to stooge for anyone

The story became almost as familiar as George Washington chopping down the cherry tree: Half-batty New York gangster Ben Siegel came to a sleepy little desert town, got a look at the sawdust-strewn Old West gambling joints, and had a vision of a European-style casino resort with ultramodern amenities and big-name entertainment; he convinced a cadre of partners back East to invest in his project, then endured all sorts of costly problems getting it built—some of which were clearly due to his inexperience in such undertakings (for instance, Siegel was neurotically hygienic, and his hotel incurred huge cost overruns when he insisted that each toilet have its own sewer line); the hotel, the Flamingo, finally opened the day after Christmas, 1946, and it was a disaster—inexperienced dealers suffered big losses, and without any rooms to stay in (only the casino, restaurant, and showroom were finished), the winners took their money home with them, leaving the joint high and dry; Siegel's partners, already incensed with the escalating cost of building the place, began to feel as if they'd been taken; they ordered Siegel executed and took over the hotel, which not only turned into a stunning success but became the model for the next half-century of Las Vegas moneymaking enterprises. Like Moses, he never saw his promised land realized.

Great yarn—the founding fable of Las Vegas—and parts of it were even true. A few crucial details were missing: The Vegas Strip already had two thriving resort casinos (the Last Frontier and El Rancho Vegas) when Siegel arrived; the Flamingo was already under construction when he muscled himself in on the deal for a controlling percentage; the East Coast mob had already infiltrated Vegas a few years earlier through ownership of several downtown joints and the telegraph service that helped bookies keep track of horse-races around the country. But the basic shape—that a single visionary crackpot with a taste for the high life recognized a little western watering hole as the locus of an American Monte Carlo in the desert—carried the weight of both fact and myth nicely. Benny Siegel did, in fact, invent Las Vegas, insofar as Las Vegas meant glitter, glamour, and hedonistic escape.

Frank knew Benny. When the gangster came West to organize Los Angeles's inept crime syndicate (known back East as the Mickey Mouse Mob) and rub elbows with Holly-wood swells, Frank, typically, delighted in the chance to brush up against real mob muscle, and he would bore friends afterward with talk about the hits Siegel had contracted for Murder Incorporated. Frank liked Benny's idea about turning Vegas into a vacation spot. In 1946, when the Flamingo was under construction, Frank announced in a Vegas paper that he was planning to build a resort casino with its own radio station (a decade later, Frank launched a similarly chimerical Havana casino, in which he was to be partnered with Tony Martin and Donald O'Connor, among others). And Frank had coincidentally been on the spot at a weeklong convocation of mob bosses in Havana in 1947, when the potentates of organized crime decided that Benny Siegel needed to be eliminated.

But Frank's association with Las Vegas took some time to develop. Though he enjoyed visiting the city to gamble and party through the late forties, he didn't perform there until 1951, at the nadir of his career, when he was booked at the Desert Inn in a gesture of kindness on the part of owner Wilbur Clark. The D.I. remained Frank's Vegas home for the next few years, and it was surely there that he became aware of the details of the new casino resort opening on the site of the old LaRue Club, just a half mile or so down the road, midway between the D.I. and the Flamingo. The owners and builders of the new place used Clark's hotel as their base of operations during construction, and they leeched plenty of Clark's best employees when their joint finally opened. They called it the Sands, and it would become the quintessential Las Vegas casino of its era.

The Sands set new standards for Las Vegas with just its look. The exterior was pointedly Moderne, with a gigantic, strikingly styled sign sticking out over the road and an eye-catching series of angled arches serving as an entryway; inside, it was dimly lit and burnished in deep wooden tones more reminiscent of a sophisticated London gambling club than the sort of bright, lively playground evoked by such rivals as the Flamingo and the D.I. Moreover, the Sands drew upon patrons' familiarity with a famously swank New York landmark, the Copacabana, importing the legendary nightclub's renowned Chinese menu and hiring away its single most important human asset, assistant manager Jack Entratter.

Entratter was one of the great showmen of his time. A hulking six-foot-three bear hobbled by a childhood bout with osteomyelitis, he was twenty-six years old and a bouncer at the Stork Club when he signed on at the Copa in 1940. For the next twelve years, Entratter, Nice Guy to manager Jules

Podell's Thug, was beloved of the stars who played the Copa, offering high salaries and deluxe accommodations such as personal suites in the hotel above the club. Entratter's arrival in Las Vegas signaled to the biggest entertainers in the business that the Sands would be their new home in the desert. As soon as they were contractually free to do so, Frank left the D.I., Dean Martin and Jerry Lewis left the Flamingo, and such performers as Danny Thomas, Lena Horne, Tony Bennett, Nat King Cole, Red Skelton, and Milton Berle all began appearing regularly in Entratter's showroom. (There were weirder acts, too: Edith Piaf, Tallulah Bankhead, Ezio Pinza, Señor Wences, Van Johnson, who sang a very little, and the immortal duo of Robert Merrill and Louis Armstrong all performed at the Sands within its first six months.) "He was our love," said Jerry Lewis of Entratter. "We wouldn't go anywhere in Vegas but where Jack was." Virtually from the moment it opened, the Sand's Copa Room became the town's undisputed top nightspot.

If the decor, chop suey, and famous faces made the Sands feel like a western satellite of the Copacabana, the financial setup of the operation made it seem even more so. The Copacabana had been owned, in the public record, by Monte Proser, but it was widely known that Proser's interests were a front for the real ownership, which included mob boss Frank Costello and such confederates as Joe Adonis. Proser was a classic front man, a relatively legitimate guy paraded out in front of the authorities to give the club the appearance of being owned by benign parties. The Copa had a few others— Podell, a bootlegger and armbreaker well known to the police, and, eventually, Entratter, who was rewarded with points of his own in the club as his role in booking it expanded.

Even if the real percentage of his ownership was, like Proser's, far less than it was reported to be, Entratter still had a sweetheart deal. He was a great front man, with a brilliance at ingratiating himself with performers and a golden touch at showmanship—his chorus line, the Copa Girls, was as famous as Flo Zeigfeld's had been in its day. Working for Costello at the Copa allowed him to flourish as an impresario and live in an extremely comfortable style. Besides, he knew how the world worked: His older brother had run with Legs Diamond during the flashy gangster's heyday and had been killed, in fact, in a shoot-out. This rare combination of criminal acquaintance and showbiz expertise made Entratter a perfect manager for the Copa—and his bosses there correctly surmised that he'd be even better at the Sands.

If it initially surprised some observers that Entratter would leave the Copa for the Sands, they hadn't understood the potential of Las Vegas as a money-earner for the mob—or the need for experienced front men. True, the Flamingo was built and run by mobsters with almost no recourse to window dressing like Entratter, but the notoriety Benny Siegel earned for the place made its real owners uneasy. Since then, virtually every hotel built on the Strip was the property of some group of gangsters, but not so as you could show it on paper. The Thunderbird was connected to criminal financial whiz Meyer Lansky; the Desert Inn was run by Moe Dalitz, a onetime bootlegger and racketeer with ties to organized crime in Cleveland and Detroit; the Stardust was the dream project of Los Angeles gambler Tony Cornero (the only Italian-American ever to build a casino on the Strip) and, with Cornero's death (of natural causes, yet!), was commonly believed to have been taken over by a combination of Chicago mobsters and the Desert Inn group.

The Sands, as befitted the newest and most refined jewel of the desert, had remarkably varied ties to the Boys, as the mob came to be known in Las Vegas. Pieces of the hotel were secretly held in New York, New Jersey, Chicago, Boston, Kansas City, Los Angeles, Texas, St. Louis—just about anyplace there was a group of gangsters worthy of the name. If the other Strip hotels were like little mom-and-pops run by the various out-of-state mobs in competition with one another, the Sands was owned by a syndicate so egalitarian in its ownership as to be tantamount to an honest-to-pete corporation.

Chief operating officer of this shadow enterprise for the hotel's first decade—unofficially, of course—was Joseph "Doc" Stacher, a major player in the New Jersey rackets almost since their inception. By the time he was thirty, Stacher had been arrested at least ten times in Newark and had once been rousted in a Manhattan hotel room along with Benny Siegel, Louis "Lepke" Buchalter, and Jacob "Gurrah" Shapiro. In the fifties, he weathered denaturalization proceedings and an indictment on illegal gambling charges stemming from his involvement in a casino near Saratoga Springs, New York. At the same time, just as the Sands was beginning to materialize, Stacher kept appearing ominously in Lake Tahoe, Reno, and Las Vegas; Las Vegas police observed him conferring with Lansky (one of his codefendants in the Saratoga Springs case), and he was seen cruising around town in a Cadillac sedan with blueprints for the Sands in tow. When the hotel finally opened, Stacher was the single biggest shareholder, though his name was nowhere to be found on any official documents; the federal government spent the next decade in unsuccessful efforts to bring his interest in the casino to the surface.

Such was the way things worked. Jack Entratter and men like him ran the place and declared themselves the owners of huge chunks of it, but Stacher and men like him were the ones who actually profited on every dollar the casino made. The Boys got their money and a certain amount of plausible deniability; the front men got glory and the trappings—if not the substance—of wealth.

Entratter wasn't the only front man at the Sands. In a stroke of genuine inspiration, the hotel's invisible owners allowed Sinatra to buy two points in the operation, thus assuring the singer's unwavering loyalty. "Frank was flattered to be invited," said Doc Stacher years later, "but the object was to get him to perform there because there's no bigger draw in Las Vegas. When Frankie was performing, the hotel really filled up."

Almost as public a figure was Jakey Freedman, a Russian-born Jew who rose from fruit peddling to oil drilling, making a fortune on the side with illegal gambling in Houston and Galveston; he was, on paper anyway, the single largest stakeholder in the joint. If Entratter represented the sophis-ticated eastern atmosphere in which the Sands wanted to wrap itself, Freedman was his utter opposite. Tiny (he stood *maybe* five foot three), favoring absurdly large western hats, string ties, and checked shirts, he gave the hotel its only touch of the Old West bullshit that typified other Nevada casinos.

He also gave it its first taste of trouble. In the summer of 1952, just before the Sands opened, Freedman was denied a casino operating license by the Nevada Tax Commission. Asked if he was hiding the ownership interests of organized crime, Freedman bristled, "I've been the star all my life. I'm not going to stooge for anyone this late."

Stooge or no, he managed to get his license, a good thing, in the long run, considering that he was the guy who, just three years later, brought to the Sands the man who would become the third key figure in its history: Carl Cohen, the Sands's longtime casino manager.

Cohen had been in the gambling business his whole life. "He was a bookie," said his brother, Mike. "I won't lie. Wherever he was, he worked sneak joints and was a bookie. He loved to gamble. He was always in the gambling business."

He was born in 1913 in Ohio, where he first learned the ins and outs of his trade in illegal gambling clubs run by the

Mayfield Road Gang under the proctorship of Moe Dalitz. Cohen's knowledge of the gambling racket—"There wasn't nothing you could pull over on him," his brother boasted—coupled with his intimidating physical presence (like fellow shtarker Jack Entratter, he stood decidely over six feet and regularly carried 250-plus pounds), made him an ideal candidate for advancement in the casino business. Within a decade, he was running the entire casino at El Rancho Vegas, which had passed down to Jake Katelman's nephew Beldon upon the founder's death. Cohen prospered at El Rancho, respectful always of the prerogatives of the Boys and of such esteemed guests as Howard Hughes, for whom he kept a hotel cabin permanently reserved.

It was Cohen's willingness to cater to Hughes that wound up leading him to the Sands. One night in 1955, Sophie Tucker was making one of her frequent appearances at El Rancho, and the joint was mobbed. As Beldon Katelman wandered through the pits and the showroom looking with favor upon the fruits of his success, he noticed Cohen paying special attention to a motley character dressed in jeans and tennis shoes—an eyesore in the midst of the high-rolling splendor. Katelman took Cohen aside and ordered him to expel the geekish-looking fellow; Cohen refused (it was Hughes, of course). The argument, right in the middle of the bustling casino, escalated until Katelman took a poke at his casino manager. Retaliating, Carl busted his boss on the jaw, sending him sprawling among the feet of his guests, and then turned and walked out of the joint; not a single security guard lifted a finger against him; half of the dealers, none of whom could stand Katelman, either, walked out as well.

A few hours later, Cohen's phone rang. It was Jakey Freedman calling to say he understood Cohen needed work and he should come and see him in the morning.

Cohen showed up at the Sands the next day still agitated.

Freedman asked him if he wanted something to eat. "When Carl was mad," his brother remembered, "he ate with both hands and he didn't give a shit about nothing." Freedman picked up the phone and called room service for a half dozen bagels with lox and cream cheese. "Make it a dozen," Cohen told him.

After knocking back the bagels with a few pitchers of coffee, the two men got down to business. Freedman spoke frankly: "I need a man of your caliber who knows the business and has a following. I don't want this joint to fall on its face." Cohen said he'd have to consider it. He conferred with his bosses back East—the people whose percentage in El Rancho he'd been covering for—and got the okay, provided he really was the boss of the casino. Accepting Freedman's offer, Cohen took five points in the operation, expanded the playing area to make work for the dealers who'd walked out of El Rancho Vegas with him, and brought along all his best high-rolling customers, including Hughes, who told him, "Wherever you go, I'm going with you."

Freedman died in 1958, and the Sands was—on paper, anyway—put into the hands of Entratter and Cohen, who turned it into the most magnetic and sparkling operation on the whole of the booming Strip. They came up with all sorts of elegant touches—an actual floating crap game in the swimming pool, a manicured putting green, electric carts transporting guests between the casino and the two-story buildings that housed their rooms. They set up reservations offices in Beverly Hills, Houston, Mexico City, and other towns likely to funnel gamblers to Vegas. They also expanded the allure of the joint to high rollers and celebrities by upping Sinatra's percentage in the operation from two to nine points and selling Dean Martin a 1 percent piece. With Sammy Davis Jr. and Joey Bishop already signed to long-term deals, the Sands was de facto home of the Rat Pack before the notion of a Summit ever entered anyone's mind.

For all of them, it was a family place. Cohen and Entratter lived on the premises—they had private pools off their apartments—and Frank eventually had a private suite (the Presidential Suite!) set aside for him as well. Cohen's brother, Mike, was hired on as a slot machine repairman and then as a craps and blackjack dealer. The various owners' wives and widows always vied for the staff's attention at each other's expense.

The nepotism was endless, if it occasionally backfired. Entratter brought in a nephew, who managed to get the sack after echoing Beldon Katelman's foolishness at El Rancho Vegas. Frank and the boys were cutting up with the lounge act after one of the Summit shows, and a casually dressed guy with a hat brim hiding his eyes was leaning against a wall watching them intently. Entratter's nephew had him hustled out by security. A few minutes later, an enraged Entratter came storming into the lounge ("He was a big man," recalled an employee, "but when he was angry he was eight feet tall") wanting to know which genius had just ordered Danny Kaye ejected from the joint.

Other employees were smarter. Bellmen, room service waiters, maids, valets, and anyone else who might stumble into a locked room learned to see nothing, hear nothing, say nothing. In a town full of discreet professionals, they were exemplary. A guy might catch the unforgettable sight of showbiz royalty cavorting with a trio of mixed-race hookers, or he might see New Orleans D.A. Jim Garrison getting the full four-star treatment on the arm from Mario Marino, Carlos Marcello's man on the scene. But was he gonna blow a job at the best hotel in town over gossipmongering? The Sands was so special that it was almost beyond reproach.

They called it "A Place in the Sun," but the joy of it for most of the more famous guests was the promise that it held of shadows. Cohen catered to the high rollers, with secret rooms where there were no betting limits. Entratter stroked the stars. "Whatever Frank Sinatra wanted, Mr. Entratter always gave it to him," said one employee, while another put it more bluntly: "Entratter feared Frank."

He had good reason. Frank's first two points in the casino were purchased over-the-counter in a fashion that the gaming commissioners couldn't object to. But the other seven points weren't quite so clean. Word was that Vincent "Jimmy Blue Eyes" Alo, yet another confederate of Meyer Lansky with ties to the Genovese family, had made a gift to Frank of the additional seven points the singer owned in the hotel. Alo's name appeared on no documents concerning the hotel, but he was apparently tightly connected to it, a fact that Entratter knew all too well. After he'd built himself his private apartment on the hotel grounds, Entratter was visited by Alo, whose interest in the Sands was partially comprised of ten of Entratter's twelve points. Entratter feted the gangster in his own apartment, which he'd had filled with showgirls, chateaubriand, Dom Pérignon, and Cuban cigars. Alo fumed: "I should have left you a headwaiter," he told Entratter in front of his minions. "You come over here and spend millions of dollars. You smoke your big cigars. You dress in your two-thousand-dollar suits. And you're nothing more than lackeys. . . . I should send you all back where you belong." Entratter was stunned into silence, and he tiptoed around Alo, his emissaries, and his buddies—like Sinatra—ever after.

This was the setting Frank chose for his big buddy movie— Gomorrah with the vice all legal, just reaching its popular zenith, its sleek new pleasure palaces celebrating Las Vegas's role in the atomic age just as its downtown sawdust joints evoked the pioneer past.

The Rat Pack Summit capitalized on the buzz around the city and around the Sands, but it also helped create and spread it. It availed itself of the city's iconography to give itself soul and context, but it became one of the central myths of the city and expanded its aura crucially. And it became one of the key rescuing events in the life of a city that seemed always on the verge of going bust.

At the dawn of the sixties, the Las Vegas gaming industry wasn't quite so stable as the city's reputation led outsiders to believe, but it nevertheless carried the potential to explode into something truly huge. In the previous decade, the Strip had gone from four major casinos to thirteen, and the city had risen to such prominence as a vacation destination that civic leaders had built a lavish convention center amid the resorts. The resident population was booming—schools and city services were overburdened—and the transient population of tourists had grown to rival that of such fabled spots as Miami and Los Angeles.

Still, for all the overheated atmosphere, there was trouble. Some major hotels failed—the Royal Nevada and Moulin Rouge, most spectacularly—and the value of others was grotesquely overinflated, with cash-flow problems at the Stardust, Dunes, Frontier, and Riviera actually hitting the papers. This didn't necessarily bother all interested parties. The mobsters behind the overvalued casinos knew how to profit from such disparities and, in fact, had helped to create them by skimming profits. But for the civic leaders not party to the backroom shenanigans jocularly known as casino management, the situation was frightening. The cost of building materials rose dramatically, and the local tax base— even with hefty taxes on tourism—was uncertain (to this day, the city has never successfully incorporated the golden miles of the Strip). It seemed to many observers that the glorious growth that had swelled the city through the fifties could pop like a soap bubble; in many respects, it was just a sleepy western town, a place where the grocery stores accepted casino chips and people would give strangers lifts along the road on particularly scalding days.

The federal government, which had so frequently fostered the growth of the city through public works projects such as the Hoover Dam and national defense sinecures like Nellis Air Force Base and a subsidized magnesium mining industry, suddenly seemed antagonistic, snooping around the ways the town did business like it never had before. The feds were after the mob, and they'd begun to look into how things worked in Vegas.

This wasn't the first time the government had made a grand posture of busting up the Vegas rackets. Estes Kefauver had visited the city in 1950, sniffing around and making noise so he might get nominated for president. But the mobsters behind the casinos weren't cowed by the show; they'd seen him too often around dames and racetracks to fear that he could truly hurt them.

In 1957, however, another probe began—and this time it was followed quickly by events that gave it some teeth. In January, the U.S. Senate unanimously voted to open an investigation of labor racketeering and impaneled a committee headed by John McClellan and featuring, as the presumed voice of the workingman, the liberal senator from Massachusetts, Jack Kennedy—who, the mob figured, was also nobody to worry about, what with his daddy's bootlegging connections to Raymond Patriarca and Frank Costello and his own fondness for the ladies.

In May, though, somebody took a shot at Costello in an apartment house foyer on Central Park West. The mob kingpin's expensive haircut was given a new part with a .38 slug, and he was rushed to the hospital in a bloodied daze. Detectives arriving at the emergency room searched Costello's pockets and turned up a wad of cash and a piece of paper inscribed with an impressive series of numbers totaling $651,284—which happened to be the exact amount taken in by the brand-new Tropicana Hotel during its first twenty-four days of operation. Up until that moment the mob had been connected to Vegas mostly by whispers and innuendos; this was a genuine smoking gun—handwriting analysts identified two casino executives' penmanship on the paper.

That November came the biggest jolt of all. A highway patrolman in Apalachin, a New York lake district hamlet, noticed lots of big cars with out-of-state plates converging on an estate owned by Joseph Barbara Sr., a local soda bottler. He knew about Barbara's lengthy rap sheet, and he knew that Barbara had recently placed an unusually large meat order with a butcher and reserved a large number of nearby motel rooms. Still, he had no legal reason to raid the place. He did, however, have the right to stop and check any vehicle on a public road, so he set up a little checkpoint on the sole access road to the estate—just him and three deputies.

A local fish peddler leaving the mansion after a delivery got a whiff of what was going on, made a U-turn, and ran into the house yelling that the cops were outside. A mad melee ensued, with most of Barbara's guests—more than one hundred all told—bolting from the house. Some ran into the woods, others jumped into limos, Lincolns, and Caddies and tried to run the roadblock. Sixty-three men were rounded up for questioning: Genovese, Profaci, Bonanno, Galante, Lucchese, Trafficante, Scalise, Zerilli, Civella—a coast-to-coast who's who of mob bosses. The next day, the FBI, which had sworn throughout the Kefauver ruckus that there was no such thing as a nationally organized syndicate of criminals, began its Top Hoodlum Program with the express aim of busting the mob. Naturally, Las Vegas became a focal point of their investigations.

Within a year of the debacle at Apalachin, there was sufficient heat on organized crime in Nevada that Governor Grant Sawyer instituted a state gaming commission to oversee the gambling industry and certify the owners and key executives of all casinos. At first, this was seen as a merely perfunctory demonstration of zero tolerance, a sop to show the feds that the state was toughening up on the mob. But then the Gaming Commission got big ideas: Without telling anybody what it was doing, it began making lists of mobsters from around the country who'd been rumored to have connections to Las Vegas; eventually, the names of eleven of these men—residents, mostly, of Chicago, Los Angeles, and Kansas City—would be entered in a volume known as the Black Book, a list of people forbidden to enter the grounds of any casino in the state; even the coffee shops would be off limits. Laughably feeble though the gesture may have been, it was good P.R.: Nevada, the state's Mormon powers hoped, was showing the world that it could clear itself of bad guys on its own and be a legitimate (in every sense of the word) rival to Miami, L.A., or Honolulu as a tourist mecca.

But despite the high-profile cleanup efforts, the mob was brazenly insinuating itself into the town more wholly than ever before. In part, it was doing so out of necessity: Almost exactly one year before work on *Ocean's Eleven* began, Fidel Castro marched into Havana and seized the casinos that had for more than a decade earned millions annually for the mob. Havana, where every sinful indulgence was available to Americans for pennies, had long worried Nevada gambling interests who feared competition from Cuba's decidedly looser atmosphere; in April 1958, the state Gaming Board barred anyone with a Nevada gaming license from operating in Cuba.

But now that Nevada had won the war against its Caribbean rival, it had to accommodate the refugees it created. The mob, after all, wasn't going to get out of the gambling business just because it had lost its Havana casinos. Instead, it sought to bolster its declining revenues with increased profits from Vegas. The city became by default the onshore home of all the vices for which Havana had been such an ideal remote repository; Vegas was, as far as organized crime was concerned, a banana republic.

Enabling the mob to build up its Vegas holdings was a bottomless new source of funding—the Central States Pension Fund of the International Brotherhood of Teamsters. In 1959, International president Jimmy Hoffa, just over one year into his reign, began to turn the pension fund into a pile of play money for the mob to do with as it pleased in Las Vegas. Using Teamster money, mob-connected interests built hospitals, golf courses, small businesses, and new hotels; existing hotels switched hands and underwent expansion and renovation. The Fremont, the Dunes, the Stardust, Caesar's Palace—all these hotels were built, bought, maintained, enlarged, or in some other way capitalized with the money that started flowing through Hoffa's hands as the fifties came to a close.

And as the new decade dawned, Frank Sinatra and his cronies merrily set about creating even more business for their larcenous friends by creating the kind of gaudy splash that only entertainers can provide, a prospectus, a come-on, a P.R. even that was equal parts movie, nightclub engagement, and billboard for the zeitgeist of a swinging new age.

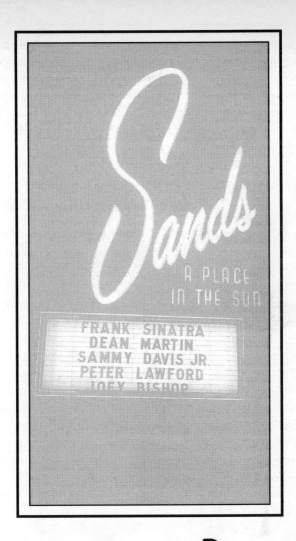

Sands
A PLACE
IN THE SUN

FRANK SINATRA
DEAN MARTIN
SAMMY DAVIS JR.
PETER LAWFORD
JOEY BISHOP

part 3

greatest straight man, one of the most original comic personalities ever in the business.

Zarathustran drama, intoxicating romance, grab-you-by-the-throat authority: That was Frank's bag.

Dean's was making the audience his friend—*especially* compared to how they felt watching Frank or Jerry. Dean took the edges off of Jerry's hysteria and Frank's egoism. He made each one go down easier. Standing beside each of them with a look of bemusement and mild shock, he was *us*—but cool and breezy and quick-witted and easy on the eyes: entertaining even on his own. Frank could never catch up.

Take the time Frank came on Dean's TV show and the two of them did a medley together: black stage, no props, tuxes, a swing beat. Frank was singing his bit when Dean broke out into a little jog, his face a blank. Then Dean sang his bit without breaking stride; he was going to do this jogging thing all the way through, apparently, and with a Buster Keaton face on, to boot. Frank stared with a drifting gaze: He hadn't a clue how to hold his own. He ad-libbed terribly: "What are we—in training? For what?" But Dean never, not even when he was singing, gave over. He was hilarious; Frank drowned.

Take the night at the Sands with Sammy when Frank sang "Too Marvelous for Words" and threw in a few extra beats: *"You're much much much much too much."* Dean wouldn't let that go. The rest of the night, he'd be mixing drinks and moving stools and listening to the others sing and ad-libbing between set pieces, all the while barking off little *much much muches* like he had Tourette's. Frank had merely been in a groove and ventured a little improv; to Dean, it was good for five to ten laughs.

The press liked to say that only Joey could make jokes at Frank's expense and live to tell about it, but Dean did it for decades and Frank was forever in awe of him for it.

This was one of the reasons Dean would always be in—and

Sammy, too, for that matter. Yes, they were pallies and brothers and all that crap, but they could do things that Frank couldn't and *wished he could:* comedy, dancing, winning over a crowd with a raised eyebrow or a "who dat?" look. (Peter and Joey, in this regard, did nothing special and were easily discarded.)

Frank was *cool* in the sense of *remote.* Dean and Sammy were *warm* in the sense of *comfortable.* When Frank took the stage it was an annunciation; people came to worship, weep, get quivery in the genitals, feel their hearts stop. When Dean and Sammy were with him, it was a party; you went to enjoy yourself.

Alone, Frank couldn't relax: He was insistent, a perfectionist, a lionizer of himself and his art. His audience adored him and feared him and envied him and lived through him, but they didn't exactly *like* him—and as a singer he never particularly cared if they did.

But his career came to be more than just his singing; it became his absent family—both the one he never had as a boy and the one he'd dumped for Ava. He'd surrounded himself with these guys to stave off loneliness, sure, but he could have (and *did* have) mere flunkies for *that.*

Dean and Sammy, though, were brothers *onstage* and *in movies* and *on records;* they weren't brothers who were really thumbbreakers or yes-men, or brothers who were so powerful that it was *you* who actually wanted something from *them.* They were guys who did the same thing as you and made it easier and more fun: golf buddies the world would pay good money to watch you play with.

Seeing him hang out with them, play their ringmaster, *relax* with them, suddenly the world didn't any longer just *behold* Frank: They *liked* him.

He didn't just *like* them: He *needed* them.

*

Stupid as it sounded, they called Frank the Leader. This was years after he was the Voice, Swoonatra, and the Lean Lark, and before he became the Chairman of the Board, Ol' Blue Eyes.

Sammy they called Smokey—because he smoked a lot, not because of his skin.

Dean was Dago—Dag for short—and they'd actually call him that in the act until Joey (of all people) walked off, complaining that Frank wouldn't want to be called "dago" offstage; Frank agreed, so it became a private thing. (Dean, of course, didn't give a rat's ass what anyone called him, and he simply called everyone "pallie" even if they were strangers, presidents of his bank, or people he knew for thirty years.)

Joey didn't have a nickname but Peter had a few: Petah, the Brother-in-Lawford (Frank's inspiration), and Charlie the Seal, because, they told reporters, he had a smoker's cough, but just as likely because his bad arm caused him to clap funny or because he liked to go down on women.

Actually, they were all Charlies, Charlies and Chicky Babys, which is another thing they called each other. (These were good things to be, as opposed to, say, being a Harvey.)

To be a Charlie was to be in. Milt Ebbins, Peter's manager, was Charlie Bluecheese because he never sat in the sun. Sammy called himself a million Charlies—Charlie Humble, Charlie Suave, Charlie Dapper, Charlie Star, Charlie Boor; his Swedish bride called him Sharlie Brown.

She was his broad, his clyde, his gasser; he was all locked up with her; he was electric.

This was really how they talked: an insider's game that was meant to exclude the Harveys and the bunters. Frank had picked some of it up riding buses with jazz orchestras, Sammy brought some of it over from the Chitlin Circuit, Peter picked up some of it from the surfers on Santa Monica State Beach, and some of it they just made up.

Clyde, for instance, could be anything or anyone—good or bad, it didn't matter: "Pass the clyde" when you wanted the salt; "How's your clyde?" as a form of greeting (much less particular than "How's your bird?," which was also a greeting but specifically anatomical); "I don't like her clyde" for a broad with a fat ass; "Let's lose Clyde" to get rid of a Harvey.

They needn't have worried about the Harveys. When they wanted to cut somebody out, they could do it by talking in their code. Journalist Stephen Birmingham once sat patiently while Charlie the Seal bragged about how their fame had spread abroad: "Like, we were getting off the boat the other day in Le Havre, and this French dame—this French reporter— comes up to me and says, *'Etes-vous un Rat?'* Luckily, I speak French, but I don't dig *'Etes-vous un Rat?'* She's asking me, am I a Rat? I don't dig. Then I dig. She's asking me about the Rat Pack, you dig? But there's no word in French for Rat Pack, you dig?" ("I told him I dug," Birmingham sighed.)

Even the term "Rat Pack" was pregnant. Frank didn't like it—or the insinuation that he was aping Bogie. For a while they were the Clan until they remembered they had a black guy and two Jews with them. Frank liked to call it the Summit. It didn't matter. It was like the mob: If you belonged, you didn't ever have to refer to it directly, and if you didn't, you sounded like a fool or worse talking about it.

It wasn't enough to drive the right car, wear the right clothes, screw the right broads, be on the same stage, or be admitted to the holy steam room or a party in the Springs. You had to talk like you belonged: certain words, certain rhythms. It added to the atmosphere, but it was also a make-or-break thing with them, separating the true insiders from those around them who were merely tolerated.

In 1961, Frank finally started his own record label and he called his first album *Ring-a-Ding-Ding*. It was a swell record filled with lively, cheeky music that lived up to the insouciant title, a phrase that he'd interpolated a couple of years earlier into a version of "I Won't Dance" and had lifted, apparently, from comedian fat Jackie Leonard. (He had to lift it from somewhere, because he could not, to a demonstrable certainty, scat. On his 1949 recording of "It All Depends on You," his vocalese passages sounded like nothing so much as a kid blowing bubbles in milk with a straw.)

Ring-a-ding-ding: the sound of coins falling into his lap, the sound of telephones bringing new offers of sex or business, the sound of turnstiles, new cars, rocket ships, bra straps, Zippo lighters, champagne corks, election booths, color TVs, hi-fis.

Everyone had a nickname, but all the words were his.

Some things you
don't want to know

Peter first stumbled across the idea that became *Ocean's Eleven* on the beach in front of his house in 1955. B-movie director Gilbert Kay told him about a yarn he'd heard from a gas station attendant: At the end of World War II, there'd been a group of G.I.'s who'd done a few smuggling jobs for the army. Kay thought that a reunion of such a squadron of cat burglars could serve as the germ of a heist story set, say, in Vegas. Peter agreed, imagining the film as a vehicle for William Holden. ("I never dreamed of Frank," he said later, "because—well, because we hadn't been speaking for nine years.") But Kay, who had a couple of stinkers to his credit, wanted to direct the thing, and Peter didn't like it *that* much; he told Kay thanks but no thanks.

By the summer of 1958, though, Kay hadn't managed to sell the idea to anybody else, and, remembering Peter's enthusiasm, he peddled the story to him again, this time without attaching himself. Peter jumped, investing five grand of his own money and five grand of Pat's and buying the story outright. The timing was truly cagey: The Lawfords had just mended fences with Frank, and they told him about their newly acquired property at a time when his Dorchester Productions still owed Warner Bros. a film as part of a deal it had cut the year before. Frank, predictably, loved the idea of a caper movie with a Vegas backdrop, and in July 1958, Warner Bros. agreed that he should develop the movie further (Jack Warner cracked that they should forget the script altogether and pull off the job).

The studio assigned Richard Breen, a crime film specialist, to come up with a script, provided that he passed muster with Frank. Breen and Sinatra first came together that September; "they had a very friendly meeting," one of Jack Warner's assistants reported. Breen had pulled quite a fast one to get the job; he'd never been to Vegas, but he "carefully concealed this fact from Sinatra." After a few research trips to the city, he'd gotten several key sequences mapped out and won Sinatra's confidence: "Frank seems in fine fettle and very cooperative," Warner was told. The producer felt good enough to attach director Lewis Milestone, set a starting date of February 1959, and consider a few potential costars, including Jack Lemmon—unaware, apparently, that Frank had already hatched his scheme to turn the picture into a Rat Pack home movie.

Breen and Milestone worked together throughout 1958, screening such caper films as *The Killing* and *The Lavender Hill Mob* for inspiration and calling Billy Wilder in as a script doctor to help them figure out the spine of the story. But Sinatra was still unsatisfied with the script (in one early version, his character was named, bizarrely, Pepe DeMaio). The shooting date was pushed back, and Breen was replaced by Daniel Fuchs, who was in turn replaced by Harry Brown and Charles Lederer, who got final credit for a script based, the world was told, on an original story by Jack Golden Russell and George C. Johnson—two guys who'd been involved so early in the process that they never actually worked for Warner Bros. on the picture.

It was an awful lot of writers, especially given the extremely shaggy shape of the finished product. Milestone admitted as much once the shoot was on. "There is little now left of the original, other than the Las Vegas locale," he told a reporter, adding that Dean turned to Frank one day during filming and asked, "You will give me a chance to read the script before we're through shooting it, won't you?"

As things stood, the finished product hardly resembled a traditional caper film with the requisite tight timing, perilous coincidences, and narrow escapes. Not only did Dean and Sammy get musical numbers, but several scenes were camped up, others led nowhere, and still others seemed plainly improvised, the sort of stuff kept in by a filmmaker primarily for the amusement of his buddies—or his boss. When it was all over, the film had mutated so far from the original concept that it was nominated, despite not really being very good, for a Writers Guild award—as Best Comedy!

While the screenplay was undergoing its patchwork genesis, Frank was casting his buddies and cutting them deals. Peter had been willing to sell the picture outright to Dorchester and Warner Bros., but Frank took care of him—just as he had in Puccini—by giving him $20,000 for the story, plus $300 per week for the shoot, plus—and this was the biggie—one-sixth of the gross: a phenomenal back-end deal which resulted in nearly a $500,000 profit on the Lawfords' $10,000 investment. Dean got $150,000 flat out; Sammy got $125,000; even guys like Richard Conte (more than $8,000 per week) and Cesar Romero ($5,000-plus per week) got healthy. (Some who were rumored to have parts, such as Jackie Gleason, Tony Curtis, and Milton Berle, never showed; others, such as Shirley MacLaine, Red Skelton, and George Raft, worked for scale.)

Frank got $30,000 for the story, $200,000 to act, and one-third of the gross—not to mention, of course, all that he stood to make as a 9 percent owner of the Sands, which was guaranteed to be packed with high rollers during the five weeks the Rat Pack planned to spend in Vegas working on the film.

February was traditionally the nadir of business in Las Vegas, so the town went out of its way to welcome the production. Police chief R.K. Sheffer read over the script drafts—with heart in throat, no doubt—for accuracy; special editions of the Las Vegas newspaper welcomed the production; the owners of the five hotels featured in the film—the Riviera, the Sahara, the Flamingo, the Desert Inn, and the Sands—accommodated the actual filming and made rooms available to the 225 actors, extras, and crew members who stayed in town on Warner Bros.' tab (the company dropped nearly $20,000 a day in out-of-pocket costs during the five weeks). The town positively boomed. The Sands, with only two hundred or so rooms to its cluster of two-story garden buildings, turned away eighteen thousand reservation requests during the first week of the Summit alone.

Milestone and three dozen advance men converged on Las Vegas on January 12. Five days later, Frank flew in from New York (his luggage got lost in the confusion attendant on a rare southern Nevada snowstorm), and the Lawfords arrived by train with Peter's manager, Milt Ebbins, and Frank's secretary, Gloria Lovell. Sammy and Joey arrived the next day; Dean rolled into town two days later with his wife and his factotum, Mack Gray.

Work began with three days of shooting at the Riviera. The earliest call was for 5:30 p.m., and no actor had to be on the set for more than three hours. On the first day of the Summit, January 20, there was no filming done at all. Thereafter, Milestone usually got one Rat Packer at a time, occasionally two, having the whole quintet at his disposal only once—to film the closing credits on a workday cut short by high winds. Most days found a single member of the Rat Pack on the set for about three hours, usually from about 3:00 p.m. to 6:00; Sammy and Peter had the most frequent morning calls (9:00 or 10:00 a.m.), with Sammy easily spending the most time in front of the cameras throughout the month. After they finished at the Riviera, Frank worked only six more days, only two of which lasted more than two hours (he even skipped town for a few days to tape a TV special in Hollywood); the only time anyone was filmed in the wee small hours was when Frank showed up one day at 5:00 a.m. for about two hours of work. Other than that, only Joey ever had a call before 9:00 a.m.— once.

So it really wasn't the film-all-day, perform-all-evening, drink-all-night scene that has become the legend of the Summit and the making of *Ocean's Eleven.* There's no doubt that there were twenty-four-hour hijinks—"They were taking bets we'd all end up in a box," Peter recalled—but precious few hours were actually given over to Milestone. Indeed, when the brief filming days and the relatively short stage shows are added up, nobody really put in more than a six-or seven-hour day the whole month. Oh, sure, it *looked* like a lot of work—a high-profile film shoot and titanic nightclub engagement all in one—but it was cushier than, say, shooting a western in the desert or playing a series of gigs on the road. What with all the amenities and the attention, it was more like a premiere party held while the film was still being made: a P.R. event aimed at boosting the box office. The whole world watched the Summit unfold in the entertainment pages of newspapers and magazines, and when the film came out, they dutifully lined up as if to kiss St. Peter's bronze toe.

Of course, not all of it was for the public. Take Sunday, February 7, when the boys entertained and partied with a Democratic presidential hopeful, Peter's brother-in-law Jack

Kennedy. Kennedy was blitzing the West in the lull before the big eastern primaries. He had a complete entourage with him, including his youngest brother, Ted, and—in an era of press coverage so cooperative it was virtually comatose—he was at least as busy dallying with Peter and his chums as he was currying favor with Nevada's political powers. Kennedy and his party were ensconced at the Sands and held court there: drinking and schmoozing in the lounge, dining on Chinese food in the Garden Room, holding press conferences, attending fund-raising receptions, and, of course, digging the scene in the Copa Room as the Rat Pack entertained.

During each show Jack attended, Frank introduced him from the stage with a bunch of sugary bullshit; Jack stood and took a bow; Dean waited for the applause to die down: "What'd you say his name was?" Big laugh.

There was more. On the night of February 8, just hours before he boarded an early morning flight to Oregon, Kennedy attended a soiree in a private room at the Sands. Strictly inner inner circle. Sammy was there. So was Peter.

As Sammy remembered it, "Peter took me aside and whispered, 'If you want to see what a million dollars in cash looks like, go into the next room; there's a brown leather satchel in the closet; open it. It's a gift from the hotel owners for Jack's campaign.' I never went near it. I was also told there were four wild girls scheduled to entertain him and I didn't want to hear about that either and I got out of there. Some things you don't want to know."

Amid all this carrying-on, Kennedy also apparently managed to start what turned into a serious, long-term affair. Frank had summoned Judy Campbell, a mixed-up twenty-six-year-old divorcée he'd been sleeping with on and off, to visit for the weekend. He introduced her to Jack and made his Sands apartment available to the two of them for a private lunch.

Judy was a good listener. Dean liked to drop by her L.A. apartment and talk; he'd even enlisted her help in spying on his wife, whom he suspected of having an affair with his manager (she wasn't). Campbell was, rarely for a woman in Frank's world, independent, always swearing that she never took gifts or money from her men and even staying down the block at the Flamingo during the Summit after having been invited by Frank to stay in a free room at the Sands. She was also, in a fashion, true. When visiting Hawaii with Frank and the Lawfords, she was shocked when Peter made a pass at her: "Don't worry, Frank will never know," he assured her, but she got huffy and blew him off.

The thing was, Frank truly wouldn't have minded. In fact, he thought Judy was a pretty good time; in the coming months he kept trying to pimp her to half the world: Desi Arnaz, Joe Fischetti, bandy-legged Jack Entratter, and a weaselly-looking guy in Miami who called himself Sam Flood. She gave them all the high hat, vexing Frank to no end: "The things you could have if you weren't so fucking stupid," he eventually snarled at her. "Wake up and realize what you've got in the palm of your hand." He didn't, however, know that she was saving herself for Jack. By the time the candidate left Vegas, they'd already made plans for a rendezvous in New York.

The Summit fostered all kinds of romances. Frank, for instance, was becoming more serious about dancer Juliet Prowse, who visited the hotel several times as the two neared engagement.

And Sammy had stars in his eyes, too. At the end of 1959, his gaze fell upon May Britt, a Swedish starlet, in the commissary at 20th Century-Fox, and he was thunderstruck. She was playing in a remake of *The Blue Angel* and waiting out a Mexican divorce. Sammy was warned that she had ice water in her veins—her chief escort around town was her mother—but one look at all that leg candy convinced him he had to try. He concocted an elaborate end run: a big party for Dinah Washington to mark the end of a nightclub engagement. Sammy called May to invite her, and she asked if she could bring her mom—then showed up with a date. He tried again, asking her over for one of his big hey-kids-let's-all-get-smashed-and-watch-a-movie nights—and inadvertently got her sick on orange brandy. Nevertheless, she found him charming, and she gladly accepted his invitation to visit the Summit when he called her from Las Vegas.

But this was still Las Vegas, a town where the beloved Nat King Cole could find himself unwelcome at the front door of the Tropicana ("I don't care if it's Jesus," said a thick-necked doorman when he was told whom he was bouncing. "He's black and he has to get outta here"), where Sands management was once forced to drain the pool after a few southern high rollers caught sight of Sammy swimming in it. So Sammy couldn't exactly let it be known that this very white actress was visiting the hotel to see him. He turned to the Leader: One afternoon in the steam room, he asked Frank to beard for him and let it be known that May was his guest: "Sure, Charlie, she's my guest."

Yet another of Sammy's amorous schemes seemed to fizzle when he met May at the plane only to discover she had brought along her mother ("Now she brings her mother," he groaned to himself), but the visit went well. Before May returned to L.A. Sammy worked up the courage to kiss her (she had to take off her high heels to give him an angle). He spent the rest of the shoot in an adolescent swoon, trying to screw up the guts to call her and imagining the best (*She loves me!*) and worst (*She hates me!*) all at once.

*

Even if she'd've been recognized, May Britt was about as unspectacular a star as made the trek to Vegas for the Summit. An unimaginable pantheon of stars partook in Frank's ecstatic desert bacchanal, from Lucille Ball to Kirk Douglas, from Jack Benny to Cyd Charisse, from Ingemar Johansson to Milton Berle, from Peter Lorre to Cantinflas—a riot of famous mugs. It was the hottest ticket Las Vegas had ever seen, probably the hottest ever. (And at $5.95 it included dinner!)

Nevertheless, the Sands felt some sort of obligation to promote it. You couldn't get a ticket to the thing, but every day the Vegas papers carried ads for it: "Star-Light, Star-Bright, Which Star Shines Tonight? It's a guessing game, and you'll be a winner at the show-of-shows." Hotel publicist Al Freeman even sent out press releases—surely the most superfluous such documents of all time—to grab up headlines.

Frank and the boys did their share of drumbeating as well, for purely humanitarian reasons. On February 7—the day Jack Kennedy arrived in town—they moved the Summit over to the newly built convention center for a benefit performance to mark Four Chaplains Day, a local event commemorating the deaths of four Nevada clergymen of diverse religions who perished in the World War II torpedoing of the USS *Dorchester*; the money raised by the show helped pay for a monument in the martyrs' honor.

It was never the same thing twice, but it would most of the time go like this: Dean, say, would be introduced by Joey, say: "Direct from the bar . . ."

He'd saunter out with a cigarette. After the ovation, he'd turn to the conductor: "How long I been on?" Then he'd sing, or at least he would start like he was singing, but with ridiculous words: "When you're drinking" (not smiling, see?), or "The Gentleman Is a Tramp," about how he was bad with money. Strictly for laughs. He was always funny—really funny—but most people were nevertheless surprised to see how easily laughs came to him, even without that monkey he'd started out with.

After a few minutes, he'd introduce Sammy or Frank, who'd sing a number or two straight (good thing, 'cause neither could ad-lib).

Then they'd schlep Joey and Peter out, they'd fetch the bar cart, and from then on in it was a travesty: Somebody would start a song, the others would blast it out of the water.

Some nights, they'd focus a bit more. Frank—and only Frank—would sing for real: three, four numbers. But most of the time it was strictly shuck-and-jive—with a decided air of hazing.

Sammy was the preferred whipping boy. Frank and Dean— big *Amos 'n Andy* men, apparently—loved to do darkie dialect and goad Sammy about being black, being Jewish, having one eye: all that funny stuff. Sammy, like a courtier to Ivan the Terrible, would bend over laughing and make sure his liege saw it: his face stretched in desperate mirth, literally slapping his knees, yet not a sound coming out of his mouth.

Sometimes he'd arrive onstage in a business suit or a sports coat and slacks—only to be upbraided by Frank for not wearing a tux: "Now you go get yourself into a dinner coat like the rest of us!"

Sammy would turn on him: "What're you, *Esquire* magazine? I'll change my suit when I'm good and ready!"

Frank'd give him a beady-eyed glare. "And when will that be?"

Sammy'd shrivel up like Jerry Lewis: "I'm ready . . ." and slink off the stage.

When he returned, it would be, apparently, to sing. They'd put a pinpoint spot on him, and he'd try a ballad:

"What kind of fool am I . . ."

"Keep smiling so they can see you, Smokey"—Frank from offstage, and the crowd roared. (He had other surefire lines: "Hurry up, Sam, the watermelon's gettin' warm"; "Why don't you be yourself and eat some ribs?"—jokes funny only in that you couldn't believe somebody trying to get a laugh with them, but Sammy would double up every time.)

Sammy'd get another number going: "She's funny that way . . ."

Dean's turn: "What way is she funny, Sam? What way? What way? I might go over the house . . ."

Or they'd do impressions. Sammy was famous for this—he did all the usual guys, plus novelties like Billy Eckstien, Vaughn Monroe, and Al Hibbler—but Dean could do an okay Cary Grant and Clark Gable, and Frank, well, Frank could do Cagney at least as good as a school kid.

There'd be dancing: again, Sammy's area, but Peter had been in all those MGM musicals, so he'd do a bit, too, with Sammy: "Shall we dance? Shall we lay down some leather, shall we dance?" He was no cripple up there, but he didn't make anyone forget Will Mastin, either; Sammy took pity and reined himself in.

And jokes: nonstop shtick with a Vegas bent. Frank, looking up like he just realized something: "You know, I never heard anybody in this town say, 'Hey, I just came from the Thunderbird!' " Dean, mixing a drink: "How'd all these people get in my room? Oh well, I guess I'll fix me another salad." Joey to Frank: "Stop singing and tell people about all the good work the Mafia is doing."

Joey wrote a lot of it—another reason Frank had him along. And Frank, so dismissive of Milestone and the movie script, protected the comedian's work. When Peter wasn't thrilled with a bit about pretending to be a busboy, Frank spat daggers: "Do it how Joey says or get the fuck off the show."

There were musical bits they'd worked out, familiar tunes

rewritten with special lyrics by Sammy Cahn, or multipart versions of crowd-pleasing songs like "The Birth of the Blues." Joey would get a chance to croon, and they'd all pretend to be offended at the nasal whine of his voice and make him leave the stage; even big Jack Entratter would get up there, wheezing along with them and reading the words off of dummy cards.

And there were bits they dreamed up on the spot—Peter, Joey, and Frank walking across the stage in underwear with their pants folded over their arms and serious expressions on their faces while Dean sang straight—a real laugh. And one they trotted out for years: Frank or Dean would lift Sammy up like a fireman holding a baby and say, "I'd like to thank the NAACP for this award."

Frank and Dean and Sammy had a ball because they were doing a shambles of their own shows: What, was *Variety* gonna say they were out of voice?

Joey was the traffic cop—and the one unmistakable sign that this was a show and not a glimpse into their private lives.

And Peter, who could barely do this sort of thing, let alone live (though he'd been doing an occasional act, if that's what you'd call it, with Jimmy Durante in New York and Vegas for a few years), well, he persevered.

"I always thought that Peter felt uncomfortable," said Joey, and everybody knew it. The joke around town went like this: A couple of low rollers get tickets to the Summit; they're lined up outside the Copa Room and one turns to the other and asks, "Who's the star tonight?" and his buddy says, "With our luck, it'll be that Lawford."

But the point was never a great show—though the critics, believe it or not, fell over themselves praising it. The point was showbiz, or, rather, showbiz as event: the ultimate you-hadda-be-there that seems even more fun as the years pass, especially to those who never had the chance to be there: Paris in the twenties, Berlin in the thirties, Greenwich Village in the fifties, the Rat Pack Summit.

By mid-February, the Las Vegas portion of *Ocean's Eleven* had wrapped; the final Summit show came a few days after that. On February 18, the whole traveling satyricon regrouped at Warner Bros. studios in Burbank for five more weeks of shooting.

Things should've gotten easier for Milestone at this point, what with no groupies nosing about, no gamblers so transfixed by the action that they wouldn't move to accommodate the film crew, no late-night shows squelching the cast's work ethic, and—most important—no desert separating the set from Jack Warner and his flunkies, who could now drop in and watch what was going on at any time. But the deportment the Rat Pack had displayed on the stage of the Sands had spilled over into their work habits.

Frank, predictably, was worst. As Peter recalled, Frank's attitude toward filmmaking had changed drastically since the two had made *It Happened in Brooklyn* together a dozen years earlier. On that film, Peter said, Sinatra "took direction beautifully, listened, contributed, and was generally extremely professional about the whole operation." By 1960, Frank's on-set demeanor had radically changed: "He had reached the point where he would tear handfuls of pages out of the script and allow the director only one take of a scene." His petulance, Peter said, directly harmed the film: "I remember once the sound man kept complaining about an unusual number of low-flying airplanes, which he was picking up through his earphones. . . . Well, after about the fourth take, which was unheard of for Frank, he said, 'Aw, fuck it! Everyone knows they're airplanes.' Indeed! But flying through a bathroom?"

On a lesser scale, Milestone had to put up with water pistol fights, squirting seltzer bottles, and even cherry bombs (which, comically, gave Mack Gray a case of the jitters). Discipline was so lax that Milestone eventually allowed people to use cue cards rather than bother them with learning their lines. Frank took a few days to cut some tracks with Nelson Riddle; Dean played the Sands as a solo and then missed some work on the movie when he agreed to substitute for Jerry Lewis, who was to follow him in the Copa Room but had exhausted himself in Florida filming a movie; Peter raced off to Israel to make *Exodus* for Otto Preminger. It was pure chaos.

When the picture finally wrapped on March 18, Dean and Frank each still owed Milestone a day's work, which he'd have to get from them later that spring: The Rat Pack Summit had already resurfaced in Miami. Nevertheless, Milestone brought the picture in at $2.037 million, nearly $100,000 under budget. His Job-like fortitude and the subsequent financial success of the film earned him a plum assignment on his next picture: MGM's misbegotten remake of *Mutiny on the Bounty*, two years of hell during which Marlon Brando nearly put his director in an early grave; sixty-seven years old when the thing finally premiered, Milestone never completed another film.

Frank may have been the headliner and the producer, but Peter was the one who had discovered the property, and Peter would be the most active in it to the very end. He kept an eye on Milestone's cut and dashed off several memos to Jack Warner with suggestions for changes. He didn't like Sammy's solo number, for instance: "Musically, which is not my department, I think it would be stronger to have Josh sing only. . . . I don't believe the dance is strong at all." And he had very strong opinions about how the robbery sequence should be reworked: "I think a great sense of urgency and excitement could be added to the whole section prior to the explosion by very simply adding a few inserts of wristwatches showing the progress of time during that period. . . . I personally was confused as to where we were in the evening."

For all his sincerity and effort, he was ignored. There really was no use trying to put too pretty a finish on the film. *Ocean's Eleven* was never really a *movie* movie: It was a publicity event, and the studio was sharp enough to see it that way.

The premiere was a gigantic affair that rivaled the Summit for headline-making power. On August 3, in a break from what had become a steady routine of campaigning for Jack Kennedy, the Rat Pack reunited for a brief, final redux of the Summit (curiously Frank's only appearance in Vegas between January 1960 and June of the following year). Everyone was in attendance: Dean, who was already appearing at the Copa Room; Joey, who flew in from Chicago where he was engaged in a nightclub gig; Sammy, taking a break from a Canadian club date; Peter; dozens of supporting actors and bit players from the film; and the usual assortment of hangers-on and glad-handers: Leo Durocher, Joe E. Lewis, Danny Kaye, Sophie Tucker, George Raft, Louis Prima, Keely Smith, Diana Dors, Barbara Rush, Tony Curtis, Janet Leigh, Nick the Greek—a perfectly representative snapshot of the cream of Vegas royalty circa 1960.

An entire evening's revelry was staged as a buildup to a midnight screening of the film: a cocktail party for the five dozen or so reporters invited on the junket; a dinner party and show in the Copa Room; a parade of convertibles up the Strip; and a live performance in front of the Freemont Theater. Ten thousand civilians crammed Freemont Street for a gander at all the high-toned flesh; the entire contingent of the city police force and the Clark County sheriff's detail was on hand, with all but emergency leaves canceled.

It was another tremendous boost to the town—Jack Paar

had the festivities filmed for a special—but there were grumblings nevertheless: Longtime Vegas showbiz columnist Ralph Pearl attended the one-shot Summit and griped "their horsing around with race and religion has finally gotten out of hand. Mix an abundance of blue material with that and you have a highly inflammable situation." Pearl admitted that the audience seemed to like the material—in fact, he confessed, "I'd be a fat, old hypocrite if I said I didn't enjoy their act. It's like eavesdropping on a stag party with binoculars"—but the very fact that he voiced some reservations at all was notable. After all, the city's famous "Welcome to Las Vegas" sign had been covered with an *Ocean's Eleven* banner to mark the premiere.

It was their town, and everybody knew it.

The only singer

For the first three days of March 1960, Frank worked a schedule that simply defied comprehension.

He had been back in Los Angeles for two weeks since the conclusion of the Summit, and he was still reporting to Lewis Milestone's set every day to do the studio work on *Ocean's Eleven*. From about 10:00 a.m. to well past dinnertime each day, Frank went, however lackadaisically, through the paces of the film; it was his single busiest week of the entire production.

Then each night, he made his way to Hollywood and Vine and the Capitol Records tower, where, recovering from the heady bombast of the Summit, immersing himself more and more fully in the Kennedy campaign, putting in long days as star and producer of a major Hollywood film, he recorded some of the most lavish and gorgeous singing performances of his entire career.

Nelson Riddle had written dramatic orchestrations of songs that Frank had sung in the forties under the musical direction of Axel Stordahl, grand, romantic ballads such as "I've Got a Crush on You," "You Go to My Head," "Fools Rush In," "Try a Little Tenderness," "How Deep Is the Ocean?" In recording them again during a whirl of activity that would have paralyzed a less frenetic or expansive spirit, Frank sang of love not with the anguished, suicidal edge of, say, *Only the Lonely* or *No One Cares,* but rather with a fullness and confidence of heart that was just as transporting as his agonized saloon songs and perhaps even of a rarer stripe. The music he recorded those three nights was vibrantly orchestral—strings and soft solos dominated, with none of the mischievous trickery of a Sinatra-Riddle swing album— but no instrument could equal Frank's voice, which by sheer will of heart and mind could sweep listeners out of their bodies. Although he had seemingly mined these songs to their fullest in the forties, he somehow found something more in each of them, transforming them from lush, hopeful stirrings of youth to ripe, gratified affirmations of maturity.

This was acting, of course. His nonfictional life held none of the pure romantic satisfaction that this music bespoke; it was far too crammed with fleeting raptures, dazzling prospects, and quick, distracting activity. But the music wasn't part of all that; it was music in and of itself that he loved, the perfect marriage of his voice, a song, an arrangement, a band; he could, uncannily, lift himself out of his own life and sing— and take us all with him.

How else explain how these overwhelming sounds emerged from a man living such a life?

How else explain a soul capable of such godly breadth?

More: The material recorded those early nights of March was finally released later that year as part of an album that took its name from a song that Frank didn't record until April (after the Rat Pack reunited in Miami for another Summit), a song that struck him as so trivial and pointless when he first heard it that he lifted the sheet music off the composer's piano with his fingertips and dropped it to the floor like a dirty Kleenex.

Over the subsequent weeks, Hank Sanicola (who really could play the piano) kept noodling with the song, which he thought Frank should record, whenever Frank was nearby. Finally Frank broke down: "What is that cute little thing you keep playing?" Sanicola handed him the music. It was "Nice 'n' Easy," by Lew Spence and Alan and Marilyn Bergman. Frank cut it and released it as the kickoff track for the eleven other songs, giving him a moderate little hit single, a new signature tune, and, inevitably, further proof of the seeming infinity of his talents.

No one else could have done it, certainly not Sammy or Dean, thoroughly respectable singers when—and this was hardly always the case—they were given the right material, collaborators, and conditions. It was music that had provided Frank a leg up in the world, and, despite all the carousing and skirt-chasing and movies and politics and careerism and foofaraw, it was music that was still at the core of his identity. Others might sing as a career, as an avocation, as a means of communicating something to the world; Frank sang as if to commune with the music, as if to dissolve what was worldly about him—his body, his money, his authority, his things— into pure aesthetic form. He could do things in music—fast music, slow music, giddy music, wrenched music—that no one else could do, presumably because he was more intimate with the art than anyone else who'd ever lived.

The songwriters, musicians, engineers, and producers with whom he worked over the decades *always* spoke respectfully of his knowledge of their shared work. He didn't know any theory—he could barely sight-read—but his instincts were impeccable, the best, perhaps, of any singer of the century. Part of it was song selection, part of it was style, part of it was sheer chops, part of it was the ineffability of talent. And he kept it up for decades, changing sounds, changing his very voice, always setting the standards in style and performance, remaining vital for more than thirty years until he gave up trying and took up singing oldies in stadiums and in duets with artistic midgets. Even then, a barrel-chested belter giving the crowd something it was stunned to find out he still had, he was peerless.

He didn't necessarily respect his talent in the same ways as, say, an opera singer. He would frequently light a cigarette at the start of a number and smoke it during the song; he would make a point of sipping Jack Daniel's during his act; and he could let his carousing impinge on his constitution. Recalling the recording of *All Alone* in early 1962, an observer said, "Frank looked like hell when he came in. It was as if he'd just been to nine orgies." But this, too, was part of the act: Shouldn't a singer of woeful ballads have a touch of alcohol and nicotine in his voice? Shouldn't the man who sang the mournful waltzes of *All Alone,* one of his most underrated and beautiful records, have sounded weary and wan? Other singers could be placed in a mood; Frank *became* it.

And more: Frank Sinatra simply *was* twentieth-century popular singing. His voice and manner became the center to which all else was relative. Some singers would be jazzier than Frank, some would be rawer, some would avoid his influence by choosing models from gospel, blues, folk, or country, but it didn't matter: They performed in a world comprehended by a grammar and a logic that Frank had invented. Phrasing, microphone technique, musical acting, stage decorum, recording method: Whatever he did became King's English. Everyone was more like Frank or less like Frank—even those who came before him like Crosby and Astaire and Armstrong and Fitzgerald, even those who ignored him like Hank Williams and Patsy Cline and those who sought to vanquish him like Elvis and Mick Jagger and

Johnny Rotten. Without Frank, no one would have an idea of what a popular vocalist should do or be. He was the Only Singer.

Which had to be very, very strange for Dean and Sammy. Compared to the aesthetic rigor that constituted Frank's mission in life, their acts were, well, acts, *lounge acts*, actually, more novelty than epiphany. Silver poets, they each found a little something in Frank's act they could do something with, expanded it with a personal spin, presented it in inimitable, repetitive, familiar styles, and made perfectly respectable careers onstage and in the recording studio. In a sense, they owed him their very lives.

Dean very assuredly would not have had a singing career had there not been a Frank Sinatra. Two years the younger, he was swept to the top in the rage for Italian boy singers that Frank incited. He had a mellower tone than Frank—he sounded more like Perry Como, actually—and there was that curious low warble in his voice, an atavism of the Neapolitan singing he'd grown up listening to on the Victrola; he also liked to slur his sibilants into a slight lisp, making up in manner what he lacked in depth of heart. He sang more novelty stuff than Frank—Italian songs, country and western, duets with Jerry Lewis, for chrissakes—and, of course, he had the drunkie thing going and truly had no work ethic. But from song choice to presentation to attitude, his act was Frank—triple-A Frank, maybe, or Frank Lite, but Frank.

With this difference: Something about Dean's singing always stayed within him. You sensed that *he* was enjoying the song—maybe exclusively—and that he didn't necessarily care if anyone else did, not even the putative lover to whom he addressed such songs as "All I Do Is Dream of You" and "I'll Always Love You." There was a self-satisfied element to his phrasing, a smugness, even a touch of the lascivious. In a few of his love songs, he sounded vaguely contemptuous, like romance was something that made him want to take a shower. You could imagine him flicking a cigarette on his girl; in his hands, a song like "Standing on the Corner" sounded like the interior monologue of a rapist ("You can't get arrested for what you're thinkin'. . . ."). He always had the grace and bonhomie to pull it off—audiences loved him—but his critics were correct to so frequently note the disdain with which he seemed to hold his audience, especially when he was performing live as a solo. When in later years he wouldn't even condescend to finish songs he'd started, there was no denying the impression that he was only concerned with himself.

Sammy, on the other hand, seemed willing to spend himself completely on the audience, yet he was just as informed by an aspect of Frank's art as was Dean. If Dean, like Vic Damone, Tony Bennett, and Eddie Fisher, was born of Frank the Crooner, Sammy, like Bobby Darin and Buddy Greco, was a son of Frank the Swinger. For Sammy, the sheer dramatic actorliness of Frank's singing was a jumping-off point for an act that transformed sincerity from something you conveyed with just your voice to something you communicated with the feet, the face, the hands, the knees, the hips. He provided a link between Al Jolson and Michael Jackson, a man gifted with a variety of awesome talents, none more impressive than the ability to marshal them all in the service of a single, overpowering emotion. What Frank could sell with a whisper or a roar, Sammy used his whole being to put across. Ballads, saloon songs, swing numbers, novelty tunes, he wrung them all, completely.

In the curious juxtaposition of his tiny frame and his deep, woody voice, in his struggles against racism, gossip, and slander, in his triumph over physical trauma and social obstacles, he became a curiously heroic figure, and this made each song he sang seem a challenge that he would conquer through sheer will. Like Frank, he believed deeply in the redemptive power of music, but where Frank thought it unseemly to do anything but *sing* a song, Sammy attacked it with his life. Audiences with whom he had nothing in common as people found themselves empathizing with his struggle and victory; to root against Sammy as he went up against a number was pure bad faith. He was a man naked against the elements with only his heart and voice to keep him alive.

This might've been why he was so restless, trying so many types of material—show tunes, blues, Latin numbers, standards, rock. He was always looking for a new fight, another piece of the world that hadn't submitted yet to his assault. He became known, over time, more for the idiosyncrasy of his métier than for the depth of his expertise in any area, as an eclectic rather than, as Dean and Frank, a specialist. And his specialty was being himself more than anyone else could ever be: "I Gotta Be Me," "A Lot of Living to Do," "What Kind of Fool Am I?," "Yes I Can." What was this but propaganda of the soul, pure ambition exactly like that which Frank expressed in his own more precise fashion?

Sammy never forgot Frank telling him to find his own sound; it was given as career advice, the counsel of an older brother to a younger. Frank certainly felt no threat from Sammy, but he may have been uneasy at seeing the neediest part of his own act presented by Sammy in such a raw, bald form. Sammy was a fabulous mimic (as, by the by, was Dean), and Frank, who could barely do a decent Kingfish, didn't care for the spectacle of his cerebral passion being alchemized into something so physical, earthly, and brash. Frank loved Sammy's act as a counterweight to his own, but when it was too close to his own, it made him queasy. This, of course, was the risk Sammy took every time he took the stage—the risk that made his art so thrilling—but Frank was nevertheless right to resist it.

Worthless bums and whores

The Pan Am clipper landed in Havana on February 11, 1947, filled with snowbirds out to enjoy the balmy climes and not-so-discreet temptations of one of the world's most exciting cities—mambos, rum, jai alai, cigars, casinos, sex shows, cheap flesh.

Among the gay throng, three well-dressed men stood apart. Two bore a distinct air of menace, mitigated, maybe, by fine clothes and grooming. The third, the slightest of them, had a softer mien; like one of the larger men, he carried a briefcase. A few years later, a photograph would be published of the three of them disembarking from the plane.

A car took the three men to the Nacional, the grandest hotel in the Caribbean. There they signed a register book. The big men were Joe and Rocco Fischetti of Chicago and Miami, cousins of Al Capone and brothers of Charlie "Trigger-Happy" Fischetti, one of the chief inheritors of Capone's crime empire. Rocco ran gambling rackets for his big brother, while Joe, weaker and a tad soft in the head, kept an eye on nightclubs, restaurants, and other quasi-legit operations.

the execution of Benny Siegel for embezzling construction funds and failing to turn the hotel quickly enough into a cash cow.)

The conclave was carefully watched by agents of the Federal Bureau of Narcotics, the only department of the federal government then convinced of the reality of an organized crime syndicate. Those agents suspected that the briefcase that Frank carried off the plane that day was filled with $2 million in cash earmarked for Luciano. In an effort not so much to discredit Frank as to draw national attention to the problem of syndicated crime, information about the events in Havana was leaked to the press. Within a few days, Frank was hit with a number of highly critical newspaper columns which fingered him for consorting with known criminals and charged him with being a bagman for the mob. The sweet, skinny crooner with the bow ties and the pretty wife was now being mentioned in the same breath as the nation's most vicious killers.

Frank tried to fight back. To charges that he ran with a bad crowd, he responded, "I was brought up to shake a man's hand when introduced to him without first investigating his past." He admitted being on the same plane as the Fischettis, and he even admitted having met Luciano, although he once again ascribed it to his good manners: "As so often happens in big groups, the introductions were perfunctory. I was invited to have dinner with them and while dining, I realized that one of the men in the party was Lucky Luciano. It suddenly struck me that I was laying myself open to criticism by remaining at the table, but I could think of no way to leave in the middle of the dinner without creating a scene."

Later, Frank said, after a gambling and nightclubbing excursion, he hit the Havana Casino: "We passed a table at which were Luciano and several other men. They insisted that we sit down for a drink. Again, rather than cause a disturbance, I had a quick drink and excused myself. These were the only times I've ever seen Luciano in my life." (The statement went unchallenged, even a few years later when police ransacking the gangster's Naples, Italy, home turned up a gold cigarette case engraved "To my dear pal Lucky from his friend Frank Sinatra.")

As for the bag with the $2 million stuffed inside it, Frank laughed: "Picture me, skinny Frankie, lifting $2 million in small bills. For the record, one thousand dollars in dollar bills weighs three pounds, which makes the load I am supposed to have carried six thousand pounds. . . . I stepped off the plane in Havana with a small bag in which I carried my oils, sketching material, and personal jewelry, which I never send with my regular luggage." (Dollarbills? Oils?)

The ugly denouement to the trip came in April, when Frank came across Lee Mortimer, entertainment editor of the *New York Daily Mirror*, at Ciro's nightclub in Hollywood. Writing for an organ of the right-wing Hearst newspaper chain, Mortimer had for several years taken issue with Frank's public stands on racial harmony and had expressed a personal distaste for Frank's singing and the reaction it provoked among the bobby-soxers. He'd also been among the loudest and most caustic voices in the rumpus about Frank and the mob; in a review of Frank's recent film *It Happened in Brooklyn*, Mortimer even referred to the star as "Frank (Lucky) Sinatra."

Frank had long been threatening to get Mortimer, and the sight of the columnist in his own California stomping grounds outraged him. Words were exchanged, or maybe not: Frank said Mortimer called him a "little dago bastard"; Mortimer denied it and said Frank called *him* a "fucking homosexual" and a "degenerate." Whatever, Frank up and decked the guy, who went to the hospital to be treated for bruises and then filed criminal charges for assault and battery and a civil lawsuit for $25,000.

Frank got murdered in the papers. Mortimer was a little prick, everybody knew that, but the press wasn't happy with having one of its own smacked by some cocky star, even if they were on his side; they let him have it. The pressure from national newspapers and his own bosses at MGM to put the matter behind him became untenable. When Frank's claim that Mortimer had used ethnic slurs against him dissolved in an absence of witnesses to back it up, he paid the columnist $9,000 and admitted in open court that "no provocation really existed" for the fisticuffs.

For the rest of his life, Frank and his family would explain away the attack on Mortimer by claiming that the columnist initiated the decades-long assumption that Frank was chummy with mobsters; one friend even reported visiting a cemetery with Sinatra and watching him gleefully piss on Mortimer's grave.

True, Mortimer had spread the Havana story, and Frank answered questions about that trip for years. But from his repeated, ferocious protest against having his name mentioned alongside those of Mafiosi, you'd've thought he was the only entertainer ever to brush up against Mafiosi—or that, the record to the contrary, he didn't like the contact.

In fact, just about every American comic and singer who had a career before the rock 'n' roll era worked for and met gangsters. From New Orleans, where a branch of the Mafia appeared at around the time Dixieland was born, to Chicago and Kansas City, where jazz and organized crime grew up together, to the nightclubs of New York and the showrooms of Las Vegas, the histories of the mob and showbiz were interlinked.

Dean knew gangsters: His hometown was filled with mob-run casinos, speakeasies, and brothels, and he himself worked as a dealer in sneak joints and as a singing waiter and entertainer in nightclubs with shadowy silent partners. He and Jerry Lewis had played the Copacabana in New York, the Riviera in northern Jersey, the Chez Paree in Chicago, the 500 Club in Atlantic City—mob joints all. They came to know the owners and their front men; even, a tad dangerously, their women.

The mobsters tolerated Jerry, but they *loved* Dean; they courted him, seeking his company in saloons and casinos and on golf courses. But he had no more desire for their favors or their company than he did to have Frank drag him around by the nose. Frank Sinatra, Frank Costello, Franklin Roosevelt: It was all the same to him. A drunken mob soldier once came up to him blubbering, "I have so much respect for you, so much respect," and kissed him on the cheek; Dean wiped his face and gave the man a withering look: "Keep a little for yourself, huh, pallie?" Dean knew that the world for such men was a one-way arrangement; he was smart enough never to be disrespectful or insubordinate—asked to make an appearance, he usually complied—but he kept his distance and tried to maintain strictly professional relationships with any gangsters who wanted to get closer.

This wasn't Sammy's problem by a long shot. Aside from Frank himself, no one in the Sinatra orbit would've been happier to accommodate gangsters than Sammy—not because they were gangsters so much as that it was just his nature to be accommodating. But no matter his manner, the mobsters that he encountered in nightclubs and casinos treated him with contempt. Sammy was a "nigger weasel" to Sam Giancana, who threw cherry bombs under his chair and belted him in the belly for suggesting that he oughtn't force Shirley MacLaine to try his spaghetti if she was dieting. Others followed suit: Jules Podell, one of Frank Costello's front men at the Copacabana, once took the wind out of Sammy's sails when he'd let his act go on too long by shouting at him, loud enough for the audience to hear, "Get off my stage, nigger!"; Joe Fischetti, Frank's Florida buddy, once summoned Sammy to a Miami Beach Teamsters convention that he'd said he was too busy to perform at by hissing at him, "Nigger, you get your ass down here even if it means you have to sprout wings to fly."

Tough crowd: They scared the shit out of Peter, who was sufficiently titillated by the spoor of gang muscle to dine in Los Angeles with Chicago mob attorney Sidney Korshak but cowered in the corner of a Copacabana dressing room when a couple of thick-necked guys in fedoras walked in on him and Jimmy Durante and wanted to know why Bobby Kennedy was being so hard on their friends. ("I was watching those guys," he spoke out brazenly when the coast was clear, to which an observer responded, *You* were watching them? They'd chew you up and spit you out!")

Even Joey wasn't immune to their pull, entertaining at the wedding of one of Sam Giancana's daughters—presumably on the arm.

But none of these guys had Frank's connections. He liked to think of himself as an almost-made guy—though a lot of his gangster pals thought he was too soft and had too big a mouth to fit the profile. He was chummy with New Jersey rackets king Willie Moretti back in Hasbrouck Heights, and had even been counseled by the older man to keep his first marriage together at a time when Moretti was dying from a dose of syphilis he'd contracted by straying from his own. Frank had helped set up Joe Fischetti as the entertainment manager of the Fontainebleau, assuring the Capone cousin a check every week whether he'd done any work to book the current act or not. When Frank's career was in the toilet, he was booked almost exclusively into joints owned by gangsters and had a testimonial dinner thrown him by L.A. hood Mickey

Cohen; when he went into the gaming business, it was through partial ownership of mobbed-up casinos and even a mobbed-up racetrack, Berkshire Downs (aka Hancock Raceway) in Massachusetts; he cut radio commercials gratis for a mobbed-up car dealer in Chicago; he played gigs at a couple of slash-and-run operations operated briefly by the mob as legitimate nightclubs in New York and Chicago; he was photographed with killers, underbosses, and dons.

It wasn't always a mutual respect society. Frank was taken as a chump by mobsters on more than one occasion. In the forties, he was shaken down by a boxing writer and onetime member of his entourage named Jimmy Taratino, whose scandal rag, *Hollywood Night Life*, presaged *Confidential* and all subsequent supermarket tabloids. The paper was funded by Mickey Cohen and, in exchange for economic support totaling $15,000, it *didn't* run any of the stories it had unearthed about Frank's philandering (Taratino was eventually convicted of extortion for scams like this).

Decades later, Frank was suckered into paying a $10,000 initiation fee and performing a few concerts on the arm for a group of gangsters led by Jimmy Fratiano, who had set the bait of offering to make him a Knight of Malta; they got some Hungarian blowhard to front the ruse and gave Frank scrolls and flags and medals, which he accepted with solemnity. It was a sham: All the money from his initiation fee and his free shows was divvied up by the hoods.

Frank knew 'em all—Santo Trafficante, Carlo Gambino, Benny Siegel, Johnny Rosselli, Johnny Formosa, Paul Castellano, Aniello DellaCroce—a pantheon of gangland stars that outshone those chummy with just about any other entertainer.

But no mobster had closer ties to him than Sam Giancana, the ferret-faced Chicago don whose life was to become so intimately linked with Frank's and, eventually, Jack Kennedy's.

It's tempting, in retrospect, to tell the whole thing as if it was Frank's idea: that Frank knew what he was doing when he mixed these men as his brothers; that he consciously tried to bring the mob into the White House and drag the president into the shadows; that he didn't think of himself as merely a source of income and amusement for Giancana and of sex and laughs for Kennedy; that he thought he'd united these two earthly potentates out of the sheer force of his will and personality just as he had Sammy and Joey and Peter and Dean.

But you had to figure that even he wasn't quite so brazen. Frank had pushed around producers and directors and columnists and the occasional studio boss or record company executive, but he'd never played in this kind of league before. Frank liked to sip Jack Daniel's and bully busboys and hookers; maybe he'd punch out a photographer. Giancana was a torturer and murderer with seventy arrests on his record, including a murder indictment at age eighteen (the chief witness to the crime turned up dead himself the day after the charges were filed). He had a grade school education and millions of dollars; he was a little, unappealing man who slept with beautiful women and commanded the loyalty of men who could physically tear him apart; and he was so cunning and distrustful that he frequently flew from Chicago to L.A. and then drove to Las Vegas to collect his portion of the money the mob skimmed from casinos there. You had to figure that *he* was the one pulling *Frank's* strings, that he was the guy who reckoned he'd use Frank as a bridge to the Kennedys.

In some respects, Giancana was a typically ruthless mobster who rose to the top out of sheer guts, greed, and callousness. He'd been born in 1908 in the Patch, a dirt-poor Italo-American ghetto in Chicago, and he'd run from his early youth with a gang called the 42s, a bunch of geniuses who'd misremembered the number of men in Ali Baba's fabled crew when naming themselves. The 42s stole and raped and beat and extorted and, when they needed to cover up those trespasses, they bombed and killed. They were keen on automobiles: They stole 'em, they joyrode in 'em, they outran the cops in 'em. Giancana, whose lunatic antics so surpassed those of his hoodlum friends that he got the nickname Mooney, which was itself shortened to 'Mo' or 'Momo,' was the best wheelman in the gang; he was involved in business well beyond his years simply because he could be counted on to bring everybody back from it untouched.

Giancana's way with a car got him noticed by the big mobs in town; before long he was driving for Machine Gun Jack McGurn, one of Al Capone's most feared henchmen. Service to McGurn meant Giancana met the other powers who'd succeeded Capone: Charlie Fischetti, Tony Accardo, Jake Guzik, Frank Nitti, Paul Ricca. In time, with enough bodies in his wake and enough rackets under his iron-fisted control, he became their peer and successor.

By the fifties, his reputation as a killer and earner put him on top. Among his coups: commandeering Chicago's numbers rackets from black gamblers, spreading the gambling interests of the Chicago mob throughout the Midwest and into Las Vegas, diversifying into businesses like shrimp fishing in the Caribbean and semilegitimate concerns as far-flung as Mexico, South America, and Iran. He was, friends of Giancana's liked to quote Meyer Lansky as saying, "the only Italian who handles money like a Jew." He carried a business card that read:

NO ADDRESS	NO PHONE
RETIRED	
NO BUSINESS	NO MONEY

On the back was a carefully worded script: "Under the Fifth Amendment to the Constitution of The United States, I respectfully decline to answer, on the grounds that my answer may tend to incriminate me": a real character.

For all his ferocity, Giancana was strangely domestic and even dainty. Tony Accardo, his predecessor on top of the Chicago Outfit, was known as Joe Batters in recognition of his use of a Louisville Slugger as an instrument of negotiation; he chopped wood and mowed his lawn to let off steam. Giancana, on the contrary, collected Dresden figurines, sterling tea services, oil paintings. His suburban Chicago home was stuffed with fine antiques and rugs—a Louis XV mahogany piano was the centerpiece—and whole sets of Meissen china. He golfed—his backyard was mown exactingly into a putting surface—and he loved to shop for jewelry, in which he had understated, discriminating taste—no gaudy pinky rings for him.

Well, there was *one* pinky ring, a star sapphire friendship ring given to Giancana by the only one of his many Hollywood acquaintances he could stand: Frank Sinatra.

Giancana flat out used just about every big star who came his way. He was contemptuous of anyone who made a gaudy living yet still had money troubles, as did so many celebrities he'd met. "Don't ever be star-struck by all that movie baloney," he told his half brother. "They're all worthless bums and whores." Yet still he was drawn to their company—maybe more than was smart. His open affair with singer Phyllis McGuire put him in the newspapers and made his more discreet mob partners worry, and rightly so, since it made him an easier target for the feds; he carried on with singer Keely Smith and bragged to his half brother about schtupping Marilyn Monroe and lesser Hollywood lights. For male stars he had almost no use at all, but in Sinatra he felt he'd found a man's man, a guy who had real class and knew how to party, a diamond, he assured those around him, amid the dross of Hollywood.

Their friendship went back to the fifties, when Giancana staged charity benefits in Chicago as a sop to his patient, sickly little wife. Big guns turned out: Dean and Jerry, Tony Bennett, Bob Hope, Jimmy Durante—filling Chicago Stadium every summer for some rinky-dink Catholic charity that no one had ever heard of. Frank met Giancana through his appearances at these events, and, as was his wont, he courted the don. They hit it off; when Giancana was arrested on a forged driver's license rap in 1958, cops found Frank's private phone number in his wallet.

The gangster and the singer were together frequently throughout the early sixties. They golfed and partied in California, Nevada, Chicago, Miami and Hawaii; they spent Easter together in Palm Springs and dropped in for dinner with Frank's parents in New Jersey; Giancana visited the Madison, Indiana, set of *Some Came Running* and was a permanent fixture on the set of *Come Blow Your Horn,* in which Frank had given Phyllis McGuire a small part.

The Hollywood crowd around Frank was appalled by the relationship. Giancana was, Peter Lawford said, "really an awful guy with a gargoyle face and weasel nose. I couldn't stand him, but Frank idolized him because he was the Mafia's top gun. Frank loved to talk about 'hits' and guys getting 'rubbed out.' And you better believe that when the word got out around town that Frank was a pal of Sam Giancana, nobody but nobody ever messed with Frank Sinatra. They were too scared. Concrete boots were no joke with this guy. He was a killer."

Nobody in showbiz read it right. To them, Frank was a mob intimate. But to those around Giancana, Frank's solicitude was an embarrassment and a joke. In March 1961, Giancana was in Miami for the Floyd Patterson–Ingemar Johannson heavyweight championship fight—as well as a series of meetings with Johnny Rosselli and intelligence agent Robert Maheu at which plans to assassinate Fidel Castro were discussed. They stayed at the Fontainebleau, and Frank happened to be playing at the hotel; he called Giancana's room constantly, trying to arrange a visit. Giancana stalled, mocking the singer to his cohorts. Finally, though, he agreed to meet Frank for a drink, telling the others, "We're going to have to see him sometime. Might as well get it over with now, but watch what you say because the guy's got a big mouth."

In the bar, Frank shook Giancana's hand. "I see you're wearing the ring," he said.

Giancana said he always wore the token of Frank's friendship, but Frank wouldn't believe him: "Oh, no you don't," he said. "I heard you hadn't been wearing the ring. I heard you never wore it."

Joseph Shimon, one of Maheu's operatives, was also at the bar, and he couldn't believe what he was hearing. "It seemed so ridiculous to me," he remembered. "He was talking like some frustrated little girl with a broken heart. Finally, I couldn't help it. I said, 'What is this? Are you two bastards queer for each other or what?' Sam fell off his chair laughing, but Sinatra was very embarrassed and turned his back on me."

In Ciro's, Shimon might've wound up, like Lee Mortimer, on his ass.

In front of Giancana, Frank, worried that he might louse up a big connection, was the one too afraid to talk.

The place was on fire

Miami was one of their playgrounds, and like everything else they touched then, it was golden.

The late fifties found the city in the midst of a boom the likes of which it hadn't experienced in thirty years. Air travel had made south Florida accessible to New Yorkers for quick weekends; Frank virtually advertised it, standing on a tarmac on the cover of *Come Fly with Me*, one thumb jauntily arched toward the TWA jetliner behind him. With Havana, once the East's premier party spot, closed by revolution, Miami offered an unrivaled brew of flesh, surf, sun, and elegance—there weren't casinos, true, but you could drink the water.

Like Vegas, Miami had a strip of fabulous hotels—the Eden Roc, the Diplomat, and, especially, the Fontainebleau, the gaudy Moderne pipe dream of architect Morris Lapidus, the most expensive, expansive, and exciting jewel of the city's glittering string. The Fontainebleau catered to the biggest shots and had the biggest stars under contract, the Sands of Collins Avenue. It was the luxe of the luxe in a town that specialized—perhaps, in the absence of legalized gambling, even more than Vegas—in spoiling guests.

It was also a celebrity magnet, its clubs and hotels offering high fees and, like Vegas, a place for entertainers to relax and watch one another work. In January 1960, for instance, just as Dean was making a resort movie at the Sands with Frank and the rest of them, Jerry Lewis directed himself in a film at the Fontainebleau, *The Bellboy*. Two months later, when *Ocean's Eleven* wrapped, Dean, Peter, Sammy, and Joey descended on the hotel, where Frank was nearing the end of an engagement. The five of them extended the Summit with a few nights of wild, improvised shows and another big-time production, not a film this time but a truly special special for TV. (Sammy was, at the time, under contract to the rival Eden Roc, but Frank convinced his bosses to free him up for the shows by agreeing to dine at the Eden Roc—along with all his chums—and create publicity for it throughout the week.)

Frank had scored a coup, perhaps the only one in all of showbiz capable of even equaling the shows at the Sands and the impending release of *Ocean's Eleven:* He had secured rights to the first post-army performance of Elvis Presley, an hour-long special for ABC to be shot in Florida with him and various of his cronies. Elvis would only appear twice, briefly, but it was a hugely anticipated pop moment.

At first blush, it was a quixotic thing for either star to do. Elvis didn't need to stand beside Frank to reclaim his audience; he might even, working alongside a performer old enough to be his daddy, look a bit dated; and if Frank was really *that* big, Elvis should have been chary of sharing his brilliant return with him: He was a rival.

From Frank's point of view, it was even stranger. He had to pay for it through the nose, for one thing: Elvis's people milked Frank for $100,000 for a mere ten minutes of Presley's time ("You should make in a year," said Sammy Cahn, whom Frank asked to produce the special, "what Frank is losing on this show"). Too, Frank hated rock music; Elvis was one of those "sideburned delinquents" he'd railed against a few years earlier, an upstart who'd edged into Frank's record sales and glory. And the two had no natural rapport, not as singers, not as icons, not even as men. Poor, southern, and white wasn't one of the guises Frank ever tried on for size, and Elvis actually idolized *Dean* among older singers of standards.

But Elvis was in that spring of 1960 the only star who shone with anything like Frank's intensity, and his return from a two-year absence was a big, big draw. To put the two of them together made a twisted kind of sense: Elvis could accept Frank's attention as an emblem of his place at the acme of showbiz, and Frank could both augment his hepcat credentials and have a hit, at last, on TV.

Lord knew he needed one: His three most recent shows, also ABC specials, had all flopped. This would be his last show in his current contract, and, like an athlete about to go free-agent, he wanted to make an impression on potential new employers. So he didn't care how much he had to fork out or whom he had to pretend to be happy to see to do it; it was show business, yes, but it was business, too.

The atmosphere around Miami's mini-Summit shows and the "Welcome Home Elvis" special was as charged as it had been in Vegas two months earlier. The town was crawling with Rat Pack adjuncts like Jack Entratter, Skinny D'Amato, and Texas oilman Bob Neal, a skirt-chaser of such renown that Jack Kennedy once greeted him with "My God, Bob Neal! That's the man we'd all like to be!" Desi Arnaz was in town, and Nancy Sinatra, and even Sam Giancana, who sported himself by tossing cherry bombs under people's chairs, a diversion that so amused Frank that he joined right in, even when Peter and Sammy were Giancana's defenseless victims. (Frank seems to have caught the fireworks bug from Giancana: Mia Farrow later remembered him frequently stuffing his pockets with cherry bombs before hitting the town, apparently intending to avoid the press by creating explosive diversions.)

Giancana was in town for more than just shenanigans,

however. Operation Mongoose, the CIA-Mafia cabal against Castro, was gestating, and he was speaking to a frightening stew of conspirators interested in recovering lost property in Cuba. Moreover, the Chicago Outfit had had some interests in Florida ever since Capone took up vacationing there; he could check up on a few things, call it a working holiday.

Whenever he hit Miami, Giancana immediately hooked up with Frank's old buddy Joe Fischetti, a handsome, enigmatic figure known around town as Joe Fish. Fischetti was one of the Fischetti brothers who visited Lucky Luciano in Havana with Frank just after the war; his older siblings, Rocco and Charlie, were capos in Chicago, the city that became theirs after their cousin Al Capone went to jail and lost his marbles. But Joe had neither the muscle nor the brains to pull his weight at home; like Fredo Corleone, he was sent somewhere warm to keep watch of things under the protective eyes of the local mob—the Trafficante family of Tampa in this case. Joe ran a few restaurants, kept tabs on—and pieces of—little Miami vices, and was always ready with a broad or a place to crash or somewhere to stash something—or someone—you didn't want found. He was Chicago's guy in Miami and, as such, Frank's guy there, too. And he was as reputable as, say, Johnny Rosselli; you could let him meet good company and not worry about what he might do. He was, as far as the IRS was concerned, a restaurateur and hotelier who received a regular salary from the Fontainebleau as entertainment director. But his position with the hotel was strictly a no-show affair that amounted to little more than his guaranteeing that the hotel had access to Frank's services. He got more than a grand a month on the books: pure tribute.

And since it was Joe Fish's town, and it was Joe Fish's hotel, the summiteers got treated right. When somebody at the front desk made the mistake of putting Joey Bishop in a suite on the seventh floor (Frank and the rest were up on fifteen), Frank called downstairs and threatened to walk unless that was changed. Joey, happily ignorant of the fuss, was preparing for the night's show. "I'm in my room, writing some material," he remembered. "Six bellboys came running in. They didn't take out my clothes. They took out the drawer with the hangers and everything. I thought the place was on fire."

After three nights of Summit shows, the "Welcome Back Elvis" special was staged. Dean, making more movies than even Frank, skipped town for L.A., but the rest all appeared, even Peter, who was a bit of all right as a song-and-dance stooge for Sammy. (The wan show's highlight turned out to be their "Shall We Dance?" number from the Sands, with Frank and Joe butting comically in and giving the hour its only touch of Summit spontaneity.)

The hour was built inanely around the conceit that Frank was "giving Elvis back" the two years he'd lost to the service by introducing him to songs and showbiz events he'd ostensibly missed. While the structure did afford Sammy and Frank the chance to sing some recent hits, the show was continually dragged down by dull production numbers, inane emcee patter read by Frank and Joey with a clumsiness that bespoke indifference rather than breeziness, and a bizarre and depressing routine featuring Nancy Sinatra as part of a human time machine—three young dopes who marched in a kind of lockstep and handed out pieces of paper describing the next historical moment to be presented.

Elvis made a brief appearance at the beginning, sauntering out in his army threads to a shrill, frenzied greeting from the live audience; he ended the opening number by singing a chorus, with special lyrics, of "It's Nice to Go Traveling," the brilliant final cut from Frank's *Come Fly with Me* LP. As a finale, he came back, this time in a tuxedo (complete with western bow tie), to trade numbers with his host: Elvis sang

"Witchcraft," Frank did "Love Me Tender." Frank won the singing hands down, but it was Elvis's night.

What the hell: When the show aired two months later, the ratings were the best ever for a Sinatra show; he wouldn't croak from a little magnanimity.

If the "Welcome Home Elvis" show enabled Sammy to catch up with his old buddy Elvis—the two had once been early casting choices to play opposite one another in *The Defiant Ones*—it also forced him to deal with one of his bêtes noires: the virulent racism of Miami, a city that, like Las Vegas, beckoned him with lucrative and prestigious work opportunities, then treated him with disdain as just another black face.

By 1960, Sammy had himself risen high enough in the world—and was standing close enough to Frank—not to have to stay in the black ghetto across the Intercoastal Waterway from the fabulous hotels of the Miami Beach strip; like everyone else on the show, he was welcome to stay at the Fontainebleau and had similar privileges next door at the Eden Roc. But the rest of the city was a dicier prospect; as in Vegas, he tended to entertain himself indoors a lot.

More and more, Sammy was beginning to resent the whole thing—the slurs and ad hoc integration and limitations. And he was beginning, for the first time in his life, to see the struggle less as a matter of *Sammy's* being accepted than as one of an entire race's being shown a table in the nightclub of life.

Ever since he'd left the army, he felt racism with painful depth. Treated as a subhuman since boyhood because of the color of his skin, he'd grown to loathe his own flesh; he would occasionally squeeze his hands together just to see what it looked like to be, briefly, white. It wasn't an uncommon feeling, he knew: "I really have at least subconsciously wished, like probably every other Negro, that there was *some* way I just wouldn't have to go *through* all of it."

He had always been in favor of integration, naturally, but by his own admission it had been only his own acceptance into the wider, whiter world that interested him. "I didn't give a damn about no race cause," he said. "I knew about the problems, but I just didn't care. I didn't care about nobody but me." He was a curious sort of pioneer, breaking down barriers that almost no other black man would ever encounter—"Long before there was a civil rights movement I was marching through the lobby of the Waldorf-Astoria, of the Sands, the Fontainebleau, to a table at the Copa. And I'd marched alone. Worse. Often to black derision" —but doing so for selfish, even ignoble reasons.

He'd always gambled on good manners and talent to get him past barriers, and he'd had his face bashed in for his efforts—sometimes literally. Still, at the end of the day, no matter how hard he'd fought or entertained, he was shunted to the side, to the back, to the colored part of town. "Colored, colored, colored," he shouted to himself in anger. "Why do we have to live *colored* lives?"

Injustice anywhere was plainly awful, but in Sammy's case especially, it was truly perverse. Few performers of any race ever so thirsted for showbiz glory and fewer still so deserved it. Sammy was a man infected by a bug—a bug that mostly preyed, it so happened, on whites, and he turned the disease into a staggering talent that curiously tilted toward white models. He perfected imitations of Cagney, Bogart, Cary Grant; he could sing *and dance* a la Fred Astaire; he admitted to "emulating the white stars"; Frank famously called him on it: "You've got to get your own sound, your own style. It's okay to sound like me—if you're me."

And that was *onstage*. Offstage, he ran so readily in the fast life of showbiz—a *white* fast life—that he became a constant target for the worst kind of racist smears. For years, he was demonized in the gossip press as a consort of glamorous white stars, sometimes rightly, often wrongly, and once, with Kim Novak, wrongly at first but so intriguingly that the two consummated the affair just to savor the exotic taboo that they'd been accused of violating. In the black press, he was excoriated, conversely, for ignoring his blackness: "Is Sammy Ashamed He's a Negro?" blared a headline; "Look in the mirror, Sammy. You're still one of us," sneered an editorial.

He couldn't, it often seemed, please anyone except the audience immediately in front of him. Attacked on all sides, he once chose the most foolish, immature solution imaginable: Out at the Silver Slipper on the Strip one night in 1958 on a drunken gambling binge, he proposed marriage to Loray White, a dancer he'd once gone with; she accepted; he shouted it out to everybody and even stood for pictures. Then he went home to sleep it off.

When he awoke, he got a glimpse of the magnitude of what he'd done: Not only was he engaged to the first pretty black woman he'd found, but the same black journalists that were lambasting him as an Oreo a few days before were now ringing him up for details of the wonderful news. He would have to go ahead with it. Against the wishes of his dad and his uncle, he arranged to marry the dancer, then quickly divorce; she would be induced to go through with the charade by money and career favors.

It was such an awful hoax, such a crass, hypocritical gesture, that he got drunk again on his wedding night, clutched his fingers around his bride's throat, and squeezed. Within a few weeks of the farcical wedding that was meant to make his life easier, he had fantasies of gunning his sports car off a Hollywood Hills road and killing himself in some moonlit canyon.

He had tried to serve everyone—white bosses and audiences and icons, black audiences and journalists—and it had nearly been the end of him. Now, however, with Jack Kennedy his friend and Frank his *padrone,* he felt he could do more and do it more honestly. Time was ripe.

In March 1960, in the midst of the Rat Pack Summit and days after Kennedy left town, Las Vegas NAACP officials presented an ultimatum to the casino owners of the Strip and Freemont Street: Let us have the same access to your establishments as whites or we will take to the streets; you have two weeks.

The city was riding a glorious crest; Sammy was everywhere, and Frank had his back; the eyes of the world were on them. The casino owners tried to negotiate, they tried to bribe, but they finally had to cede. At 6:00 p.m. on the day of the deadline, after intense brokering by crusading *Las Vegas Sun* publisher Hank Greenspun, the NAACP, the Las Vegas chief of police, the Clark County sheriff, and Governor Grant Sawyer signed a deal to bring down segregation barriers at all hotels and casinos in the city and on the Strip. It was called the Moulin Rouge Agreement, in honor of the hotel in which it was signed.

The irony in naming a civil rights accord after the Moulin Rouge was bittersweet. If Vegas is a Roman candle, always exploding with dazzling new delights, then the Moulin Rouge hotel and casino might have been its brightest-ever rocket, a little pocket of Las Vegas as wild as Harlem, Beale Street, Central Avenue, or the French Quarter.

Built in 1955 way out in a no-man's-land between the black shanties of Westside and a few hardscrabble white developments off Bonanza Road, the Moulin Rouge was the first fully integrated casino and hotel in Las Vegas. It was a place for the town's five-thousand-odd blacks to gamble, drink, and carouse, for wealthy blacks from around the country to have a deluxe place in the sun of their own, and for entertainers not welcome at the segregated casinos to stay and party in splendid comfort.

It was high time, as Sammy could attest. When he'd rolled into the city a decade earlier to play the Last Frontier as part of the Will Mastin Trio, he split $350 with his dad and uncle and was otherwise unwelcome; except for their dressing room, the stage, and the back of the hotel, where they stood waiting each night for a taxicab, white Las Vegas was off limits to them. They could drink and gamble and dine out in skanky makeshift joints on the unpaved streets of Westside, they could sit—quietly—in the back row of a downtown movie theater, they could visit black-only whorehouses, churches, and stores, but the razzle-dazzle of dice and lights and ice cubes and perfume and plunging necklines—the Las Vegas that was even then a paradise on earth—that was out. And Sammy, so painfully aware of being accepted as a performer and rejected as a man, ate his heart out over it, gazing out the dirty window of his despicable little rooming house at the glow radiating from the Strip.

Back then, even the biggest black stars got shafted in Las Vegas. It was a Jim Crow town, plain and simple, and all the more awful for being not some Deep South backwater but a major entertainment center and a vacation spot for people whose opinions mattered so much in showbiz. Black show-people grew used to ill treatment as they traveled throughout the country, but they had never experienced Vegas's strange combination of big-time facilities and salaries and Mississippi backwater segregation. Sure, they'd been treated the same as they got in Vegas—and far worse—in little burgs everywhere. But they needed to be a part of Las Vegas—just as they needed to be part of New York and L.A.: It was where the showbiz was.

But it was also segregated by both official and unofficial policy. The people who ran the city—Mormons, Italians, Jews—always claimed that *they* weren't the racists; they blamed it on the Texan high rollers on which so much of their business relied. But they weren't necessarily averse to setting limits on other groups, either. They didn't need black entertainers in their showrooms nearly as much as black entertainers needed to show that they could play Vegas crowds, create buzz, and earn Vegas money.

It didn't matter if you were Louis Armstrong or Will Mastin, Pearl Bailey or Sister Rosetta Thorpe, the Mills Brothers or Tip, Tap and Toe; sunset either found you working on a hotel stage or back in Westside where you belonged. Even the majestic Lena Horne, the second-ever headliner in the history of the Flamingo, wasn't allowed in the public areas of the hotel, and ultimately stopped coming to Las Vegas altogether, despite the fact that the town's "cabarets," as she called them, paid the best salaries of anywhere. "I never liked the atmosphere," she remembered diplomatically.

It hadn't always been that way. Before World War II, there were so few blacks in Vegas—and, truly, so little going on at all—that the town was integrated as a matter of course. In 1941, for instance, Pearl Bailey got off a train at Union Station, walked into a Freemont Street casino, and put down a bet; nobody thought to stop her. But by the end of the war, when a booming magnesium industry brought thousands of black workers from the South—and when the first big-money resorts in town began to blossom—a less liberal atmosphere descended. If Pearlie had tried to place that same bet the next time she was in town—at the Flamingo in 1947—she would've been asked to leave the joint by somebody comfortable calling her "nigger."

And that was for headliners—who were the only blacks permitted to play in the city at all. Black lounge acts, musicians, dancers, chorus girls, singers, and comics without big names weren't even considered worthy of the right to be humiliated by the bosses of the best hotels. Almost every black act that played Vegas was a major one; new talent was almost completely denied the town as a proving ground. The Will Mastin Trio, for instance, barely qualified, and it was only when Sammy became a star that anyone considered hiring them regularly.

Not that Sammy's making a hit in Vegas was some kind of integrationist success story; it may not even have been a showbiz rags-to-riches tale. It might have been even rarer—a true marriage of souls. Sammy was in perfect harmony with the excess of the place—the whole of showbiz in one pint-sized fireball. He was never more alive than when he was performing there, wringing an audience limp—he aimed at no less, in fact—then wandering out to drink and smoke and bet far too much money and grab every pretty girl that walked by; just the sort of excessive, spree-bent guy the town thrived on. Success in Vegas—wowing a star-choked crowd— mattered as much to Sammy as making a hit in New York or L.A.; the town became one of his shrines and he, in turn, one of its great prophets. And as his star rose gradually, with one or two others who shared his plight, he set about to make the place more accommodating for himself and—what the hell— for those alongside and behind him, too.

Like him, a handful of black entertainers broke through one at a time. They were superstars, they were brash young men, they were brotherly with the entertainment directors and casino managers and hotel presidents: They belonged. They had to be cagey and sly and daring and gutty—but they did it.

In 1955, Sammy and his pop and uncle broke the color line at the Last Frontier. Over the years, other black headliners had been permitted to live in gilded cocoons while performing at the hotel, but the Mastins were given rooms, allowed to have family members in the audience, and granted access to the casino. Management found out that letting a guy like Sammy wander the pits could be profitable, especially just after shows let out, when the sight of a hot star gambling big money tended to encourage onlookers, drunk on charisma, into rash, house-friendly bets of their own.

At roughly the same time, just across the road, Harry Belafonte integrated the Riviera through a string of subversions. Taking the initiative of jumping into the swimming pool and placing bets at a blackjack table without asking first if it was okay, he was accepted by adoring crowds and *then* by the bosses—who didn't approve but couldn't complain with the way things turned out.

For the most part, though, the absurd, hurtful charade continued unabated. An *Ebony* reporter in town to do a story on a black entertainer was allowed only to watch a show from the wings and talk to the star in a private dressing room before being whisked from the Strip to Westside. Light-skinned black balladeer Herb Jeffries showed up for an engagement at the Sands unaware of the segregationist policies—as was the new hotel employee who'd booked him and arranged for his room. At first, management was prepared to show him the door, then relented and gave him a room but no access to any other parts of the hotel; moreover, he was told, his accompanist would have to stay in Westside. "If he does, I do," Jeffries declared, introducing pianist Dick Hazzard to Sands executives: Hazzard was white.

It was ridiculous, it was insulting, and it would have to stop—at least for the big stars. In 1957, Nat King Cole, a mainstay at the Sands, got the green light from Jack Entratter and Carl Cohen: While he was in town he could do anything in their place that he wanted to, anything any white person did. He couldn't necessarily visit any other joints, but the Sands was his. By that time, Sammy had moved to the Sands as well, partly out of love of Frank, partly because the Sands was the acme of the Strip, partly out of his own well-deserved star status, partly because it was more sophisticated, and, by extension, more welcoming, than any other place in town.

Except, of course, the Moulin Rouge, that fabulous paradise owned, ironically, by a syndicate of Jews from New York and

L.A.—with two points thrown to heavyweight champ Joe Louis in token of his services as front man and greeter, his first such sad gig in town.

From the day it opened in 1955, the Moulin Rouge was a sensation. It didn't book acts as famous as those that played the Strip hotels—it couldn't afford them—but it drew those same performers, after hours, for fabulous, star-studded jam sessions. If Louis Armstrong couldn't drink and party and schmooze at the Sands—and he *couldn't*—he'd head over to the Moulin Rouge for the 2:00 a.m. show, with its fabulous Watusi dancers, and beautiful can-can girls, and Lionel Hampton entertaining a mixed-race crowd that might include Frank, Sammy, Dean, Bob Hope, the Dorsey Brothers, Nat King Cole. Showbiz, so well integrated, flocked to the place. "People knew the rest of the town was so wrong," reflected the hotel's entertainment director, Bob Bailey, "and everything at the Moulin Rouge was so right."

The place was as handsome as any hotel on the Strip. From the outside, it resembled the Sands, with a big cursive sign atop a sort of artfully perforated pylon. The inside was done up in a Parisian motif, with gilded chandeliers and ornaments, lavender ceilings, and murals of the Pigalle. It was built during a boom time—the Hacienda, the Dunes, the Riviera, and the Royal Nevada all opened that same year—but it so stood out among its peers that it made the cover of *Life* magazine.

It lasted six months.

You'd hear whispers over the years that the Strip hotels, fearful of loss of custom to a celebrated new rival, leaned on the banks that had written short-term loans to the Moulin Rouge's owners, that the notes were called back, that a sinister cabal wiped out paradise. But the pettier truth is that the hotel was undercapitalized—there were legitimate mechanics liens against the place—and the town had overbuilt besides: The Royal Nevada, which broke no taboos, went belly-up almost as fast and strictly for financial reasons; the Dunes and the Riviera struggled out of the gate.

Still, those other hotels meant nothing to anybody, whereas the Moulin Rouge was an Eden, and fate and the gods, it seemed, had conspired to reveal it and then close it away. In 1957, it reopened, with another white owner, barely surviving, eventually losing its liquor license when it was revealed that black customers had to pay more for drinks at the bar than whites. The resultant cry of racism leveled at the city's one fully integrated casino was strange, hurtful. To many of those trying to break Las Vegas's color line, the Moulin Rouge became an embarrassment; it had been a transitional vehicle, and once their sights were set higher, they abandoned it as a distasteful compromise—a separate-but-equal joint.

The last meaningful glimpse of the hotel as a part of the Vegas scene was that day in March 1960 when the Strip's major resorts finally agreed to open themselves to black customers, the day the Moulin Rouge Agreement, the first major step in ending Las Vegas's awful racial history, was signed.

It was, of course, hardly an instant sea change: As late as 1966, Sammy, an acknowledged Prince of the Strip, could complain about being asked, "Stay in your suite as much as you can between shows, OK?" ("At least they're *ashamed* of it now," he sighed), forcing him to turn his rooms in the Aqueduct building of the Sands into a seraglio of evanescent delights—wild parties, private movie screenings, near-orgies.

In all, a decade of pressures, investigations, protests, and legislation would be required before the once-and-for-all integration of state gaming facilities and resorts was complete from patrons through employees. But the Moulin Rouge Agreement was the start. After that moment, little Sammy could feel able to confront big Jack Entratter about segregation.

He did it, too. When integrationists threatened to picket the Strip hotels at a time when Sammy would, coincidentally, be performing at the Sands (they wanted more black employees at the major casinos), Sammy stuck his neck out, walking into Entratter's office with an ultimatum: "You're going to get picketed and it's going to be very embarrassing, because I'm going to be on the picket line. . . . I'm not going to, quote, be in a hospital recuperating from mild pneumonia and exhaustion, end quote. I'll be right out front, walking back and forth."

He wasn't asking for the world— "Nobody's saying take out an ad in *Ebony* magazine saying, 'You're Welcome at the Sands'" —just some fairness. Entratter, to his credit, came through. Eventually, Sammy played to mixed-race audiences, and customers at the Sands would see black faces—however scattered—among the employees of the hotel.

For Sammy, even to make such requests of Entratter was a sign of a raised consciousness. And soon afterward, when civil rights leaders began to ask him to lend his presence to protests, petitions, and marches, he joined Belafonte, Sidney Poitier, Ossie Davis—acknowledged leaders—and he did the right, selfless thing, flying to Selma and staring down Bull Connor and his thugs.

He didn't spend the night—he didn't dare—but he made himself visible: an icon of white showbiz, a very prominent black man, linking arms with Martin Luther King Jr. and declaring solidarity with other people who had skin like his.

Frank never marched; Peter, Joey—never; Dean joked about it: "I wouldn't march if the Italians were marchin'."

But Sammy, finally on top of the world and awakened to the opportunity to help others reach his status, stepped outside of himself for the first time in his life without thinking of what he, personally, would get out of it.

Frank had told him to be his own man: When he finally embraced his race, when he declared blackness to be his "religion," he was just that.

Almost the end of frankie-boy

By the time the Miami Summit and the Elvis show were over, politics was more the order of the day than showbiz. Virtually from the moment that John Kennedy left the Sands with his satchelful of cash, Frank was among his most avid supporters, volunteering not only his time, money, and talent but that of everyone within his orbit.

"Frank snapped his fingers, and people fell into line," recalled Peter's manager, Milt Ebbins. "He'd get on the phone to somebody and before you knew it he'd be saying, 'Gotcha down for ten thousand,' and that would be the end of it."

Lawford, of course, was already enlisted in the campaign, but Frank put the finger on all his chums, among whom Sammy was the most receptive. "My role was 'Let Sammy take care of all the ethnic people,'" he remembered. "Wherever I was playing, a campaign official would give me a list of rallies and cocktail parties at which I could sing a song or just mix and shake hands and add to the excitement that was building around the figure of JFK." He caught a buzz off the communality of the joint effort. "There were always groups huddling, planning activities, and it was exciting to be there, everybody knew you and you knew everybody and you were all giving yourselves to something in which you deeply believed." He enjoyed brushing up against Jack—"John came out of one room as I arrived and it was 'Hi, Sam . . .' with two jokes and he was off into another room"—but he was wary of kid brother Bobby: "Bobby was not as enamored of the group, or of show business, as John was," he reflected. "He was courteous, appreciative, but all business, and I had the feeling that though he recognized our value at rallies he also saw a negative that our flashy show business association brought to the campaign."

Not everybody was as quick as Sammy to follow Frank's lead. Shirley MacLaine, so liberal that she'd petitioned the governor of California to stay the execution of Caryl Chessman, saw Jack Kennedy for the calculating political schemer that he was. Even after being personally politicked by Jack in a convertible on Mulholland Drive (she thought for sure he was about to get frisky), she preferred the idealism of Adlai Stevenson. Frank tried to talk her out of it. "He said Jack knew how to use power and Stevenson didn't," she remembered. "He said it took greater courage to go for Jack because he was more political, which might be more suspect, but was more effective." But she held firm until the Democratic race was decided.

As for Dean, Frank probably knew better than even to try. Dean made it clear that he had no more interest in presidential politics than he did in local water district elections. He'd met Jack Kennedy in Chicago about a decade earlier when he was still with Jerry, and the three of them scammed broads together. He wasn't terribly impressed with the guy then, and he certainly wasn't willing to jump onto Frank's bandwagon, even if the Rat Pack *had* been renamed the Jack Pack. As far as Dean was concerned, power was the ability to be left alone.

Who needed to go beg votes for some spoiled *irizaccio?* He'd show up. Period.

But Frank did swell elsewhere in Hollywood, bringing such high-wattage liberals as Judy Garland, Angie Dickinson, Tony Curtis, and Janet Leigh aboard. They hosted fund-raisers for the campaign throughout Los Angeles, several of which were held at Peter and Pat Lawford's beach house, including one that fermented to such a madcap pitch that Teddy Kennedy delighted the assembled movers and shakers with a belly dance.

That, of course, was just the sort of thing that Kennedy's political opponents were hoping the presence of Sinatra in the senator's campaign would provoke. Estes Kefauver, Lyndon Johnson, and Hubert Humphrey were Jack's chief rivals for the Democratic nomination, and their organizations tried to draw as much attention as possible to the intimacy of Kennedy and the Rat Pack. It had to be done just right: They couldn't exactly discuss the relationship of a promising opponent with the most popular entertainers of the day out loud—they might as well have sent money to Kennedy's campaign themselves—but they could quietly remind key supporters that the senator's friends included Sinatra and, worse, Sammy, political poison in the South.

The race remained perilously close for months, requiring that Frank and his cronies be kept under wraps. After the Summit, for instance, a Kennedy team descended on Vegas to spirit away photographic evidence of Jack's having partied with the boys. They didn't want the world to learn how close the candidate was to Sinatra: "We wouldn't let him campaign openly in the primaries," said a Kennedy aide. "We couldn't even let Peter Lawford in because of the Rat Pack image."

Frank was allowed to make a single public contribution, a novelty record of "High Hopes," his hit tune from the previous year's film *A Hole in the Head*, rewritten at Jack's request by Sammy Cahn with special lyrics for the election—"Everyone wants to back Jack/Jack is on the right track." Perfect, optimistic fun, it became the unofficial anthem of Kennedy's bid.

Still, even at arm's length, Frank could bring sufficient heat onto the campaign as to threaten its viability. There was his decision—just after the Rat Pack Summit—to make a film of *The Execution of Private Slovik,* a World War II story about an American G.I. put to death for desertion; Frank would produce, direct, and star. For screenwriter, he made a bold choice: He would defy the Hollywood blacklist by hiring Albert Maltz, his old *The House I Live In* collaborator, who had been jailed for refusing to testify before Congress about communist infiltration of the film industry and had been living in Mexico since 1951.

There were already holes in the blacklist. Otto Preminger and Kirk Douglas had both hired Dalton Trumbo, another member of the Hollywood Ten, to write *Exodus* and *Spartacus,* respectively. And Trumbo and several other writers had continued to produce work for Hollywood throughout the previous decade under assumed names, even winning Academy Awards, pseudonymously, for their screenplays. So Frank's decision wasn't some kind of thunderbolt.

But neither Preminger nor Douglas was intimately linked in the press with a presidential campaign, and if Hollywood was ready to forget the Red Scare, the rest of the nation, and the conservative press in particular, weren't.

Frank—or somebody close to him—realized that there might be a political cost to Jack Kennedy once it became known that Maltz had been hired; they deliberately waited until after the New Hampshire primary of March 8 to announce it. Frank was still in Miami then, and Maltz, who'd acceded to a delay in the announcement of his employment even though he was eager for its squelching effect on the blacklist, called him there from New York. "I asked him openly if he wanted to delay because he was raising money for Kennedy," Maltz remembered, "but he said, 'No, I support Kennedy because I think he's the best man for the job, but I'm not doing anything special for him.' So I suggested we make the announcement right away, and he said fine."

Kaboom: On March 12, the *New York Times* reported that Maltz was working for Frank. Within days, conservative pundits across the nation (many working for the rabidly anti-Red Hearst chain) were denouncing the decision ("Dump Maltz and get yourself a true American writer," read an editorial in Hearst's *New York Journal-American*); a Senate subcommittee declared that it would start looking anew into communist infiltration of the film industry; and Hollywood's number one flag-waver, John Wayne, chimed in: "I wonder how Sinatra's crony, Senator John Kennedy, feels about him hiring such a man."

This sort of stuff brought out the scrapper in Frank. He took out an ad in the Hollywood trade papers declaring his prerogative to hire whomever he chose and adding that both he and John Kennedy were their own men: "I do not ask the advice of Senator Kennedy on whom I should hire. Senator Kennedy does not ask me how he should vote in the Senate."

But the uproar would not die. More editorials and denunciations followed. General Motors threatened to cut its sponsorship of a TV show being produced by Peter's company and of three specials Frank was set to make for ABC-TV ("Fuck 'em," said Frank of the auto giant, "there'll be other specials"). Colonel Tom Parker threatened to pull his gold mine, Elvis Presley, from Frank's "Welcome Home" show. Frank's kids were needled at school.

Then, most alarmingly, Catholic priests around the nation spoke out against Frank in their Sunday morning sermons, going so far as to accuse Jack of softness toward communism.

"God, was that a mess," recalled Peter Lawford.

Joe Kennedy had sat silently by watching the spectacle, but when the cardinals of Boston and New York told him that Jack could lose the Catholic vote if such prominent supporters as Sinatra were insensitive to the church's position on communism, he called Frank on the carpet.

"It was almost the end of Frankie-boy as far as the family was concerned," Lawford remembered.

Old Joe was blunt: "It's either Maltz or us, make up your mind."

And for one of the very few times that anyone could remember, Dolly's boy caved. Maltz was paid his entire fee—$75,000—and let go. Frank issued a public statement declaring that he was bowing to "the reaction of my family, my friends, and the American public" in firing the writer. In the wake of the fiasco, he neither spoke with Maltz nor pursued the film further. But he maintained a relationship with the Kennedys, who were satisfied that they could control him.

Most of the time. In an ugly coda to the Maltz affair, Frank ran into John Wayne a few days later at a Hollywood night-club. Frank, into his cups, called out to the hulking western star: "You seem to disagree with me." Wayne backed away, "Now, now, Frank, we can discuss this somewhere else," and friends separated them. But Frank wasn't done. He hissed at a nearby newsman—"I guess you'll write all this down!"—and then caused a melee in the parking lot, attacking a valet with the aid of Sammy's bodyguard Big John Hopkins and screeching away in Sammy's Rolls-Royce after shouting, "Tell that guy not to sue me if he knows what's good for him! I'll break both his legs!" Sue him that guy did, and Frank settled the mess out of court.

It was exactly the sort of thing that had the Kennedys worried.

If Frank wanted to pitch in, he would have to do so in other, quieter ways.

The most exciting
assignment of my life

The Making of a President, 1960: Through March and April, the talk went back and forth, back and forth, between the Kennedy camp, the Outfit, and their liaisons, Frank Sinatra and Judy Campbell—one savvy and proud enough to think he was not an instrument of powerful men but their peer, the other a fetish object almost entirely unaware of the glutinous web she'd been sucked into. Jack Kennedy assured both Frank and Campbell that he was relying on them; Sam Giancana pretended to want nothing but their friendship. And perhaps neither of those princes of power realized that they were on a collision course that would traverse the bodies of their two starry-eyed go-betweens.

Their first collaboration came that spring. The May 10 primary in West Virginia was shaping up as one of the most crucial moments in Jack's burgeoning campaign. Though he'd beaten his strongest opponent, Hubert Humphrey, in Humphrey's backyard state of Wisconsin, Kennedy's religion and privileged northern background worked heavily against him in an impoverished state that was only 5 percent Catholic.

The Kennedy family launched one of its vaunted wall-to-wall assaults on the state, with Bobby virtually taking up residence there, the sisters and wives hosting teas with local women, and Jack even pressing a mine safety bill in the Senate. Joe Kennedy sat down with Richard Cardinal Cushing in Boston and made up a list of Protestant churches in the state to which to donate money ("What better way is there to spend campaign money than to help a preacher and his flock?" the cardinal asked). Franklin D. Roosevelt Jr. showed up on the stump and told the coal miners, whom his parents had fought to grant the right to organize, that "my daddy and Jack Kennedy's daddy were just like this," holding up two entwined fingers to get his patently untrue message across.

Even less honest, of course, was the help that flowed from Frank and his pal Giancana, who, with his large sums of untraceable cash and connections to the West Virginia political machine, suddenly had the chance to become a kingmaker. He was already well known to the Kennedys, of course. Over the years, Old Joe had sought favors from him, and Bobby had mercilessly grilled him in front of the McClellan Committee hearings the previous June. Giancana, like so many other mobsters before him, responded to every question by invoking the Fifth Amendment, even laughing as he did so, provoking Bobby to ask, "Are you going to tell us anything or just giggle? I thought only little girls giggled." It made great TV, and it added to the public impression that the Kennedys were the mob's worst nightmare.

But that was for the public—part of the hypocrisy of politics. Privately, Giancana believed that he could buy some security for himself by aiding Jack's campaign; he even had Frank's word on it. So when he was asked to help in West Virginia, he forgot Bobby's preening and set to work. He gathered a $50,000 war chest, using money, it was whispered, from the ever-flowing Teamsters Central States Pension Fund, and dispatched Skinny D'Amato, who knew all the sneak joints in the state, to distribute it.

It was an uphill struggle. The anti-Catholic prejudice in Appalachia was no myth, as Bobby Kennedy learned to his shock when he came to Wheeling to register Jack for the primary—"They actually shrunk up against the wall, as if such a Catholic might be contagious," recalled a campaign aide. Tavern owners had to be bribed to put Sinatra's "High Hopes" pastiche on their jukeboxes; D'Amato had to forgive gambling debts beyond the money he spread around. "We're gonna have to buy every fuckin' vote in the state," Giancana groaned. Humphrey's people were spreading around their own lucre, despite their guy's sniffling that he couldn't "afford to run through the state with a little black bag and a checkbook." When it came down to it, Humphrey spent plenty and the Kennedys just plain outspent him. As one small-town politico told the local Humphrey organization, "You gave us five and Kennedy came in with ten."

All the spending proved worth it: Kennedy won 60-40, and Humphrey responded by quitting the race. Jack was now the Democratic front-runner, and Giancana reckoned it was largely his doing. So he determined to keep a careful eye on his investment: That hot number that Jack was doing? Divorced, Liz Taylor looks, friend of Frank's? Momo had his hooks in her but good.

Frank had introduced Judy Campbell to Giancana in Miami. The mobster introduced himself as Sam Flood. He courted Campbell with assiduous consideration, reserve, and modesty. He sent her yellow roses each and every day, but he respected her desire not to be given gifts of significant value such as cash, trips, or jewelry. She said she took him for a widowed old businessman, even though she knew that he was friendly with Sinatra's shady Miami buddy Joe Fish, that he was treated with astounding deference wherever they went, and that he had lots of friends in Chicago with thick necks, broken noses, and names like Potatoes, Crackers, Monk, Smokes, Teets, Nags, Fifi, Horse, Needles, Cowboy, Turk, and Dutch. Maybe she didn't recognize him for what he really was: As she wrote with plausibility after his death, "Outside of Chicago, in 1960 how many people had heard his name?" But by the same token, she couldn't have been exactly the wayward Catholic schoolgirl her memoirs would make her out to be.

Campbell had been part of a swinging Hollywood scene during her marriage to actor Billy Campbell; she'd rubbed elbows with swells in Beverly Hills, Las Vegas, Palm Springs, and Miami; she'd gotten intimately involved with several powerful men, including Jack, who was famously married, and Frank, who'd tried unsuccessfully to introduce her to the pleasures of three-way, interracial sex (she once lay in bed with him pretending to sleep while a black prostitute performed oral sex on him). Moreover, she was a savvy judge of her surroundings. She was sensitive to the ways in which the wives of men like Dean, Peter, Jack Entratter, Sammy Cahn, and Jerry Lewis (who wanted to sleep with her and gave her a meaningless job as bait) snubbed each pretty new girl on the scene. And she was especially keen on reading Frank's moods and his deeply fractured sense of himself: "He wants to be so many people," she observed, "that he doesn't know who he is."

She went along with it all not because she was naive but because it was too rich to resist. She was granted a spectacular lifestyle that seemed to harmonize with the tenor of the times and beat the hell out of living off a modest inheritance and pretending to make a career as an artist. She simply denied, even to herself, that, like Frank, she was a plaything to both Giancana and Jack Kennedy, something they used and discarded willy-nilly.

And Frank was no different: As Johnny Rosselli said bluntly

of Sinatra's standing with the Kennedys some months later, "They treat him like a whore. You fuck them, you pay them, and they're through."

The Kennedys had, in fact, kept Frank and his pals at arm's length until they were assured that Jack had the nomination in his pocket, and then they enlisted them in an all-out electoral blitz. But the Democratic National Convention would mark the big public arrival of the Rat Pack on the bandwagon.

On Sunday night, July 10, 2,800 people attended a $100-a-plate dinner at the Beverly Hilton. Frank had beat the drum and turned out a dazzling array of celebrity flesh: Sammy and Peter, of course, and Judy Garland, Angie Dickinson, Janet Leigh, and Tony Curtis, as usual, but also Shirley MacLaine (who had finally hopped the bandwagon), Milton Berle, George Jessel, Joe E. Lewis, and Mort Sahl.

The following day, Frank and Sammy, along with Curtis and Leigh, led the assembled convention in the national anthem. When Sammy was introduced, a chorus of boos rose up from the Alabama and Mississippi delegations. He was staggered; what should have been a crowning moment had become yet another slap in the face.

"I focused on a flag in the back of the hall and clung to it, standing there, torn to shreds inside, hurt and naked in front of thousands of people, in front of the world," he remembered. He tried to maintain a posture of dignity, but he began to cry.

Frank could sense his anguish. "Those dirty sons of bitches! Don't let 'em get you, Charlie," he said.

But the bigots had hit the mark. After choking his way through "The Star-Spangled Banner," Sammy left the convention hall. Frank and the others stayed on to politic, taking the floor to mingle with the delegates and tilt the vote toward their man—who was so sanguine with the inevitability of his nomination that, at least according to Peter and Judy Campbell, he spent his time in L.A. lining up trysts with on-again, off-again flames like Campbell and Marilyn Monroe.

On the night of the eleventh, the night of Sammy's shame, Jack tried to involve Campbell in a threesome with another woman; offended by the suggestion and shocked at his bizarre sense of priorities—"I would think you had enough on your mind without cooking up something like this," she told him—she left, avoiding him for the rest of his stay in town. Quick to recover, Jack saw Marilyn the very next afternoon and then dined with her at Puccini's, Frank and Peter's Beverly Hills restaurant. At the table with Peter and Kennedy aide Kenny O'Donnell (who'd driven the flustered Campbell home the night before), Marilyn joked about how Jack had been "very democratic" and "very penetrating" with her during some private time they shared earlier in the evening.

The following afternoon, Jack, Bobby, and Old Joe sat watching the convention on TV from the Beverly Hills mansion of Joe's old showbiz friend Marion Davies, entertaining a steady flow of labor leaders and political bosses from around the country. Frank was there as well, serving as bartender and greeter. But when the actual balloting got under way, Frank returned to the convention hall, where he anxiously monitored the activity.

As the Wyoming delegation cast its votes, putting Kennedy over the top, Frank went wild, jumping up and down and slapping Peter on the back. "We're on our way to the White House, buddy boy," he shouted. "We're on our way to the White House!"

The following night, one of Frank's little touches fizzled. Comedian Mort Sahl, invited by Frank to address the convention before Jack's acceptance speech with, presumably, an anti-Republican routine, threw in a few jibes at the Kennedys: "We've finally got a choice, the choice between the lesser of two evils," he told a surprised audience. "Nixon wants to sell the country, Kennedy wants to buy it." (After which, the comedian was forever blackballed by Sinatra, surprising no one.)

Later in the evening, Peter threw a party for the nominee at his Santa Monica home. Jack's voice was gone from all the talking he'd been doing—he ordered his daiquiris from the bar by writing down what he wanted—but he perked up when Sammy walked in, bearding for him with Marilyn on his arm. The candidate and the screen goddess soon cozied up, and Sammy, once again, drifted away.

The Kennedys, frankly, would've preferred it if Sammy had just disappeared altogether. If Frank was apt to stumble on occasion and threaten the dignity of the campaign, Sammy was a bad-luck magnet who was in all likelihood doing more actual harm than good merely by showing up. In a general election against Nixon, Jack didn't have to try terribly hard to win the black vote (or, what the hell, the Jewish vote), but he desperately needed the southern vote, and Sammy genuinely imperiled his ability to get it.

It was more than just his being black: It was the romance with May Britt, which had blossomed beyond all probability into something serious. In March, after the interiors on *Ocean's Eleven* were through, Sammy caught up with her in New York, where she was filming *Murder, Inc.*, and they decided to get married. It was a risky venture, Sammy knew: Anytime his name had been linked with a white actress in the past it had proved an ugly scene. But this was the real thing, and he banked on May's being Swedish and a movie star of sorts to buffer the inevitable public outcry at their union. Still they kept it under wraps among their Hollywood cronies, lest word leak out to *Confidential* or one of the gossip queens.

In May, Sammy flew to London to appear in a royal command performance before Queen Elizabeth (he was in top

183

form, flooring the crowd on a night that found Nat King Cole drowning in flop sweat) and sticking around for a nightclub engagement at the Pigalle. Sammy always loved to affect British airs, and he took to London readily, sporting Savile Row suits complete with bowler hats. He was also delighted to discover when May visited him there that few heads were turned by the sight of an interracial couple—in part, of course, because he wasn't as well known in the U.K. as at home, but certainly because of different racial standards as well.

That all changed when word of their increasingly public courtship made its way to the States. Headlines back home started asking when Sammy and May would marry, and, rather than live with speculation and innuendo, Sammy foolishly called a press conference to announce the engagement. Among the unusually passive Fleet Street reporters in the audience was an American wire service reporter who peppered Sammy with obnoxious, provocative questions: "Are you announcing it over here because you're afraid to do it at home?" "What happens if you find you can't go home?" "Isn't this the first marriage between a Negro man and a blonde, white movie star?" "How would Miss Britt feel if her kid turns out to be black—you know what I mean?" The British writers couldn't hoot the man down, and Sammy finally lost his cool: "Buddy, I've known what you've meant for forty-five minutes. Now as far as our children are concerned it would not matter to us, in terms of our love for the child, if it were white, brown, or polka-dot."

Oh boy.

Aside from a small but ugly protest outside of the club during the remainder of Sammy's gig—Oswald Mosley's fascist thugs picketed the place with placards reading "Go home, nigger" and "Sammy, back to the trees"—the press conference meant nothing to most British observers: an American nightclub performer marrying a Swedish starlet.

Back home, however, the press ran with Sammy's "polka-dot" comment for days, and he returned to a shit storm. First there was the convention, where he could at least ascribe the catcalls that wounded him to traditional southern bigotry. But a few weeks later—after invitations went out to an October 16 wedding at which Frank had agreed to stand as best man—he was greeted outside of the Lotus Club in Washington, D.C., with a reception even uglier than the one in London. More pickets: "Go back to the Congo, you kosher coon," "What's the matter Sammy, can't you find a colored girl?" and, insanely, a charcoal-colored dog wearing a swastika and emblazoned with a sign that read, "I'm black too, Sammy, but I'm not a Jew."

There were death threats, bomb threats, ugly phone calls. He got bags full of hate mail: "Dear Nigger Bastard, I see Frank Sinatra is going to be best man at your abortion. Well, it's good to know the kind of people supporting Kennedy before it's too late. [signed] An ex-Kennedy Vote." Someone sent him a cartoon clipped from a right-wing newspaper. In the first panel, Sammy stood posed as a butler offering JFK a tray of fried chicken and watermelon; in the second, he sat next to Kennedy eating; the caption read, "Will it still be the *White* House?"

These, of course, were extreme responses, and Sammy did what he could to shield May from them—turning her into a prisoner of hotel suites and room service meals when he even dared let her accompany him on the road.

But his timing had truly been awful: Southerners opposed to Kennedy's election were making great hay out of the inference that Jack countenanced interracial marriage, and Frank was getting hammered for acceding to so public a role in the wedding. (Oddsmakers in Vegas were laying three to one that Frank would bail and have Dean take his place.)

"I combed the papers every day," Sammy remembered.

"The already stale news that Frank would be my best man continued making the front pages and too often by 'coincidence' right next to it were stories about Frank campaigning for Kennedy."

In early September, he found himself back at the Sands for the first time since the Summit and began to consider the corner in which he'd painted himself and his mentor.

"I could imagine the pressure Frank must be under," Sammy thought. "He must have eighty guys telling him, 'Don't be a fool, you've worked hard for Kennedy, now do you want to louse him up?' He must be getting it from all sides. And the worst of it is it's understandable." Without conferring with May, he decided to relieve Frank of his duty and delay the wedding.

Tremulously, he called Sinatra in Palm Springs and told him that there were problems with the banquet room, with the rabbi's schedule, anything.

"You're lying, Charlie."

He fessed up: "Look, what the hell, it's best that we postpone it 'til after the election."

Frank got quiet. Sammy could hear a party going on elsewhere in the house. "You don't have to do that."

"I want to. All the talk . . ."

"Screw the talk!"

"I know, but it's better this way."

Awash in relief, gratitude, sorrow, shame, Frank spoke in a near-whisper: "I'll be there whenever it is. You know that, don't you?"

"I know that, Frank."

"You know that I'd never ask you to do a thing like this. Not your wedding. I'd never ask that!"

"That's why it's up to me to be saying it."

"You're a better man than I am, Charlie. I don't know if I could do this for you, or for anyone. . . ."

Frank, Dean, Sammy, Peter, and Joey. (*Archive Photos*)

The Voice in a crowd: Frank leaves a New York high school in 1945 after delivering a talk on racial justice. (*Archive Photos*)

Prince of tides: Peter prone on a long board in Hawaii with the great surf champ Duke Kahanamoku.(*Archive Photos*)

His way: Dean meets the press backstage at the Sands. (*Sands Hotel*)

Cool breeze: The Will Mastin Trio
(Mastin, Little Sam, Big Sam, left to
right) out on the town.
(*Archive Photos*)

Sammy jokes with Frank, who wears
his *Kings Go Forth* publicity togs;
Sammy would be booted from
Frank's next war film, *Never So Few*,
for dissing his Leader in the papers.
(*Archive Photos*)

An adult paradise: The Sands in 1952, complete with parking spaces out
front on the Strip and a naked skyline. (*Sands Hotel*)

The Sands's famous floating crap game: The empty sky beyond the diving board is today choked with thirty-story hotels. (*Sands Hotel*)

Jakey Freedman with Kim Novak. (*Sands Collection, UNLV Library*)

Carl Cohen and wife, Fran. (*Sands Collection, UNLV Library*)

Everybody comes to Jack's: Humphrey Bogart puts the touch on Jack Entratter, while Lauren Bacall and Judy Garland dish the dirt, in a candid moment of bacchanalia during the legendary "Rat Pack" weekend. (*Sands Hotel*)

Jack Entratter with consummate lounge lizards Ernest and
Mary Hemingway. (*Sands Hotel*)

Lauren "Den Mother" Bacall's thirty-second birthday, September 1956:
Jack Entratter and Kim Novak look on; Humphrey Bogart took a pass on
the festivities, spending the weekend on his yacht with his son instead.
(*Sands Hotel*)

Dean signs up:
At Judy Garland's
1955 Long Beach
concert, Dean sits
beside his wife, Jeanne.
Debbie Reynolds is in
front. (*Archive Photo*s)

Nowheresville:
Frank, Dean, and
Mack Gray kill time
in Madison, Indiana,
while filming *Some
Came Running.*
(*Archive Photos*)

Pallies: Filming *Some Came Running.* (*Archive Photos*)

Happiness, perhaps: Sammy's marriage to Loray White. The celebrants include Joe E. Lewis, Harry Belafonte, and Donald O'Connor (left to right). (*Archive Photos*)

All together now: Peter, Sammy, Frank, Joey, and Dean. (*Archive Photos*)

The Summit: Dean, Joey, Frank. (*Sands Collection, UNLV Library*)

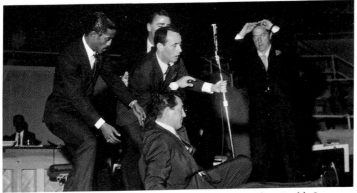

The Summit: Sammy, Peter, and Joey erect, Dean sprawling, Buddy Lester looking for a cue. (*Sands Collection, UNLV Library*)

The Summit: "Shall We Dance?" A promotional poster for the Four Chaplains benefit is visible behind the bandstand. (*Sands Collection, UNLV Library*)

Ocean's Eleven: Sammy the garbage man greets Joey the porter. (*Archive Photos*)

Two kings: Frank and Elvis in Miami, March 1960. (*Archive Photos*)

Opening night on Fremont Street: Dean, Shirley MacLaine, and Joey at the Las Vegas premiere of *Ocean's Eleven*. (*Archive Photos*)

Peter and Frank sort things out; Sammy wisely demurs. (*Archive Photos*)

Happiness, for real: May and Sammy on their wedding
day, commemorating the ceremony . . .

. . . and holding a press conference. (both *Archive Photos*)

Got scotch? The boys try a new look on the set of *Sergeants 3*. (*Archive Photos*)

Frank and Dean arrive in London, May 1961, just before putting the kibosh on Peter's plans for a tony cruise. (*Archive Photos*)

One too many? Dean, Sammy, and Frank at the Coconut Grove, the night the Rat Pack trampled Eddie Fisher's act, summer 1961. (*Archive Photos*)

Peter, Pat, and Frank arriving in London, 1961.
(*Archive Photos*)

His own man: Sammy at the March on Washington, with Anthony Franciosa
behind him to his right, June 15, 1963. (*Archive Photos*)

The one laugh Frank could always get, on the set of
Robin and the Seven Hoods, 1963. (*Archive Photos*)

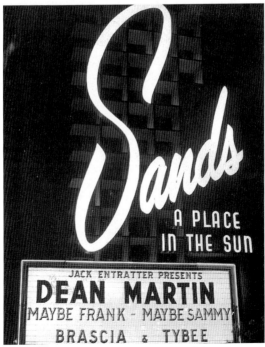

Mannered spontaneity: A Sands marquee of the early 1960s.
(*Sands Collection, UNLV Library*)

Frank contrite: Speaking through clenched teeth, Frank tells a reporter in Beverly Hills about the melee at the Sands, 1967. (*Archive Photos*)

"Shall We Dance?" redux: Peter and Sammy in Swinging London to make *Salt and Pepper*, 1967. (*Archive Photos*)

"You've been doing it, haven't you?"

Frank put the phone down without another word. A minute passed, with Sammy dying inside.

The next thing he heard was Peter, all business: "Frank can't talk any more."

Sammy said nothing.

"Charlie?"

"Yes, Peter?"

"Charlie, I . . . it's beautiful of you."

They said goodbye.

And now he had to break the news to May—an even harder call. He reached her in an ebullient mood: She was all caught up in the excitement of the presents that were starting to arrive in the mail.

He spoke reasonably: "Darling, it boils down to this. Over a period of almost twenty years, Frank has been aces high, aces up—everything a guy could be to me. There's nothing in the world he wants from me, nothing in the world I can do for him except be his friend. Ninety-nine percent of the others come and go and you act nice and help them if it's convenient, but Frank is a *friend*, and now he needs something from me, so there can be no evaluating, no hesitating, no limit."

She said she understood, but she gave him a subtle warning: "I know it's not easy to suddenly start thinking differently than you always have, and I know you're trying."

The next day, they sent telegrams to their guests announcing that the wedding would be delayed until November 13— the Sunday immediately following Election Day. Sammy's publicists put out a statement blaming the postponement on complications with May's Mexican divorce. Even though it was transparently a lie, it worked: The heat was off Frank and, consequently, Jack's campaign. The only losers were Sammy and May. When they finally did marry that November, with Frank, Peter, and Dean in attendance, there was a slight note of deflation in the air—and a pregnant bride under the *chuppah.*

Truth be told, Frank probably would've just as soon gotten Sammy's wedding out of the way, he was so damn busy anyhow. After the convention, he campaigned more publicly for Jack than he had during the primaries, hitting the Hawaiian islands in a September barnstorming tour with Peter and serving as host for the Democratic Governor's Ball in New Jersey at the end of October. Both of these were combined with work: the shooting of *The Devil at 4 O'Clock,* a Mervyn LeRoy thriller that gave him a chance to act opposite one of his screen heroes, Spencer Tracy, and a stint at the 500 Club in Atlantic City, during which he passed an evening talking shop with a couple of over-the-hill hookers at a seedy bar, finally dismissing the pair with "Oh, shit, get the fuck away from me, you pigs."

The end of August found him at the Capitol Records tower on Vine Street recording perhaps the best swing album of his life—*Sinatra's Swingin' Session!*—a collection of rollicking, spirited, loosey-goosey updates of several songs he'd recorded in the past ("I Concentrate on You," "My Blue Heaven," "It All Depends on You") and another number that constituted the most stunning display of sheer audacity in his entire recording career: a finger-popping swing version of "Ol' MacDonald" with special lyrics that transformed the "chick" of the children's version into a curvy dame. It was a completely infectious performance—sexy, confident, and charming, the work of a master artist who could whip off stuff this good, it seemed, just as easy as lighting a cigarette; it reached number 25 on the charts.

On top of all that, he was party to a big wedding in his own family. On September 11 at the Sands, he gave the hand of his twenty-year-old daughter, Nancy, to Tommy Sands, a pretty-boy pop singer who'd had a couple of Top 40 hits a few years earlier. Like Elvis Presley, Sands had enlisted in the military, and the wedding was originally meant to be held later that fall. But Frank's commitment to the film in Hawaii forced his daughter, in an ironic reversal of Sammy's fate, to move her wedding date up, and so Sands was forced to get hitched in his air force uniform, only the first of many occasions at which he would be made to feel an adjunct to his famous father-in-law.

With all this going on that summer and fall, then, it was little wonder that Frank began to show signs of wear when the election finally came around. Election Day found him holed up in his offices watching the results and keeping a telephone line open to Chicago, where he and Joe Kennedy had once again prevailed upon Sam Giancana to pull strings and see to it that Illinois's twenty-seven electoral votes—more than 10 percent of the total necessary to win—fell Jack's way. Nixon won the vast majority of the state's 103 counties, but he lost Cook County by an average of two votes per precinct—slightly more than Kennedy's statewide margin of victory. As in the West Virginia primary, any chicaneries in Chicago by Kennedy partisans were probably matched by the work of Nixon forces working elsewhere in the state; moreover, Mayor Richard Daley was just as likely to have manipulated the vote in his city as Giancana. And it was reasonable to assume that the vote in Texas, which also fell into the Kennedy column, was just as crooked as the one in Illinois. But Giancana would forever take credit for Kennedy's victory— "Listen, honey," he told Judy Campbell, "if it wasn't for me your boyfriend wouldn't even be in the White House"—and he assumed that the new president would reciprocate in kind once he took the reins of power.

That little matter still hadn't quite been settled, however, by 3:00 a.m. West Coast time, and Frank, his nerves absolutely frayed from a day of waiting, hit the roof when he watched Nixon take to the podium and refuse to concede a race that was still, technically, up in the air. In a bootless reprise of his drunken 1944 assault on Westbrook Pegler's Waldorf suite, Frank called Nixon's hotel and lambasted an operator who refused to put him through to Nixon's suite: "Do you know who this is?" It didn't matter. He slammed down the phone, went grudgingly to bed, and woke up in a new world which he was convinced he had helped build.

For Peter, who'd invested less of himself in Jack's election than Frank, the campaign was a strange, giddy season. He had headlined a number of events, including that series of Hawaiian quick hits with Sinatra that climaxed with a performance in front of nine thousand people at the Waikiki Shell. And he had shown up somewhat more than usual on TV, guesting on variety shows hosted by Frank, Perry Como, and others. He even changed his nationality so as to be able to vote for his brother-in-law, standing in Los Angeles among six hundred other immigrants on April 23, 1960, and taking the oath of citizenship. He voted by absentee ballot, spending the last days of the election in Boston and Hyannis Port with the Kennedys.

He had also contributed at least one crucial service, advising Jack on how he should comport himself on television, giving him tips on makeup, hair, wardrobe, and, most crucially, demeanor: "Don't be afraid of the camera," he told him. "Look directly into it, as though it were a friend across the dinner table. You'll be making contact with millions of people at the same moment, but each one will feel as though you're talking only to him." This counsel proved especially useful, of course, in the debates between Kennedy and Nixon, in which, famously, Jack was reassuring, confident, and positive while his opponent looked like a nervous, unshaven shyster.

But such cosmetic expertise aside, the Kennedy men never really reckoned Peter as their equal. They took him, correctly, for an intellectual flyweight, and his lack of passion for political or even financial matters made him less interesting to them than their other brothers-in-law, Sargent Shriver and Stephen Smith. Peter was an outsider as a Brit, he was an outsider as a movie actor, he was even an outsider as an only child: The very size and fraternalism of the Kennedy clan made him ill at ease. "He just didn't like that atmosphere—that big family," recalled Milt Ebbins. "At one time they rang a bell for dinner. And we'd sit down at this long boardinghouse table, the women would come out with pitchers of milk and big tubs of butter and hot bread and creamed fish and mashed potatoes, and they'd all jump on it. Peter couldn't take that. It seemed almost barbaric to him. He just sat there."

The family sensed Peter's alienation, but they sensed an undertone of condescension in it as well and decided, perhaps tacitly, to take him down a peg. In one of their famously rambunctious games of touch football (a game Peter had never played because of his nationality, weak arm, and preference for solo sports such as tennis and surfing), the Kennedy men, led by Smith, decided to "get Peter," tackling him with relish and knocking the wind out of him. Peter tried to convince himself that it was just a case of the new boy's being hazed, but he never allowed himself to feel part of the inner circle.

Ironically, Peter's sense of discomfort around the rest of the family made him close to another outsider—Jacqueline Bouvier Kennedy—whose upbringing and tastes matched Peter's nearly as much as did her sense of alienation from her husband's boisterous clan. In time, Jackie's solicitude became, curiously, Peter's strongest connection to the Kennedys. Jack and Bobby, after all, came just to see him as a pimp, the rest of the family hadn't even that much use for him, and his marriage to Pat foundered on the shoals of his adultery.

Still, his celebrity counted for something. And soon after the election, the Kennedys granted Peter and Frank the honor of planning a gala for the eve of the inaugural, a star-studded performance that would underscore Jack's sense of glamour and defray the Democratic National Committee's debts. Tickets for the show at Washington's National Guard Armory were $100 per seat and $10,000 per box. Just under $2 million would be raised, enough to defer not only the cost of Jack's campaign but some outstanding debts from Adlai Stevenson's 1956 race as well.

Frank, naturally, launched into his task with relish. He inveigled Ella Fitzgerald to fly in from Australia, Shirley MacLaine from Japan, Gene Kelly from Switzerland, Sidney Poitier from France. He and Peter convinced several Broadway producers to darken their stages for the night, freeing such performers as Ethel Merman, Anthony Quinn, and Laurence Olivier to attend. During a TV special saluting accomplished women in early 1960, Frank had renewed his acquaintance with Eleanor Roosevelt, and, though she had supported Stevenson for the nomination against Jack, he prevailed upon her to attend the gala. He got Leonard Bernstein to conduct patriotic music and Carl Sandburg to read poetry; he had special lyrics and music written for the occasion. Joey Bishop was named emcee; Dean and Sammy were slated to perform, along with Harry Belafonte, Jimmy Durante, Mahalia Jackson, Milton Berle, Nat King Cole, Fredric March, Red Skelton, Helen Traubel, Juliet Prowse, Alan King, Bette Davis, Louis Prima, and Keely Smith—an unprecedented constellation of celebrity talent.

"This is the most exciting assignment of my life," Frank

gushed. But his feelings weren't necessarily shared by his friends. Dean still couldn't be bothered with Jack Kennedy, and he asked out of Frank's to-do, insisting that he was committed to finishing a film back in L.A. Entitled *Ada*, it starred Dean as a rube manipulated by a corrupt southern political machine to become governor. The director, Danny Mann, liked Dean well enough but didn't sense that his star was so deeply committed to the picture that he couldn't have taken a few days off: "I never had a feeling that he was worried about the picture," Mann remembered. Still, it provided Dean a deft sidestep.

Sammy, on the other hand, made plans to suspend his engagement at the Latin Casino nightclub outside of Philadelphia in favor of the inaugural gala, ordered a new tuxedo from Sy DeVore, the Rat Pack's preferred haberdasher, and insisted that May, who was trying to accustom her new husband to life on a budget, hit Bergdorf Goodman for a gown to wear to the performance and a Chanel suit for the swearing-in. He was overwhelmed with having been asked to participate. It was, in his eyes, a vindication not only for himself and his talent but for everything he'd ever believed was good and true and just: "It really can happen in America," he remembered thinking. "Despite all the obstacles, still in 1960 an uneducated kid from Harlem could work hard and be invited to the White House."

They waited until practically the last minute to crush him.

Three days before the gala, Sammy was awakened in his Philadelphia hotel room by a call from Evelyn Lincoln, Jack's personal secretary. She stammered to her point: "Mr. Davis ... Sammy ... the President has asked me to tell you that he doesn't want you present at his inauguration. There is a situation into which he is being forced and to fight it would be counterproductive to the goals he's set. He very much hopes you will understand."

They didn't even have the grace to have Frank or Peter do it; they might as well have shot him in the heart. He thought of a million objections he could raise, a million reasonable arguments. He remembered Jack's joking, his smiles, his thank-yous, his "I won't forget your help. . . ." But he muttered a lame "I understand" and got off the phone, then lay back on his bed, nauseated.

Within the hour, Peter called. "They talked the President into it," he explained. "They said, 'Look, this is our first time out. Let's not do anything to fuck up. We've got Southern senators, bigoted congressmen. They see you as too liberal to start with. Peter Lawford's an actor, we've still got residue from "The Clan's Taking Over the White House." If we have Sammy here, is he going to bring his wife? We can't ask him not to bring her.' The President said, 'Okay, then dump it. Call Sam. He'll understand.' "

The snow job continued: "You'll be interested to know that Bobby argued for you," Peter went on. "'That's bullshit! It's wrong! The man campaigned!' But he was overruled. He got so angry he walked out of the rest of the discussion."

Sammy wasn't really listening anymore. He called May and told her the awful news, and for the next few days, he floated through his act numbly. The Latin Casino retracted its earlier announcement that he'd be canceling his shows, saying that "his audiences come first," or some other lie.

On the night that Frank was hosting his gala, Sammy stood in the wings in the nightclub torturing himself. "I wondered what the people would be thinking," he remembered, "looking at me onstage in Camden, knowing that the rest of the Rat Pack was in Washington. It hurt like a motherfucker." (When Jack was killed, the family invited Sammy to the funeral, but he was working in L.A. and couldn't attend. He reflected later that Jack "had not been a friend of mine," but he nevertheless made a ritual of visiting his grave whenever he was in D.C.)

*

Frank would've commiserated with Sammy if he'd've had the time, but he had whipped himself into a frenzy with the gala. He worked diligently with Peter on the scripting of the program, down to the song lyrics and written introductions of performers. He pored over details of scheduling, transportation, and accommodation. An entire floor of the Statler Hilton had been reserved for the entertainers, each of whom had received, as a token of Frank's gratitude, a silver cigarette box with an invitation to the inaugural inlaid on top (the bill for these party favors ran $90,000). For himself, Frank had ordered a custom-designed wardrobe of outlandish opulence: an inverness cape with red satin lining, silk top hat, swallowtail coat, striped trousers, a double-breasted gray suede weskit, black calfskin oxfords, white kid gloves—all in duplicate, lest he should somehow besoil himself.

He had taken care of everything, it seemed, except the weather. Early in the afternoon, snow began to fall, and it fell till evening, bringing traffic in the city to its knees. The stars who'd come to the armory to rehearse were unable to return to the hotel to change into their performance attire. The gala was to begin at 9:00 p.m., but the auditorium was only half-full at that hour.

Frank would've been agitated even without the storm— earlier in the day he'd tried to bar the press from rehearsals and then, forced to relent, banned them to a remote balcony in the otherwise empty auditorium. But pacing backstage in his fancy duds, wondering if the president-elect would be able to make it through the snow-choked streets, he died a thousand deaths. As Bill Asher, who directed a taping of the gala, remembered, "Frank was really into the juice that night, and he got mad at Peter. We had a lineup of people in the show on a big bulletin board, and Frank kept coming into the room screaming, 'Fuck Lawford! I'm not gonna do this show. I'm out!' and then he'd pull his name down off the board."

The tension was finally broken at 10:45 by the arrival of Jack and Jackie Kennedy. Frank composed himself sufficiently to escort the president-elect's wife to her box, and the three-hour show went off without a hitch. (Joey got the first laugh, looking up at the president-elect in his stage-side box and saying, "I told you I'd get you a good seat. And you were so worried. . . .")

At its finale, Jack took the stage and spoke: "We're all indebted to a great friend—Frank Sinatra. Long before he could sing, he used to poll a Democratic precinct back in New Jersey. That precinct has grown to cover a country." Peter, too, was patted on the back: "A great deal of our praise and applause should also go to the coproducer, my brother-in-law Peter Lawford. He has been a citizen of this country less than a year, but already he had learned a citizen's delight in paying off a political debt."

Such stuff had little impact on Peter, who felt sufficiently removed from the goings-on that he didn't even attend the swearing-in the next morning and dallied with a pickup on the side. But Frank reveled in the president's praise: He bought an ad in *Variety* to have Jack's remarks reprinted, and he had them pressed onto a record which he would play for hours, boring guests in Las Vegas, Palm Springs, and L.A. to tears.

On the night of the inauguration, Frank held a private party for the stars of the gala at their hotel, and he was overwhelmed with pride when Jack snuck away from one of the official balls downstairs to mingle with the celebrities for a little while. Photos of the evening, along with virtually every note and letter Jack ever sent him, found their way—framed—into a Kennedy Room in Frank's Palm Springs house. The place where Jack and Frank had spent a few days grooving in the sun some fifteen months earlier was gradually becoming a shrine.

What they were really being paid for

Ocean's Eleven had been such a lark and had made everyone associated with it such a nice piece of change that they all swore they'd have to do it again as soon as they could. That turned out to be the spring of '61, when the original Rat Pack quintet of Frank, Dean, Sammy, Peter, and Joey were reunited in the desert with supporting players and pals Buddy Lester, Henry Silva, and Sonny King, an old Times Square buddy of Dean's who somehow was excluded from the first film; they even found work on the picture for three of Bing Crosby's sons.

Dean and Frank coproduced the movie through their companies, Claude and Essex, and United Artists was chosen to distribute it as part of Frank's deal there. (As a wedding present the previous December, Frank had given Sammy profit participation in the picture, putting him on par with himself and Dean.) John Sturges, with whom Frank and Peter had worked on *Never So Few* and who had a reputation as a handy man with a western (*Gunfight at the OK Corral*, *Last Train from Boot Hill*, *The Magnificent Seven*), was given the directorial reins. The script and story were credited to W.R. Burnett, but the film was a fairly loyal remake of *Gunga Din*, the 1939 George Stevens classic based on a liberal interpretation of a few lines of a Rudyard Kipling poem. Burnett had translated the action to the American West, soon after the Civil War. Frank, Dean, and Peter were the title characters, cavalry officers and best buddies fighting the Indians (just like in Kipling—get it?) and about to be separated by the decision of one of them to get married. Joining up with them was a puppy-dog loyal freed slave (Sammy) who wanted so badly to be a cavalryman that he fetched their water and blew the bugle for them—another role suffused with the stuff of human dignity.

The film was originally intended to be called *Badlands*, and it was shot under the name *Soldiers Three*, but MGM had made its own spin-off of *Gunga Din* with that very title in 1951; the studio kept threatening action against the new film throughout the shoot, and Frank finally agreed to change the name to *Sergeants Three* during editing. (Informed of the title change, Joey quipped, "I wish you'd told me. I'd have played it differently.")

The film was shot in Kanab, Utah, a small desert town in the Monument Valley some two hundred miles from Las Vegas. There was, of course, no nightlife. "There was a Dairy Queen that was open until eleven o'clock," Joey remembered. "My advice to everybody was to get two scoops, because after that there wasn't a goddamn thing to do." And yet they found their own fun. Frank had ordered extensive renovations to the hotel that was housing the company during the location portion of the shoot and dipped into the film's budget to pay for it; with their rooms all connected by interior doors, the boys could pull pranks on each other after hours, or merely get together to watch TV, play cards, and drink.

Another leisure activity was written off to the production

as well: Call girls were shipped in and paid as extras for saloon sequences. "The man in charge, an older gentleman, very moral and proper, who had to handle the arrangements was so upset," recalled a secretary on the film. "He had to pay them more than scale and he didn't know how to figure it all out, how to designate what they were *really* being paid for."

There were other, legitimate indulgences. Uncharacteristically, Frank had arrived on the location early and insisted on being shown the rushes of the work that had been shot by an advance unit. Producer Howard W. Koch explained that the projection equipment hadn't arrived yet from L.A. "I'd say it's next to impossible," he told his boss. "That word isn't in my vocabulary," Frank said. Koch, determined to make good, recalled that Kirk Douglas was shooting his own western, *Lonely Are the Brave,* in New Mexico, and, reaching that crew by phone, he arranged to have a projector flown to Kanab, where Frank watched the footage four hours later.

Peter, for one, might've wished that Koch hadn't been so eager. He showed up in Kanab thirty pounds overweight— he'd spent the last year lounging on the beach rather than playing volleyball on it. No one had ever seen him so bloated and puffy; when the crew gathered in the basement of the local schoolhouse to watch the rushes, Frank would snicker, "There's fat boy," whenever Peter appeared. Peter immediately took to a diet with the aid of Dexedrine, losing all the excess poundage but giving his performance a strange yo-yo effect: He would look tubby in some scenes, svelte in others.

But that was the ethos governing a Rat Pack movie. Frank had always insisted these things were done for fun and money. Anyone who took them seriously was an idiot.

Joey learned this the hard way. "Before the picture started," he remembered, "Frank says to me, 'Can you ride a horse?' I said, 'I never been on a horse in my life.' He says, 'Learn how to ride 'cuz you're the sergeant in charge, you're going to be leading us. Get a wrangler. Hire the best guy you can get.' So for two months, religiously—I mean I couldn't walk, my back was hurtin', everything—I practice, stoppin' the horse dead, around barrels, goin' into a full gallop from a dead start. This is for two months. Finally I get the script and I go through it. On page 117 I am with a horse but I'm walking it. I'm holding the reins. And that's my only connection with a horse."

What we do is a rib

Everything was new that year.

Jack had his White House. Sammy had his gorgeous-blonde bride and a baby on the way. Frank and Dean were buying into a casino, the Cal-Neva Lodge in Lake Tahoe. And they were all working for a newly formed record label, Reprise, which was founded and owned by Frank. He was more than just the Leader now. He was literally their boss.

For years, Frank had been chafing under the rule of Capitol Records, the label that had signed him when he was poison in the industry and that had been home to the greatest music he'd ever recorded. He started his own company, Essex Productions, and tried to convince the world that it was a full-blown record business that merely used Capitol's distribution services, but nobody was fooled: Essex was a paper company, a tax dodge, and Capitol owned the rights to everything Frank had cut for them and everything he had yet to cut for them under a rich seven-year deal he'd signed with the label in 1957.

Capitol, Frank felt, paid handsomely in every respect except the one that mattered most to him—his freedom. Repeatedly, he kept trying to finagle some kind of independence for Essex from Capitol president Glenn Wallichs; repeatedly, he was turned down. In the spring of 1959, he even went on strike, recording nothing at all for a period of ten months and threatening worse.

During this hiatus, Frank kept trying to find a way to take complete control of his recording career. He nearly bought the Verve label for himself until it was snatched up by MGM. Finally, in 1960, he decided he'd simply start up an independent company of his own, commitments to Capitol be damned. In December, he announced the formation of Reprise Records. Reprise was touted as being particularly sensitive to the aesthetic and commercial prerogatives of its artists. All rights to their material would revert to them after a specified period (*reprise,* get it?), after which they would be free to repackage, rerecord, or rerelease it however they saw fit. (Sammy, always cash-short, sold these rights back to the company when he signed on.)

It looked a bit to industry insiders like the founding of United Artists, the original case of the "lunatics taking charge of the asylum." But Frank got his chums to jump ship with him, found a few other willing artists to record, and released a full slate of five albums the month after Jack's inauguration, including tenor saxophonist Ben Webster's *Warm Moods,* and three albums that clearly signaled the label's independent spirit: *It Is Now Post Time,* by Frank's saloon crony Joe E. Lewis, *The Wham of Sam,* one of Sammy's great recordings with Mel Torme's longtime arranger Marty Paich, and Sinatra's own thirty-minute homage to the zeitgeist he himself had birthed, *Ring-a-Ding-Ding!,* a record that came complete with its own exclamation point.

Sammy's album was audaciously dramatic, capturing the energy that he conveyed onstage with highly stylized renditions of show tunes like "Blame It on My Youth," "Can't We Be Friends," and "Thou Swell," the latter set in a wildly upbeat arrangement that exploited Sammy's brilliant articulation to its height. Paich, who became Sammy's greatest wrangler, getting several fabulous records out of the singer before losing his attention after a few years, found just the right balance between showbiz schmaltz and real jazz feeling —the core, indeed, of Sammy's whole act. There were bigger hits before and after, but *The Wham of Sam* (what a title!) was Sammy's great coming-out party on vinyl, a chance for people who'd never seen him live to get a real sense of his titanic strength as an entertainer.

Still and all, *Ring-a-Ding-Ding!* made *The Wham of Sam* sound like a collection of Gay Nineties tunes crooned to a ukulele. There was that cover: a cartoon drawing of Frank in a snap-brim hat, fingering a blue bow tie and making a high sign with the same hand. There was the title song, an insidery number by Jimmy Van Heusen and Sammy Cahn built on a meaningless Rat Pack catchphrase and sprinkled with obscure showbiz slang ("do a skull," for instance, referred to a kind of openmouthed vaudeville double take). There was the cheeky juxtaposition of "The Coffee Song" with "When I Take My Sugar to Tea." There were Johnny Mandel's foot-stomping, brassy arrangements, the most purely up-tempo stuff Frank would record until he worked with Count Basie a few years later. Like "Ol' MacDonald," the whole thing screamed out brashness, confidence, insouciance, *balls*. It was, almost coincidentally, a hit; what it really stood for was Frank's domination of the era.

He owned casinos and record companies, restaurants and vast expanses of land; he produced films and TV shows; he slept with the women of his choosing, whether they were hookers, starlets, waitresses, or Marilyn Monroe; his entourage included the most celebrated entertainers of the day; he consorted with the underworld; he helped elect a president. What was not to brag about? The world was Frank Sinatra's playground: He owned the equipment, he invited whomever he wanted to play with, and he could stop everyone cold whenever he wanted to and rivet everyone's attention with his music. There'd never been anyone in the world of entertainment with so much talent and power at once.

Naturally, this wasn't universally seen as a good thing. Frank was widely known for his hedonism, his flouting of conventional morality, his liberal politics, his temper. All of this made him anathema to many commentators in the press, not all of them kooks of the stripe who tortured Sammy. During the campaign, various showbiz columnists had attacked Frank and the Rat Pack, which was still generally known as the Clan. Longtime Sinatra nemesis Dorothy Kilgallen was, predictably, among the carping crowd—she actually quoted Jack Kennedy as saying of Frank, "He's no friend of mine, he's just a friend of Pat and Peter Lawford"— as was Ruth Montgomery, a Hearst syndicated columnist. But there were cavils as well from such presumably neutral voices as *Time* ("some of JFK's biggest headaches may well come from the ardently pro-Kennedy clique that is known variously as the Rat Pack or the Clan") and journalist-to-the-stars Joe Hyams, who reported that the Kennedys had warned the Rat Pack to start behaving like "serious citizens" and wrote a pair of unwelcome articles detailing Frank's financial affairs.

In the final stages of the election, and periodically throughout 1961, the various members of the Rat Pack sought to downplay the talk of their mutual admiration society as some sort of cabal that threatened the very foundations of American democracy and decency. Frank was first and loudest, declaring outright that there was no such thing as the Clan: "The various guilds that are part of my professional life are the only organized groups to which I belong," he pronounced through a press agent. "'The Clan' is a figment of someone's imagination. Naturally, people in Hollywood socialize with friends, as they do in any community. But we do not get together in childish fraternities, as some people would like to think. There is no such entity as 'The Clan' and there never has been. I am fortunate to have many friends and many circles of friends, but there is no membership card." Likewise, he told columnist Earl Wilson, then (but not always) in his favor, "There is no Clan. It's some guys that like each other and get along together. There are no membership cards or anything like that. This whole thing is silly."

Peter chimed in: "Now look—that Clan business—I mean that's hokey. I mean it makes us sound like children—like we all wore sweat shirts that said 'The Clan' and Frank with a whistle around his neck. They make us sound so unsavory. We're just a lot of people on the same wave length. We like each other. What's wrong with that?"

Even Dean, of all people, had something to say. "It's silly to call it anything like the Clan or the Group," he said. "If anything it's more like the PTA—a Perfect Togetherness Association."

Sammy would joke about it sometimes, asking, "Would I belong to an organization known as The Clan?" and kidding that the Rat Pack was "just a little group of ordinary guys that get together once a year to take over the entire world." And Joey, of course, got off the best line—"Clan, Clan, Clan! I'm sick and tired of hearing things about the Clan. Just because a few of us guys get together once a week with sheets over our heads. . . ."

The talk really did have a life of its own, with the same commentators who'd inspired the public fascination with the Rat Pack now reading into this "there is no Rat Pack" P.R. campaign signs that the group truly was finished: showbiz gossip waged as talmudic exegesis. Wrote columnist Sidney Skolsky, "Call it what you will—clan, group, PTA, or what have you—the summit meeting boys are going to dissolve slowly. The Clan will be no more because that's what the leader wants." Then *this* sort of writing gave rise to yet another layer of analysis, such as Dorothy Kilgallen's comment that "reports elsewhere that the Frank Sinatra Clan has disbanded, or is coming apart at the seams, are far from factual. It's still a tightly-knit organization, even if some members had to pretend to go 'underground' for obvious reasons."

Indeed, that summer showed that the Rat Pack was far from kaput. There was the shoot of *Sergeants Three*, for instance. There they were, incongruously stuck out in Fuck All, Utah; one night, they managed to break the monotony by sneaking into Vegas to hit a trifecta of sorts, bouncing from casinos where Vic Damone and Eddie Fisher were playing to the Sands, where Danny Thomas had center stage. In each joint, they broke up the headline act with their antics, grabbing the spotlight and doing bits from the Summit to the delight of audiences and, at the very least, the patient indulgence of the stars.

Two months later, they were all in L.A. finishing work on the film and they did it again, crashing Sonny King's opening night at the Slate Brothers nightclub. Dean and Frank pounded King's toes from their ringside seats, then took the stage and poured whiskey on the comic: a 100-proof baptism from the pontiffs of cool. Sidney Skolsky, who was becoming a scold, wrote that the incident felt like "a college initiation to see if Sonny could get into the fraternity known as 'The Clan.'"

Few had seen the Sonny King show, and few except self-righteous columnists cared. But a few nights later, the Rat Pack converged on a far more visible event and disrupted it to widespread annoyance. Eddie Fisher opened at the Coconut Grove nightclub in the Ambassador Hotel soon after his wife, Elizabeth Taylor, survived a serious bout of pneumonia, and columnists from all over the nation joined celebrities in showing up to support the singer.

Not long into the show, Eddie was singing "That Face" when Dean piped up from ringside, "If I were you, I wouldn't be working—I'd be home with her"—just as if it were Sammy up there. Some people laughed, and Eddie seemed tickled, and soon enough, Frank, Dean, Sammy, and Joey took the stage, drinks in hand, for a mini-Summit of lewd jokes, bowdlerized songs, ad-libs—the usual shit. Some in the audience were no doubt thrilled at the sight of such high-wattage spontaneity, but they were in the minority, and the people who'd come to see Fisher weren't terribly pleased.

"This was a disgusting display of ego," groused Milton Berle, and the press agreed. Declaring that the stunt "came off with a thud," *Variety* opined that "the audience was not amused." "Frank and his henchmen took over and ruined Eddie's performance," grumbled Hedda Hopper. "You sensed a feeling of audience resentment," tsked Skolsky. "This was the first time The Clan played to a hostile audience; the first time they received unfavorable comment in the press."

Frank seemed sincerely puzzled by all the negative attention. He spoke out in a self-defense marked by a sense, exceedingly rare in him, that he'd been stung. "We never hurt anybody, and we don't plan to," he said. "I've never seen an audience dislike what we do." Rather than accept that he and his cronies had disrupted Fisher's show, he called it "beautiful. When we jumped on stage, he broke up and couldn't sing any more. I never saw a reaction from a crowd like we saw that night—I swear it was like New Year's Eve. What we do is a rib—a good-natured kind of rib. Really we rib ourselves." (So they weren't grown-up degenerates, after all; they were kidders.)

As if to counter the bad P.R., Frank spent a lot of 1961 running around doing charity gigs—a benefit for Martin Luther King Jr. here, a trip to Mexico City to help fight child poverty there—and he began to plan for a world tour the following year: Europe, Israel, Hong Kong. It didn't fool anyone: Commentators, audiences, antagonists and fans alike still took him for some kind of seductive degenerate.

And the problem wasn't necessarily that he was mis-understood. Rather, he may simply have succeeded too well: Whether he and his buddies acted out of compulsive mega-lomania or calculated self-parody, they had riveted the eyes of the nation; everything they did was subject to intense scrutiny and apelike emulation. They were the subjects of *New Yorker* cartoons (psychiatrist to glum middle-aged guy: "What makes you think Frank Sinatra, Dean Martin and all that bunch are so happy?")—they were the popular national currency.

Studying the ins and outs of the Rat Pack became a form of Kremlinology, with gossips and journalists trying to figure out who was in, who was *almost* in, who'd been rejected. Author Richard Gehman published a paperback, *Sinatra and His Rat Pack,* listing two dozen or so of Frank's buddies, along with official titles, and classifying them all into A and AA groups; the book went into three printings. Gehman's old source Humphrey Bogart, who deplored the cant of showbiz idolatry, would've been disgusted.

In the fall, former MCA agent David Susskind kicked off the new season of his *Open End* talk show with a roundtable on the Rat Pack. Gehman was invited, along with another journalist, Marya Mannes, to decry the behavior of Sinatra and his cronies, while Jackie Gleason, Joe E. Lewis, Toots Shor, and Ernie Kovacs were called in to present the opposition point of view. It was meant to stir people up, but no one had anything really nasty or significant to say. Listening as his journalist guests admitted they admired the Rat Pack and his celebrity guests listed Frank's dozens of charitable acts, a bemused Susskind sighed, "You're making him sound like Albert Schweitzer!"

Such stuff never really sullied the Rat Pack's name. The public knew there was something *wrong* about them—hell, that was part of their allure. What it indicated wasn't approbation but adoration: Interest in the group was at such a fever pitch that the tiniest incident involving them was blown into absurd proportions. When working on the inaugural gala, Frank and Peter landed at National Airport in Washington, where they—and the sweatered dog accompanying them—were met by a military escort and led into town. A Republican congressman from Iowa decried this waste of taxpayer money, and editorial pages across the nation echoed him, ringing the alarm.

The following summer, the press took notice again when Frank showed up at the White House for a visit and was seen talking with presidential spokesman Pierre Salinger, who took pains at a Q&A session with reporters to put some distance between the singer and the president. It didn't help matters that Frank flew straight from Washington to the Kennedy family home in Hyannis Port for a weekend of sailing. In the company of Pat and Peter Lawford, Ted Kennedy, and Dominican playboy Porfirio Rubirosa and his wife of the moment, Odile, Frank and Jack cruised for hours on the family yacht, *Honey Fitz*. Salinger was once again forced to throw up a smokescreen of lies between his boss and Sinatra, insisting that Frank had been invited to Hyannis Port by the Lawfords so that he could "confer with Ambassador [Joseph] Kennedy about a souvenir recording of the inaugural gala." (In fact, that recording had become rather a hot potato, with Frank and the ambassador bickering over plans for its release until Old Joe ordered the director to cut all traces of Frank from the kinescope—a virtually impossible task that became moot when the quarrel was forgotten; besides, nobody outside of the in-group ever saw the thing, anyhow.)

These were little nothings—one-day stories that didn't

change anyone's mind about the way things were carried on between the Kennedys and their decadent Hollywood friends. Behind the scenes, however, things were much more nefarious and grotesque. There was the little betting pool that Peter and Jack had set up between themselves and some of Jack's old buddies from Choate and Harvard, the object of which was to reward the first man to sleep with a woman other than his wife in the Lincoln Bedroom. Peter won, but not by getting laid. The stewardess he enticed into the bedroom turned out to be a lesbian, but he prevailed upon her to act with him in front of Jack as if they had been intimate. Handing his brother-in-law the prize money later on, the president muttered, "You son of a bitch! I knew you'd be the one to win."

Encouraged by Jack's frequent example, Peter made a habit of bringing pickups to the White House and, as in other things, he could be at least as clumsy as graceful in handling them. There was the time he escorted a Capitol Hill secretary to an intimate dinner at the White House that wound up being reported in a chaste but nevertheless suggestive article in the *New York Times*, and the time when, at another soiree, his latest pretty young conquest revealed herself to be an employee of Arizona senator Barry Goldwater, even then considered a front-runner for the 1964 Republican presidential nomination. "For God's sake, Peter!" Jack stormed afterward. "Don't you find out who people work for before you bring them up here? *Jesus!*"

Antics like these were anathema to Jackie Kennedy. True enough, she'd made up her mind to abide her husband's infidelities, which, alas, were no different from her father's or her father-in-law's. But the pranks of her swinging brother-in-law and his depraved Hollywood friends were another matter entirely; she certainly didn't have to turn her home into an adjunct of the Sands, least of all with the Washington press snooping around. So, since she genuinely liked Peter, she focused her animus on Frank, who, at least by her arithmetic, was leeching privileges from Lawford. Frank became persona non grata in her White House, creating a sticky situation for Peter and Jack, both of whom considered him a pal and, even more, a creditor.

Peter talked the matter through with Jack. "During one of our private dinners, he brought up Sinatra and said, 'I really should do something for Frank,' " he recalled. " 'There's only one problem, Jackie hates him and won't have him in the house.' " They joked about smuggling Frank into the White House in a garbage bag or one of John-John's diaper bundles. Then Jack hit on the idea of waiting for Jackie to leave town and having his sister Eunice Shriver serve as hostess for a dinner with Frank.

According to Peter, Frank "flew to Washington for the day and a car drove him up to the southwest gate. Even without Jackie there, the President still wouldn't let him come in the front door. I don't think he wanted reporters to see Frank Sinatra going into the White House. That's why he never flew on *Air Force One* and was never invited to any of the Kennedy state dinners or taken to Camp David for any of the parties there."

Frank was smart enough to sense that he was being kept out of the center of things, however diplomatically, but he wasn't about to jeopardize his standing with the president by making a fuss over it. Instead, he pointedly scapegoated Peter, usually in ways that wouldn't leak over into his relationship with the Kennedys.

In the summer of 1961, for instance, Frank, the Lawfords, the Rubirosas, Jimmy Van Heusen, Mike Romanoff, and Bob Neal made plans to rent a huge yacht for a cruise of the French Riviera with Joe and Rose Kennedy, capped by a performance at the International Red Cross Ball hosted by Princess Grace in Monaco. En route, Frank, Peter, Van Heusen, and Milt Ebbins stopped in Paris to see Dean, who was headed off to Germany for a singing engagement. Trouble began when Peter horned in on a young woman Dean had been chatting up. In a climate in which it was considered unchivalrous for one married man to make off with the romantic conquest of another, Peter upset Frank and Dean by leaving a cocktail party with the pretty lass in tow. "Your friend's a real nice guy," Frank snarled to Ebbins, while Dean bemusedly asked, "Whatever happened to one for all and all for one?"

Frank grew further incensed the following night when, out at a restaurant in Paris with a large party, he watched from the table as Peter and Pierre Salinger had an extended talk at the bar, out of earshot of their fellow diners. Sinatra swaggered a bit drunkenly to the pair: "You guys having a private conversation? What are you talking about that you can't say in front of me?" The two tried to explain that they'd simply bumped into one another while ordering drinks and got lost in small talk, but Frank fumed and left.

The next day, when the cruise was meant to commence, Frank called Nice, where Neal had spent several thousand dollars renting a huge vessel. "I'm not going on any goddamn cruise with that lousy bastard!" he hollered.

"Which lousy bastard is that, Frank?" Neal asked.

"Fucking Lawford!" came the thundering reply. "To hell with him! I'm going to Germany with Dean!" And off he went to Frankfurt, adding a dash of Rat Pack spontaneity to one concert but leaving a gaping hole at another: When Dean and Frank turned up AWOL, Sammy performed at Princess Grace's benefit alone.

Back home, Frank's temper hadn't settled. He set about to record *Point of No Return,* the last of the four albums he had agreed to cut for Capitol in exchange for release from his contract, which still had three years to run. The sessions caught him in an extremely agitated mood. Just the previous year, while working on another of these obligatory albums, he'd thrown several tantrums, finding some minuscule thing to carp about in each take of each song. His petulance was ultimately forestalled by trumpeter Sweets Edison: Catching the look of imminent explosion in the singer's eye just as one number was ending, he cut him off with "Shit, baby, you can't do it any better than that!"—at which, however angry, Frank had to laugh.

These final recording dates ought to have had a bit of bittersweetness to them: They'd be Frank's last in the famous round Capitol tower, they consisted of ballads he'd sung for years such as "I'll Be Seeing You," "September Song," and "These Foolish Things," and they were arranged and conducted by Axel Stordahl, the elegantly reserved proctor of Frank's great 1940s solo recordings on Columbia, who was, it was widely known, in the last stages of a battle with cancer.

But Frank was so angry at having to give Capitol one more moneymaker that he virtually had to be talked into the dates by his lawyers. And when he was there his demeanor was poisonous. After greeting the orchestra collegially, he raced through the sessions, not even stopping to make sure the recordings would be usable on an album. "We were doing one take on everything, and that's the way it went," said trombonist Milt Bernhart. "After an hour he was through with six numbers, and he said goodbye and was out the door—and he did that two nights in a row. We got no more than one or, tops, two takes on everything. On several, [producer Dave] Cavanaugh came out of the booth and said, 'Frank, we had a little trouble with the bass on that last take,' but by that time Frank had torn up the sheet. 'I'm sorry,' was the way he put it. 'Next number.' You had to be there to see it."

The album turned out beautifully, actually, with the lush, mournful ballads of Frank's youth revisited in the deeper, more rueful tones of his mature voice. In fact, all four of the albums he whipped off for Capitol after the advent of Reprise—*Nice 'n' Easy, Sinatra's Swingin' Session!, Come Swing with Me,* and *Point of No Return*—would have to be rated highly among his career's work. The fact was that while he was in the midst of all the commotion he'd orchestrated around himself—the hustle, the furor, the pettiness, the glory—he was in such good voice and had such marvelous commercial and artistic instincts that he could almost, as a singer, do no wrong.

He was one talented son of a bitch.

I feel dirty

Adele Beatty
Alora Gooding
Altovise Gore
Amy Rea
Andre Boyer
Angie Dickinson
Anita Ekberg
Ann Sheridan
Ava Gardner
Barbara Marx
Betty Furness
Betty McDonald
Candy Toxton
Carol Lynley
Catherine Mae Hawn
Celeste Holm
Claire Kelly
Dani Crayne
Debbie Reynolds

"Like the food at a party, flashy girls come in a variety of shades and sizes, but it's always the same variety. They are presented as 'actresses,' that's the standard line whether they are starlets or hookers. In New York, the term is model." — *Judith Campbell Exner*

"The women, who didn't seem to mind being referred to as 'broads,' sat up straight with their legs crossed and little expectant smiles on their carefully made-up faces. They sipped white wine, smoked, and eyed the men, laughing at every joke. . . . A long time would pass before any of the women dared to speak, then under the main male conversation they talked about their cats, or where they bought their clothes; but more than half an ear was always with the men, just in case. As hours passed, the women, neglected in their chairs, drooped; no longer listening, no longer laughing." —*Mia Farrow*

"Could they see women as real beings with needs and intelligence? Did they ever communicate on a fulfilling level? I was secretly grateful that I didn't really see them as potential lovers. Had anything like that developed, I would have been in real trouble." —*Shirley MacLaine*

"It seemed to me that the married men were worse than the single ones. They were always looking, always hunting. You'd see them at parties with different girls and every once in a while you'd see them at a party with their wives. As far as I was concerned, I had made up my mind that if I got married again, I'd have to accept the fact that my husband would cheat." —*Judith Campbell Exner*

> Deborah Gould
> Diana Trask
> Dorothy Dandridge
> Dorothy Provine

Edie Goetz
Elizabeth Taylor
Evie Lynn Abbot
Eva Gabor
Gail Renshaw
Geri Crane
Gina Lollobrigida
Gloria Vanderbilt
Gregg Sherwood
Hope Lange
Ira von Fustenburg
Irene Tsu
Irma DiBendetto

"What is it Sammy's got that the girls go for? Ask that sexy redhead from *Phenix City Story*—or read it here!" —*Confidential Magazine*

"WHAT MAKES AVA GARDNER RUN FOR SAMMY DAVIS JR.? Some girls go for gold, but it's bronze that 'sends' sultry Ava." —*Confidential Magazine*

"I've never had a day-to-day relationship with a woman, to the extent that I've never even spent a whole night in bed with a woman. Never. When it was time to sleep either they'd go home or I'd fall asleep on the couch or the floor. I haven't slept in bed with anyone since I was a kid." —*Sammy to May*

"There was some sex going on, switching partners, group sex, it was there to be had if you wanted it, any kind, any way. It was free-form, and when living got too depressing, hanging out with a group like that got your mind off it, for that moment at least it fogged your brain and you didn't feel so bad. . . . Sex wasn't the point, though. *You didn't want to be alone.* Two or three people would get into bed with you and you'd fall asleep. You had physical companionship, that's what you needed, a quiet, friendly body lying next to you, and you'd sleep." —*Sammy*

Jacqueline Park
Janet Margolin
Jean MacDonald
Jean Seberg
Jeanne Carmen
Jeannie Biegger
Jill Corey
Jill St. John
Jo Ann Tolley
Joan Arnold
Joan Blackman
Joan Cohn Harvey
Joan Crawford
Joi Lansing
Joni Anderson
Judy Campbell

"On December 17, 1946, [he] had contacted [a] well-known call-house madam in an effort to talk to one [of her] call house girls. [She] was not in at the time and Lawford requested that she call him back at the Mocambo Night Club. On another occasion, information was developed that a call house girl ... was 'reportedly a frequent trick for movie actor Peter Lawford.' Another Los Angeles prostitute reportedly 'bragged' that she knew the movie star, Peter Lawford, and on several occasions (our informant) had overheard her attempting to reach Lawford by phone." —*FBI report*

"He was into oral sex. He could and did do the other, but he preferred oral sex. That's what the Cepacol was for, because most girls of my generation thought oral sex was dirty. I flatly refused to do it when we were together. That's what ended our physical relationship." —*a Santa Monica beach friend of Peter's*

"Peter was the whore's delight. Every time we traveled, every place we went, there were all these hookers. It was cheaper for him to do that. You have to wine and dine girls. Peter never wanted to get involved. It was easier to have call girls than to try and romance somebody." —*Milt Ebbins*

"Sammy had found this beautiful little model, a white girl. He fell in love with her, and they were living together while they were filming *Salt and Pepper.* Peter stole her away. Sammy came to me and said, 'That fucker, I'll never talk to him again.' I asked Peter, 'What did you do?' And Peter replied nonchalantly, 'I stole his girl.' " —*Milt Ebbins*

"If Peter didn't want to get laid, he'd get a girl to suck his cock. Every night of his life. That doesn't sound like a homosexual to me. I'd be with a girl, and the next thing I knew she'd be with him." —*surfing buddy Joe Naar*

Judy Garland
Judy Holliday
Judy Meredith
Juliet Prowse
June Allyson
Kathy McKee
Keenan Wynn
Kim Novak
Lana Turner
Lauren Bacall
Layte Bowden

Lee Remick
Lisa Ferraday
Lois Nettleton

"Dino used to fuck every human he could." —*a Steubenville friend*

"He was a bastard: all wine and candlelight, then a pat on the ass in the morning." —*a conquest of Dean's*

"Dean was too beautiful, too handsome. The women, I mean. One had to accept that." —*Jeanne Martin*

"The two of us walked into Sammy's dressing room, Frank Sinatra was there. Sammy had to leave for a few minutes, and when we were alone, Sinatra told me Dean Martin was due at any moment. He suggested that, as a gag, I should strip down to my underwear to greet him. I was hesitant at first, but I thought I was being put to a test to see if I could play in the big leagues. So I slipped out of my black-and-white polka-dot jumpsuit and greeted Dean Martin wearing my black bra, matching bikini panties, and white go-go boots. 'Wonderful, charming,' said Martin, who told me to get dressed again, 'because Frank is an asshole.' " —*a conquest of Sammy's*

"The most beautiful broads went crazy for Dean." —*Jerry Lewis*

"He was a good sex man, but his big interest was golf." —*Herman Hover, proprietor of Ciro's, on Dean*

Loray White
Marie Roemer
Marilyn Maxwell

Marilyn Monroe
Marion Dixon
Marlene Dietrich
Martha Hyer
Mary Lou Watts
Mary Rowan
May Britt
Meg Myles
Melissa Weston
Mia Farrow
Miriam LaVelle
Molly Dunne

"Frank is just plain broad nuts. He can no more not look at a dame than he could stop singing. . . . It's pathetic in a way. Once I heard him talking about a girl he'd been out with the night before. She wasn't much better than a hooker. The way he talked about her, you'd have thought she was the greatest broad in Hollywood. He was like a kid. He said, as though he couldn't begin to understand it, 'You know, I think that girl really did like me.' How do you figure it? Here he's had broads after him by the thousands all these years and he doesn't even know what they see in him." —*a friend*

"Everyone made more money when Frank played the Strip, especially cab drivers and hookers. Frank loved hookers and used them a great deal. He preferred them because he didn't have to deal with them emotionally. And he always paid them well." —*Mrs. Jack Entratter*

"He's a little twisted sexually. There are a lot of odds and ends in his sex life. He loved call girls for orgies and he liked to see women in bed for kicks, but not all the time." —*a conquest of Frank's*

"The girls were no more than toys to him. Some mornings I'd get to the house and find four or five of them in the bed at the same time, and all colors of girls, too, let me tell you." — *Frank's Palm Springs houseboy*

"He liked to make love lying on the floor listening to his own records. It was great!" —*a conquest of Frank's*

"He was real good to his girls. He gave them all parts in his movies." —*Frank's longtime makeup man, Beans Ponedel*

"Before bed, he would be so charming. The girl was 'mademoiselle this,' 'darling that,' and 'my sweet baby.' He was [a] cavalier, a perfect gentleman. You never saw anything like this man in your life. He'd jump across the room to light a cigarette. He'd fill her glass with champagne every time she took a sip. . . . It was the next day that we'd always find the other Frank, the one who wouldn't speak to the girl, who had been the most beautiful woman in the world the night before. Sometimes he wouldn't even go near her, nor would he tolerate any affectionate overtures from her. Humped and dumped. The minute the conquest was achieved, kaput. The girl could pack her bags. I saw so many of them leave his house in tears." —*Jimmy Van Heusen*

"There were a lot of women who fell in love with Frank but he'd reject them and throw them over. There's a monster in him who wants to screw the world before it screws him—hurt people before they hurt him. Then he feels guilty about being so ugly and that guilt makes him a Mr. Nice Guy and so he does favors for some of the girls he's used or rejected." —*a conquest of Frank's*

"I kept coming back to Frank because there is something

compellingly attractive about him that draws you like a magnet. I think that's why so many stick to him even when he grinds his heel into their very soul." —*Judith Campbell Exner*

"I feel dirty. I'm going to take a shower." —*Frank, after being smothered with kisses by a female fan*

Mona Freeman
Nan Whitney
Nancy Barbato
Nancy Gunderson
Nancy Reagan
Nancy Seidman
Natalie Wood
Pamela Hayward
Patricia Kennedy
Patricia Seaton
Peggy Connelly
Peggy Crosby
Phyllis Elizabeth Davis
Phyllis McGuire
Rhonda Fleming
Rita Hayworth

"I am very much surprised what I have been reading in the newspapers between you and your darling wife. Remember you have a decent wife and children. You should be very happy." —*telegram to Frank from New Jersey don Willie Moretti regarding press accounts of the Ava Gardner romance*

"You fucking no good bastard, you were going to get married and not even tell me, weren't you?"

"You know I can't tell you because you always give me hell, Mama." —*Frank and Dolly*

"Ava, why don't you tell the governor what you see in this 120 pound runt you're married to."

"Well, there's only 10 pounds of Frank, but there's 110 pounds of cock." —*John Ford and his star on the set of* Mogambo

"He always told me one of the things that fascinated him about Ava was that there was no conquest. He couldn't conquer her. That is where the respect comes. He never got her." —*Sheckey Greene*

"Frankie is enchanting as usual and, as usual, he has a 'broad' installed with whom he, as well as everyone else, is bored stiff. She is blond, cute and determined, but I fear her determination will avail her very little with Betty Bacall on the warpath." —*1/1/56 diary entry of Noel Coward*

"Some of the wives of his friends were strangely possessive toward him and not crazy about me." —*Lauren Bacall*

"Frank really dropped the curtain on me. A chilling experience. I still don't know how he did it, but he could behave as though you weren't there." —*Lauren Bacall*

"It is a known fact that the Sands Hotel is owned by hoodlums, and that while the Senator, Sinatra and Lawford were there, show girls from all over the town were running in and out of the Senator's suite." —*Justice Department document*

"Teddy says it's all Frank Sinatra's fault and he is nothing but a procurer of women for these guys. Sinatra is the guy that gets them all together. Meyer says it's not Sinatra's fault and it starts with the president and goes right down the line." —*Meyer Lansky and his wife, Teddy, discussing the sex lives of the Kennedys, as reported by an FBI surveillance agent*

"I pictured myself in Las Vegas sitting with the hookers as I had so many times before. It is 4 a.m. Frank and the other men are telling jokes and laughing loudly. A jaded piano plays the cocktail songs. The women are apart, we are wearing our best dresses, our faces are fixed right. We chat about cats, and we wait." —*Mia Farrow*

"If I had as many love affairs as you've given me credit for, I'd now be speaking to you from a jar in Harvard Medical School." —*Frank to an audience of Hollywood press agents*

Rita Maritt
Robin Raymond
Romy Schneider
Ronnie Cowan
Sal Mineo
Sandra Giles
Scottie Singer
Sharman Douglas
Shirley MacLaine
Shirley Van Dyke
Sophia Loren
Sylvia Ruzga
Toni Anderson
Toni Della Penta
Vanessa Brown
Victoria Principal
Zorita

And a cast of thousands . . .

I'm a whore for my music

It would be late, Frank would be holding court.

Maybe they had played a show earlier in the evening, and it was getting on 3:00 or 4:00 a.m., and they were in a roped-off area of a casino or a hotel or in a back room of a saloon or the most private area of a nightclub.

Maybe they had eaten dinner at his house—Italian food cooked by Frank and served on tiptoes by George Jacobs, or takeout from some showbiz clubhouse like Chasen's or Puccini.

It could be someplace on the regular route—Beverly Hills or Palm Springs or Las Vegas or Miami or New York or Chicago—or someplace on the road like London, Paris, New Orleans, San Francisco. Frank Sinatra was a movable feast, after all, and very au courant. "Frank knew piano bars that no one else knew," Shirley MacLaine remembered.

But wherever, exactly, it would be late: 3:00, 4:00 a.m.

Frank would be telling stories and needling people, teasing the women with a hint of sexual tension or the men about their clothes or their hair or their lineage, whatever.

Around him would be a group. On a good night, it would

include Dean, Peter, Sammy. It would include a couple of big guys, invariably: Hank Sanicola, Jilly Rizzo, Andy Celentano, Mack Gray, and worse and more sinister. It would include showbiz buds like Don Rickles, Tony Curtis, Eddie Fisher, Buddy Lester, Richard Conte. Broads, of course—wives, even. And there'd be these adjuncts, these supernumeraries, swelling the scene with the regularity of a stock company, friends to everybody but nevertheless not quite the real thing themselves: Sammy Cahn, Jimmy Van Heusen, Swifty Lazar, Harry Kurnitz, Mike Romanoff.

Some nights were really special, with lots of the top dogs together. Some nights it was Frank and, oh, Sammy—plus, of course, a few big guys, maybe the latest dame.

But it was something, somewhere, nearly every night. Frank needed to keep the end of the day at bay. He'd sleep until noon, or later, no problem. But until that moment of submission came, until he felt safe and calm enough to be alone, there'd be a party of some sort.

Dean didn't care for it. He'd like a few drinks, of course, a few laughs, some gambling, a girl, but the marathon of it, the effort—that he didn't need. Frank would be urging him to join some spree; Dean would beg out—a broad waiting for him, he'd say: always a good excuse—and then go back to his room and a western on TV or a comic book. And every night—for real!—his prayers.

Peter and Sammy, though, were cut just right for such nights, maybe even more than Frank. Nothing thrilled them enough, not the booze, which hit each of them harder than it ever did Frank, not the elegance or the glitter or the perfume. On the road, they might put all the lightweights to bed and then continue on with Frank in one of their suites, drinking after sunrise, when John Q. Putz was getting to work. Guys would joke that with this crowd, "a black tie evening" meant "bring sunglasses."

And yet even the most dedicated decadents couldn't quite keep up with the Leader. No one ever remembered, save for when he was all broke up over Ava, putting Frank to bed. Oh, George Jacobs did it plenty, as did, eventually, Barbara Marx, but those were private moments, more harrowing than even the closest of the chums ever saw. Socially, no one ever stayed at the table after Frank to keep up the jollity or pick up a tab. Sammy, who emulated Frank's endless late-night partying his whole life, watching movies and playing board games and even holding play readings in his homes and suites when he was too afraid to hit the town and venture the disdain of racist nightclub owners and doormen, could recall being worn to a frazzle by Frank, a man ten years his senior. He'd stifle yawns, he'd rub at his plastic eye (a sure sign of exhaustion): "At that hour, there was nothing happening anywhere that interested me as much as my bed. The thought of it made me giddy. Bed, oh bed. Bed, bed, bed, soft bed." (Weariness turned him, apparently, into Gertrude Stein.)

Not every night ended with a fade. Some exploded: Frank might get cross with somebody in a bar or restaurant and instigate a shouting match, or worse; he might brood or sulk over some perceived slight or other and then erupt hours later against food, furniture, clothing, friends, the help. Plates and telephones flew, windows broke, guns were fired, an original Norman Rockwell portrait was destroyed. And those same late-night friends who would sit patiently for Frank's teasing on other occasions would scurry into action—cleaning up, quieting up, paying off, warding away.

Some of these men would never dream of committing such acts themselves: Cahn and Van Heusen were songwriters, for God's sake, not thumbbreakers. They didn't travel with bodyguards at their backs and cherry bombs in their pockets. They didn't have police records or FBI files. They weren't prone to such outbursts, but they endured them, witnessed

them, hell, *condoned* them with their silence and their willingness to return and, inevitably, see more of them. It was the
price they paid for what they received: Frank's approval,
acceptance, aura. Somebody once called Van Heusen out on
it, the toadying and pandering and looking the other way and
buttoning up he did for Frank: He admitted with some shame,
"I'm a whore for my music."

That was a mite strong, but there was a truth to it. Beyond
Dean and Sammy, his brothers in performance and celebrity
and mien, beyond Peter, whom he curried for ulterior reasons
that the whole world tacitly understood, beyond the few guys
like Joey and Rickles and Tony Curtis and Yul Brynner and
R.J. Wagner, with whom he worked, there was that second
layer of men who were around Frank because their livelihood
depended on it. Friendship was possible, of course, and some
of these men would come to mean a great deal to Frank and
his family, but there was always this other dynamic to the
relationship—not unlike that with Peter. It was understood
that a certain deference would be paid Frank, that that
"Leader" joke was no joke. Frank's will was not to be crossed,
his choices not to be questioned. "He has hurt me more than
once, Frank Sinatra," Sammy Cahn confessed, but his favor
was apparently worth the price of the injuries.

Of all these adjuncts, Cahn and Van Heusen may have been
the oddest because they were the smartest, the most talented,
the ones who should've known better. They were remarkably
gifted in their fields, but they so tied themselves in with Frank
and his world that they were smothered even while being
rewarded.

Over time, they became Frank's house composers and, by
extension, those of the Rat Pack as a whole. Cahn went back
with Frank to the Dorsey days, and he'd written for Frank
first in partnership with composer Jule Styne and then with
Van Heusen; that latter tandem were the great songwriting

team of Frank's fifties and sixties—"All the Way," "Love and Marriage," "High Hopes," "The Tender Trap," "The Second Time Around," "My Kind of Town." Some of the material was commissioned with exacting specificity by the singer ("Ring-a-Ding-Ding," "Come Fly with Me") and some was never published—specialty material consisting mainly of Cahn's topical, often salty rewrites of lyrics for Friars Roasts, benefits, and, of course, the Kennedy campaign: "Everyone wants to back Jack/Jack is on the right track."

Feisty, ferret-faced, prematurely balding, Cahn was a Jewish New York songsmith in the mold of Berlin, Arlen, the Gershwins, a street kid with a gift, in his case, for rhyme. Van Heusen had been born Edward Chester Babcock, a native of Syracuse, New York, descended, the family legend went, from Stephen Foster. He attended a seminary and Syracuse University, writing pop songs the whole while, then became a Tin Pan Alley stalwart. He was a ladies' man and a crack test pilot, and, in the words of many witnesses, one of Frank's ideals—a man's man, strong, worldly, accomplished, discreet. He, too, had been around Frank since the forties—he'd written the music for "Nancy (with the Laughing Face)" and had been one of Frank's constant companions in L.A., New York, and Palm Springs.

As bachelors and fellow aficionados of female delights, the two songwriters reveled in the flesh that fell to them from Frank, and they happily abetted his adulteries and affairs to their constant profit. They disrespected his first marriage to the extent that they let him conduct trysts in their Sunset Strip apartments, and they witnessed his courtship of and estrangements from Ava Gardner with dispassion, always ready to commiserate with him or stop him from committing some stupid act over her. It was at Van Heusen's New York apartment that Frank slashed his wrists over Ava's absence in 1953—one of many little incidents that the composer overlooked in the pursuit of a friendship built around Frank's singing his songs.

A very few others in Frank's orbit during the early sixties had careers as independent as Cahn and Van Heusen. Whirlwind agent Swifty Lazar and restaurateur Michael Romanoff, holdovers from the Bogart Rat Pack, were men whose lives, built on sheer moxie, must've struck Frank as parallels of his own. Lazar was a renegade in the agenting business who wasn't bothered by taking cuts from both a buyer and a seller in a deal, or by peddling properties and people that weren't his to represent. Romanoff was an honest-to-goodness con man: A Russian-born Jew raised largely in orphanages in Illinois, he spent his adult life boldly impersonating the royalty of Europe, passing himself off as the nephew of the last czar so audaciously that he parlayed the scam into a $6,000 grubstake to start his famed restaurants, at which he lorded over Hollywood's elite to their exquisite pleasure. These were clearly A-list guys over whom Frank had no more control than he did over Jack Kennedy or Sam Giancana. They were happy to accept his friendship, his invitations, his custom, to engage in one-upmanship and practical jokes. But they weren't flunkies, not even close.

For the real thing—muscle, gofers, yes-men—Frank preferred big guys who could put on a suit and not get embarrassed, borderline thugs with just enough polish to pull off legitimate business. Hank Sanicola was number one through the fifties. He helped Frank manage his music interests and served as a casual accompanist, but he also had pieces of various Sinatra enterprises—until the day, that is, he literally asked Frank to let him out, luggage and all, when they were driving through the desert arguing about how to run the Cal-Neva Lodge, in which Sanicola owned points.

By then, Frank had met Jilly Rizzo in Miami Beach and had helped promote and fund his Broadway saloon by slipping him a few dollars and making the joint his unofficial New York clubhouse (it even appears in *The Manchurian Candidate*). From the mid-sixties on, no one was around Frank more than Jilly, and no one could get to Frank unless they passed through the massive wall of protection he constituted. Of course, Jilly didn't hurt anybody so's you could prove it: There were other, meaner guys for that. But a nod from Jilly could be a blessing or a curse—could get you near Frank or banish you forever—and most everyone who crossed his path was happier with the former.

Dean, too, had a wall: Mack Gray, a kind of companion, valet, procurer, bodyguard, and drug peddler who came into Dean's service after George Raft, his original boss, could no longer afford to keep him on the payroll. Like Sanicola and Jilly, Gray intimated danger and pain to anyone considering violating the space of his boss. He'd been a fight promoter before putting in twenty years under Raft. He looked the part of a hood, he even had the nickname Killer, but he wasn't quite the figure of menace he seemed. That nickname, for instance, came not because he was capable of homicide; it was a corruption of the Yiddish word for "hernia."

Gray's real name? Max Greenburg.

A Jewish thumbbreaker for an Italian singer: Even in picking his rough friends, Dean had a better sense of humor than Frank.

The Frank situation

Jack Kennedy loved sports: football, of course, and sailing and golf. He loved games like Diplomacy and Charades. And he loved trashy novels, especially espionage novels. He famously devoured Ian Fleming's James Bond books, and he enjoyed *The Manchurian Candidate*, Richard Condon's best-seller about an American soldier brainwashed by the North Koreans and programmed to assassinate a U.S. presidential candidate. It was a crackling good read, combining cold war paranoia with creepy psychological themes and a shock ending—part page-turning thriller, part satire of American mores and politics. Everyone who read it—Jack Kennedy included—thought it would make a swell film.

Two Hollywood hotshots, screenwriter George Axelrod (*The Seven Year Itch, Will Success Spoil Rock Hunter?*) and director John Frankenheimer (*Birdman of Alcatraz, The Young Savages*), got ahold of the rights to the book, and in September 1961, they approached Frank about starring in it and releasing it through his contract with United Artists, which was handling distribution of films made through Sinatra's various production companies. Frank liked Condon's story—he had already played a presidential assassin in 1954's *Suddenly*— and he expressed his interest to U.A. president Arthur Krim,

Frank had already been considering a renovation of the Palm Springs estate. Now he began a major reconstruction of the entire grounds. The main house was expanded with the additions of a banquet room able to seat forty and a Kennedy Room decorated with mementos of the president; two cottages were added to house Secret Service agents, and a communications center was installed, with five private telephone lines, teletype equipment, and enough cable to handle a full switchboard; a concrete heliport was poured, and a towering flagpole was erected, modeled after the one Frank had seen in Hyannis Port flying the presidential seal as a sign that Jack was there. Steep overtime charges were incurred so that work would be completed in time; lumber was even flown in by helicopter. "He redecorated every part of the house except his own bedroom," Nancy Sinatra recalled. The prize piece: a bronze plaque attached to a bedroom door in the main house reading, "JOHN F. KENNEDY SLEPT HERE November 6th and 7th 1960." (The dates were wrong: Kennedy's only previous overnight visit to the estate had been in November 1959; Election Day in 1960 was November 8, and Jack had been back East in the days immediately prior.)

Frank's avidity amused the Kennedys, who remembered him arriving in Hyannis Port the previous September with two loaves of bread for Joe. "It had been kind of a running joke with all of us," Peter recalled. "No one asked Frank to do this."

Which is why what followed was all the more awful for him. Without his knowing it, his entrée into Camelot, always tenuous, had eroded. All the shit that Frank had steered Jack's way—the broads, the Mafia money, the shadowy friends—was about to be shoved back in his face by the Kennedys with heartless indifference.

Jack was set to visit Palm Springs on March 24; on March 22, Peter Lawford was told by Jack and Bobby to call Frank helipad he'd had built. "He was in a frenzy," Lawford recalled.

When he arrived in Palm Springs, Jack asked Peter how Frank had taken the news. "I said, 'Not very well,' which was a mild understatement," Peter said. "The President said, 'I'll call him and smooth it over.' So he did. After the conversation Jack said, 'He's pretty upset, but I told him not to blame you because you didn't have anything to do with it.' "

But that wasn't how it went. Frank mourned the distance that Jack had placed between the two of them. "If he would only pick up the telephone and call me and say that it was politically difficult to have me around, I would understand," he lamented to Angie Dickinson. "I don't want to hurt him. But he has never called."

Among the Hollywood crowd over whom he had lorded his intimacy with the president, Frank suffered an awful loss of face—Eddie Fisher joked that Frank should have a plaque on the house reading, "JFK Almost Slept Here"—and everyone close to him who had anything to do with the fiasco incurred his wrath. Jimmy Van Heusen, who owned the house next door to Crosby's and made it available to the Secret Service, was given the cold shoulder for weeks.

But Peter—Peter was a dead man. "I was the one who took the brunt of it," Lawford remembered. "He felt that I was responsible for setting Jack up to stay at Bing's—Bing Crosby, of all people—the other singer and a Republican to boot. Well, Frank never forgave me. He cut me off just like that—just like that."

Peter tried to call Frank to make amends, but Frank refused to talk with him, telling people that he wanted nothing more than to punch Lawford in the face. He and Frank had already given up the restaurant, Puccini, that they jointly owned (after mobster Mickey Cohen had started a fistfight with Red Skelton's manager in the joint, it went on to be filled more frequently with cops than customers), but now Peter wouldn't even get considered for future Rat Pack films; worse, Peter claimed, Frank "turned Dean and Sammy and Joey against me as well."

Frank finally agreed to hear Lawford's side of the story from Milt Ebbins, the actor's manager, who explained the truth behind the snub—that Bobby didn't want Jack so close to Sinatra when so many of Frank's mob friends were under intense Justice Department scrutiny—but that did nothing to alter Frank's resolve against Peter.

"None of it worked," said Ebbins. "Frank just wrote Peter off. And Peter was destroyed. He loved Frank. He loved being a part of the Rat Pack. And all of a sudden he was on the outs."

Peter had never felt very connected to things, but now the fog that always dampened his soul and separated him from the rest of the world seemed thicker than ever. He sulked. He drank. He saw anti-Lawford conspiracies in every downward turn of his career (he claimed that Frank put in a bad word for him with Billy Wilder, costing him a couple of film roles). He was still the president's brother-in-law, of course, still a big movie star with a glamorous life. But he started dying when Frank cut him off, and it was one of the longest, ugliest, most painful deaths that could be imagined.

One of these days it'll come out

Frank's banishment from the Kennedy inner circle had been of his own making.

But it had begun, weirdly, in the Las Vegas hotel room of comedian Dan Rowan on Halloween, 1960.

Rowan had come to Sam Giancana's attention as a rival for the affections of Phyllis McGuire, the star of the singing McGuire Sisters, whom the gangster had begun to court earlier in the year—in part by having the Desert Inn tear up nearly $100,000 in gambling markers she'd run up at the blackjack tables.

In an effort to find out just where he stood with McGuire, who was said to be engaged to Rowan but had seemed pretty darn available to Giancana when he'd brushed up against her, the gangster availed himself of a new friend, Bob Maheu, a real spook, with ties to the FBI and CIA, now working in the private security business. Maheu was part of the queer mix of government, criminal, and exiled Cuban forces trying to formulate a strategy to oust Fidel Castro and retake Havana for democracy and gambling. Johnny Rosselli, Giancana's man out West, was Maheu's contact with the mob, and Rosselli introduced the two in October 1960 at a Florida meeting attended by a variety of parties interested in Castro's demise.

Giancana (who was, unbeknownst to him, the subject of the first-ever FBI wiretaps back in his Chicago headquarters) had always harbored a fascination with electronic eavesdropping equipment—he had once extensively grilled a navy man who was dating one of his daughters on the subject. He asked Maheu if it would be possible for him to bug Rowan's room and find out if the comic was making time on him with Phyllis. Maheu, using the money with which the CIA was funding the Mafia's cabal against Castro, hired an operative named Arthur J. Balletti and sent him off to the Riviera Hotel to surveil Rowan.

In Vegas, Balletti and a cohort wired Rowan's room and telephone and took up a post in a room of their own. On October 31, 1960, they took a break from their work for lunch, leaving their recording and monitoring equipment out in plain sight on their beds. They forgot to hang the Do Not Disturb sign: A maid came in to make up the room, got a look at all those sinister wires and machines, and called the cops. When Balletti came back from lunch, alone, he was arrested. Rosselli arranged for the $1,000 bail to be paid by a Las Vegas gambling buddy, and the bumbling wiretapper split town.

Rosselli himself broke the news to Giancana about the bungled operation. "I remember his expression," Rosselli recalled. "Smoking a cigar, he almost swallowed it laughing about it." Rosselli, however, wasn't amused: Unlike Giancana, who thought the CIA-inspired plot to kill Castro was a nice opportunity to take money from the government, he held out hopes that the hit could really be pulled off. The Balletti incident "was blowing everything," he said years later, "every kind of cover I had tried to arrange."

He didn't know how right he was: When Vegas authorities

had learned that Balletti was from Miami, they called the FBI in on the case, and the bureau's attentions were heightened when they learned that Maheu was connected to the caper. An effort to find out what Maheu wanted with Dan Rowan led to Rosselli, surveillance of whom began in earnest in June 1961. The following January, Rosselli was seen leaving Romanoff's restaurant in the company of Judy Campbell, and suddenly what had begun as a comical screwup in Las Vegas took on— for the handful of people who had the whole story in their heads—a truly gargantuan dimension.

For anyone who could put all the pieces together, a stunning story unfolded. J. Edgar Hoover was chief among the cognoscenti. He knew a bit about Judy Campbell: She'd been mentioned as consorting with Jack Kennedy in sketchy reports he'd received about the Rat Pack Summit; she'd been interviewed in October 1960 about her acquaintance with Sam Giancana; and she'd been connected with the president in what was clearly an ongoing sexual relationship. The sight of her in Rosselli's company enabled Hoover to draw a pattern of strings connecting Jack Kennedy to Giancana through the body of the woman to whom Frank had introduced them both—and to connect the government that was making such a decorous public show of prosecuting the mob with a shadow government that was willing to use the mob as a hit squad for a coup d'état in a foreign country.

In February, just after the announcement that Jack would be staying with Frank in Palm Springs, Hoover laid a carefully worded bombshell on Bobby Kennedy's desk outlining just what he knew about the president, Campbell, and Giancana. The following month, two days before Jack's trip West, Hoover had lunch with the president and touched on the same matter. That afternoon, Jack made his last-ever call to Judy Campbell from the White House and ordered Peter Lawford to inform Frank that there'd been a change in plans. Telling Peter that

Giancana was known to have made several visits to Frank's estate, staying in the very guest room in which the president was supposed to bunk, Jack said, "I can't stay there while Bobby's handling the investigation."

Frank was finished as a player. And it wasn't Jackie, who'd always felt Frank was too vulgar, who'd shot him down: It was his own tragic hubris—his belief that he and his friends were above morality, that his friendship could erase whatever was circumspect in a president's shacking up with a mobster's girl. Jack could ignore his wife's qualms, and even those of Bobby, who had always been made a little queasy by his older brother's fascination with showbiz types, but Hoover scared him—and Frank had inadvertently given Hoover plenty of ammunition.

If the Kennedys now found Frank's society politically untenable, the others party to the singer's audacious juggling game found his lack of juice with the Kennedy family infuriating. Frank had indicated to Giancana that the mob's assistance with Jack's election would be recompensed with an easing of federal inquiries into racketeering, but the fall of Sinatra's star in the eyes of the Kennedys coincided with an increasingly ravenous attitude toward the mob on the part of the Justice Department.

In this, Giancana had good reason to be mad. He had played ball with Jack in the West Virginia primary and in Chicago during the general election. He had gone along with the CIA loonies and their cockamamie scheme to kill Castro. He had even helped Jack keep his good name in February 1961, when an L.A. restaurateur was set to name the president, Frank, Dean, Sammy, and even Jerry Lewis as correspondents in a divorce action against his starlet wife. Jerry was the hero in that one: He prevailed upon Judy Campbell to get Giancana involved, and the don sent Rosselli to L.A. to put a muzzle on the private eye who'd dug up all the dirt.

And what did he and his pals get for all this trouble? FBI listening devices in their homes and headquarters, burly agents harassing their mistresses and legit employees (families were, by mutual agreement, off base), and byzantine legal pressure unmatched since the IRS case against Al Capone.

The FBI had begun bugging the Chicago mob in the summer of 1959 by planting a listening device in a tailor shop the gangsters used as a front; political fixer Murray "The Camel" Humphries sensed as much and used to begin his business day by declaring to an empty room, "Good morning, gentlemen, and anyone listening. This is the nine o'clock meeting of the Chicago underworld." Eventually, dozens of schemes were uncovered by illegal FBI electronic surveillance, from the corruption of Chicago politicians, policemen, and judges, to efforts to silence witnesses in cases pending against various mobsters, to the split of mob interests in Las Vegas between the Chicago mob and a Las Vegas group led by former Detroit and Cleveland gangster Moe Dalitz.

But it wasn't until the summer of 1961 that they became bold enough to confront their prey directly. Oh, there had been little set-tos over the years, but nothing to compare to the onslaught launched that summer by a group of agents, led by former Notre Dame boxing champ and U.S. marine Bill Roemer, who, among other fancies, decided they would rattle Giancana by deposing Phyllis McGuire before a federal grand jury.

One day, they learned that McGuire would be flying to New York via Chicago and that Giancana would accompany her on the first leg of the trip; they decided to serve her with a subpoena at O'Hare Airport.

The plan was for Roemer and his partner, Ralph Hill, to distract Giancana with a series of pointless questions while two other agents hustled McGuire off to a private room for interrogation.

As soon as they identified themselves as federal agents, Roemer and Hill got hit full blast with the Giancana charm: "A man can't even be left alone with his own girlfriend in this fuckin' country."

While Giancana was busy making friends, McGuire was spirited away; Giancana got back on the plane, apparently looking for her. When he came off, he was carrying her purse.

The sight inspired Roemer: "My, that purse certainly becomes you, Mo. I heard about you being a fairy but now we know, don't we?"

Giancana went white. "You fuckin' cocksucker!" he hissed. "Who do you think you're talking to? I could have Butch [Blasi, his bodyguard] come out here with his machine gun and take good care of you right now."

Roemer asked him if he was threatening a federal officer, a felony, and he backed off.

"I suppose you intend to report this to your boss," he proffered.

"Who's my boss?" Roemer asked, playing along.

"J. Edgar Hoover."

"Yes, I imagine he'll see a copy."

"Fuck J. Edgar Hoover and your super boss!"

"Who is that?"

"Bobby Kennedy."

"Might be he'll see a copy, yes."

"Fuck Bobby Kennedy! And your super, super boss!"

"Who is my super, super boss?"

"John Kennedy!"

"I doubt if the President of the United States is interested in Sam Giancana."

"Fuck John Kennedy. Listen, Roemer, I know all about the Kennedys, and Phyllis knows more about the Kennedys and one of these days we're going to tell all."

"What are you talking about?"

"Fuck you. One of these days it'll come out. You wait, you smart asshole, you'll see."

It did come out, too, but Sam wouldn't live to see it. Instead of vindication, he got harassment. The FBI began tailing him everywhere he went, sometimes with results almost as comical as the attempt to bug Dan Rowan: In Miami, Giancana was leaving a restaurant when an agent who was watching him lost his grip on a tree limb and fell to the ground at the gangster's feet; in New York, a Giancana associate was approached by another FBI agent who also, coincidentally, was named Bill Roemer, prompting Giancana, upon hearing the news, to cry out, "That cocksucker Roemer, he's all over the fuckin' place!"

A few weeks later, he was griping to one of his cohorts again, in a conversation captured by wiretap.

"I got more cocksuckers on my ass than any other cocksucker in the country! Believe me when I tell you. I was on the road with that broad [McGuire]. There must have been up there at least 20 guys. They were next door, upstairs, downstairs, surrounded all the way around. Get in a car, somebody picks you up. I lost that tail, boom, I get picked up someplace else. Four or five cars with intercoms, back and forth, back and forth."

The other man was incredulous: "This was in Europe, right?"

"Right here!" Giancana cried. "In Russia: Chicago, New York, Phoenix!"

It got to be too much for him: "This is like Nazi Germany and I'm the biggest Jew in the country," he wailed.

The only choice, Giancana felt, was to call in the marker that

Frank Sinatra had assured him he had with the Kennedys, and who better to call it in for him than Frank? Through the summer of 1961, Giancana and his associates, particularly Johnny Rosselli and Johnny Formosa, another Las Vegas operative who watched over gambling in Indiana as well, reminded Sinatra that he had promised to intercede with the Kennedys on their behalf.

And when he'd been in Hyannis Port that September, that is apparently just what Frank did. Alone with the attorney general, he wrote the name of the don of the Chicago mob on a pad, handed it across the table, and said, "This is my buddy. This is what I want you to know, Bob."

Bobby couldn't believe the balls of him; it would be one of the unforgivable trespasses that would, mere months later, make it so easy for him to give Frank the heave-ho. Of course he would pay the message no heed.

Sinatra came back to Giancana empty-handed. Unwilling to admit that he'd failed, though, he stalled them with assurances that he'd work things out. Sam Giancana was a past master at detecting bullshit, however. His increasingly agitated complaints against the Kennedys and Sinatra became a litany on FBI transcripts of conversations recorded in his hangouts.

In December 1961, Giancana and Rosselli spoke at bitter length about their situation, particularly about how ineffective Frank turned out to be. Rosselli had recently seen the singer in California.

"He says he's got an idea that you're mad at him," Rosselli reported. "I says, 'That, I wouldn't know.'"

"He must have a guilty conscience," replied Giancana. "I never said nothing."

He pondered Frank's claims to having put in a good word for him with the Kennedys. "I don't know who the fuck he's talking to," he finally said. "After all, if I'm taking somebody's money, I'm gonna make sure that this money is gonna do something, like, do you want it or don't you want it? If the money is accepted, maybe one of these days the guy will do me a favor."

"That's right," Rosselli said. "He says he wrote your name down."

Giancana was annoyed. "Well, one minute he tells me this and then he tells me that and the last time I talked to him was at the hotel down in Florida a month before he left and he said, 'Don't worry about it, if I can't talk to the old man [Joe Kennedy], I'm gonna talk to the man [Jack Kennedy].' One minute he says he's talked to Robert, and the next minute he hasn't talked to him. So he never did talk to him. It's a lot of shit. Why lie to me? I haven't got that coming."

"I can imagine," Rosselli commiserated. "Tsk, tsk, tsk. If he can't deliver, I want him to tell me, 'John, the load's too heavy.' "

"That's all right," Giancana responded resignedly. "At least then you know how to work. You won't let your guard down, know what I mean?"

He had begun to see how little pull he and his emissary Frank really had. "If I ever get a speeding ticket," he sighed, "none of those fuckers would know me."

"You got that right," said Rosselli, who then offered a little bit of advice: "Go the other way. Fuck everybody. We'll use them every fucking way we can. They only know one way. Now let them see the other side of you."

In the coming weeks, Giancana spoke worse and worse about Frank: "If he [Jack Kennedy] had lost this state here he would have lost the election, but I figured with this guy [Frank] maybe we will be alright. I might have known. . . . Well, when a [obscenity deleted] lies to you. . . ."

Giancana considered Dean a pain in the ass as well. He wanted the singer to play some nightclub dates for him and found him elusive.

"That fuckin' prima donna," Johnny Formosa complained. "You can't call him. I gotta go there and lay the law down to him, so he knows I mean business."

"It seems like they don't believe us," Giancana sighed. "Well, we'll give them a little headache, you know? All I do is send two guys there and just tell them what they're working at. Bang, you crack them and that's it. Just lay them up. If we ever hit that guy you'll break his jaw. Then he can't sing."

Formosa must've liked Dean; he softened at the thought: "Maybe none of them gotta get hurt. Maybe they'll come to their senses."

But soon enough, Formosa had grown as impatient as Giancana. At a meeting soon after, he explicitly described to his boss how he'd like to revenge himself on Frank and everyone around him.

"Let's show 'em," he told Giancana. "Let's show those asshole Hollywood fruitcakes that they can't get away with it as if nothing's happened. Let's hit Sinatra. Or I could whack out a couple of those other guys. Lawford and that Martin. And I could take the nigger and put his other eye out."

Giancana muzzled his bloodthirsty grunt: "No, I've got other plans for them."

He could've gone Formosa's way, or Rosselli's—shown them his other side. For the most part, Giancana loathed show folk: "Hollywood is the only place I've ever been, besides Washington, D.C., where everybody—men and women—are just beggin' for you to use 'em," he told his brother. He liked to use celebrities to ferry money for him—"They make great bagmen. Everybody's too busy bein' dazzled by a star and askin' for their autograph to ask what's in a briefcase"—but he looked down on them: Sammy was "a nigger weasel," Peter was "Peter the Rabbit," Dean and Jerry Lewis were "fuckin' prima donnas." Only Frank was okay: "A real stand up guy," he said approvingly, "too good for those bums in Hollywood."

"I guess I like the guy," Giancana told his brother when the subject of Frank came up. "Shit, it's not his fault that the Kennedys are assholes. But if I didn't like him, you can be goddamned sure he'd be a dead man."

As long as he was letting him live, and since he couldn't get him to deliver the Kennedys, Giancana schemed up a way for Frank and his bum friends to turn a profit for him.

It involved setting up a mini-Las Vegas in an unincorporated part of Cook County, north of Chicago. Giancana had been a silent partner in the Villa Venice, a restaurant in the area, since 1956, and he was planning to spend $25,000 to upgrade it; in the spring of 1962, he sold it from one front man to another to give the operation the appearance of a genuine makeover. Two blocks away, in a nondescript Quonset hut hidden from the road by a parking lot filled with trucks and heavy machinery, he built a plush gambling joint—carpeted and air-conditioned, with craps, blackjack, and roulette tables, and a fully stocked bar and snack shop.

The plan was going to call in favors from such heavy-duty stars as Frank, Dean, Sammy, and Eddie Fisher and inaugurate a new entertainment policy at the Villa Venice, using the attendant hoopla to attract high rollers to the nearby gambling facilities. The first one up would be Fisher, a guy for whom the widowed Giancana, curiously, had a soft spot: "There's a guy with a broken heart," he told a lieutenant, imagining the singer's grief at having been dumped by Liz Taylor.

Fisher opened the Villa Venice on October 31. The joint had been splendidly remodeled. Guests were greeted at the front entrance by gondoliers, who poled actual watercraft through an actual river that snaked into the main room. Able to seat eight hundred, the showroom was sumptuously decorated with a thick burgundy carpet and discreetly tasteful wall furnishings. The tables were dressed with fine linen, china, flatware, and stemware; flowers and maidenhair ferns served as centerpieces. Off to one side was the Venetian Lounge, a bar with a separate entrance, spiffed up with fountains and a fireplace. Upstairs, private quarters for the performers were provided—a complete suite of rooms where they could rest or play host between shows.

Everyone who came to the Villa Venice for the family-style Italian food and the top-notch entertainment paid $10 at the door just to get in; reservations were taken in minimums of ten only—a hundred bucks before you opened the door or got a piece of bread. But the *really* big dough was taken in at the Quonset hut, which was overseen by Giancana associate Rocco Potenza. Tables took bets up to $100 a pop—and higher—with some fish taking baths for as much as $25,000 in a single night.

All this activity naturally drew the attention of the FBI agents on Giancana's case. They found their way to Fisher at his downtown Chicago hotel. The bureau knew he'd given up a lucrative engagement at the Dunes in Vegas to play the Villa Venice, purportedly for free. Asked why, he hemmed and hawed, talking about his good friend Frank Sinatra. The phone rang; it was another friend, comedian Louis Nye. "That was my attorney, Louie Nye," Fisher told the agents, "and he advised me not to talk."

Following Fisher's engagement, the celebrated trio of Sinatra, Martin, and Davis came to town (they were in fighting shape; only two months earlier, they'd played Skinny D'Amato's 500 Club in Atlantic City). It was a much more elaborate affair all around. Representatives of Reprise Records came in from L.A. to set up the musical arrangements and tape the concerts for a possible live album; it was to be Frank's only pay for the gig, and he hoped to net $500,000 through record sales. In addition, Frank was demanding that Giancana book a private train to transport him and Dean to Chicago. The gangster couldn't believe it.

"That Frank," he complained. "He wants more money, he wants this, he wants that, he wants more girls. . . . I don't need that or him. I broke my ass when I was talking to him in New York."

When the gig finally opened at the end of November, it was the biggest thing to hit town in decades. Lines snaked around the block from the unlikely nightclub's doors. The Quonset hut casino was packed. The opening night crowd included a rogue's gallery of Chicago criminals: Marshall Caifano, Jimmy "The Monk" Allegretti, Felix "Milwaukee Phil" Alderisio, Willie "Potatoes" Daddano, and, of course, Giancana, as well as Wisconsin gangster Jim DeGeorge and Joe Fischetti, Frank's guy from the Fontainebleau.

Frank, Dean, and Sammy played sixteen shows in seven days, breezing confidently through the same act they'd been doing in Vegas and Miami and elsewhere since the Summit. During nonworking hours, Frank and Dean palled around the city with Fischetti.

Once again, FBI agents descended on the performers to find out how it was that they came to be available to play at the Villa Venice for free. Dean just plain ignored inquiries until he left town; the FBI had no more luck getting him to play ball than the mob did. Frank gave the agents a song and dance about how he had known Leo Olsen, Giancana's front man, since their boyhood days in Jersey and he was delighted to lend him a hand in his new business.

Only Sammy, perhaps a bit more intimidated by J. Edgar Hoover's burly white investigators, gave the feds anything to work with. They interviewed him one morning in his suite at the Ambassador East hotel downtown; Sammy was dressed only in tight black slacks, and he offered to fix the agents drinks.

They were strictly business: Why had he shown up here instead of at some paying gig somewhere else?

"Baby, that's a very good question. But I have to say it's for my man Francis."

Or friends of his?

"By all means."

Friends like Sam Giancana?

"By all means."

And what did "by all means" mean?

"Baby, let me say this. I got one eye, and that one eye sees a lot of things that my brain tells me I shouldn't talk about. Because my brain says that, if I do, my one eye might not be seeing anything after a while."

Fair enough. The agents left.

The trio completed their engagement at the Villa Venice on December 2; they would rev it all up again the following month at the Sands. By then, however, the Villa Venice was, curiously, no longer in the entertainment business. Though its debut month was a brilliant success, the restaurant had shut down regular operation and was available from that point on strictly for rental as a catering hall. It was sold; one day, it burned to the ground. *Finis.*

And its shadow owner, Sam Giancana? Federal agents listened in on him as he tallied up the take from that spectacular month. Between the nightclub and the gambling hall, the crime boss was ahead $3 million in cash: tax free.

Frank had definitely cleared his marker.

All the creeps that Frank liked to run with, all the thugs whom Dean and Sammy worked for, all the awful shit Peter was in on—guess who was the only one ever to testify at a murder trial: Joey.

It was right before *Ocean's Eleven.* He was asked out to a San Fernando Valley restaurant by a theatrical agent who ran with Mickey Cohen on the very night that Jack "The Enforcer" Whalen was rubbed out in the joint. Joey wasn't actually there at the time, but he became a witness for the guys accused of the murder, and the story that he stumbled into made for a better plot than the caper picture he made with Frank and the boys.

Whalen was a big, bruising bookmaker and legbreaker, a convicted extortionist who bullied everyone smaller than him and kissed the ass of anyone more powerful. He had been in the air force during the war, and he still had a flyboy's daring. Ordered by L.A. mob boss Jack Dragna to submit to authority, he told him off: "I'll make up my own mind whether I stay in business or not."

He was the sort of thug who'd take money from somebody who wanted to buy a little justice, then split it with the intended victim—with whom he might even turn around and take a piece out of the guy who'd hired him in the first place. He earned his nickname through a habit that made him lots of enemies: If anyone in town had a beef with a bookie who refused to pay on a bet, Whalen would track the welsher down and get the aggrieved party his money. In the disorganized mess that passed for the L.A. mob, Whalen was the kind of freelancing loose cannon that nobody wanted around but nobody knew how to stop.

Mickey Cohen, for one, couldn't stand the guy. Whalen had once literally ripped Cohen's pants off him to get at his bankroll so as to settle somebody's score. "This great big enforcing bullshit cocksucker," Cohen fumed in his memoirs. "He had no respect for nobody. Everyone knew what a vicious, bullying, rotten bastard Jack-this-so-called-Enforcer-Whalen was."

"Was" being the operative word. Whalen, who'd been warned that Cohen had a contract out on him, nevertheless showed up at Rondelli's, an Italian restaurant in Sherman Oaks, on the night of December 2, 1959, to collect a bet from one of Cohen's crew. He'd only been inside for a few minutes when he got a .38 slug in the brain.

Rondelli's was a fashionable spot. Errol Flynn, Melvin Belli, and Liberace were regulars, and the home-style food was reckoned the area's best. It was also secretly owned by Cohen. "It was trying to be run as a legitimate joint," the gangster lamented. But after the hit, its heyday was over: "This was the final come-off."

The murder investigation was strictly Damon Runyan. Cohen and others on the scene insisted they didn't see anything. "When I hear shots, I run," said one, echoing Cohen, who said he'd ducked under a table as soon as Whalen had walked in and started a fracas. Searching the premises, police found three guns in a Dumpster, none of which was the murder weapon but two of which were Cohen's.

The actual murder weapon had been spirited away by Cohen flunky Sam LoCigno, and it was Sam who Cohen decided would take the dive for the hit. This was the deal: Sam would get $50,000 and all legal expenses if he would plead self-defense, claiming that well-known bully Whalen had been hitting and threatening him; Cohen and other witnesses would back his story, and he'd get an easy sentence.

It didn't work. LoCigno was convicted of first-degree murder and sentenced to life without parole. And as for his money, "LoCigno was supposed to get $50,000," said Cohen. "To be truthful, he didn't get it."

Cohen, of course, knew that LoCigno wasn't the real killer. "The person that hit Whalen was an expert shot," he explained. "This expert shot never missed before with whatever it was." LoCigno, Cohen sighed, "couldn't hit the wall of an auditorium." But he wasn't about to reopen the case by pointing this out to the cops.

LoCigno stewed in jail, slowly realizing he'd been screwed, and finally told a priest what really happened. The priest told the D.A., who decided to seek a new trial for LoCigno and widen the scope of the case into a conspiracy to kill Whalen by Cohen and three others. The state supreme court agreed that there hadn't been sufficient evidence for LoCigno's initial conviction (police had never, for example, turned up the murder weapon), and a new trial was held in 1962 with Cohen, LoCigno, and three others as defendants.

Cohen's defense was based on common sense: "It was the hottest place in town," he said of his restaurant. "So when the move was made to knock Whalen in, would I blow up my own joint? . . . The killing was the end of Rondelli's and the good food for a lot of people."

Another defendant, Joseph DeCarlo, a theatrical agent whom Cohen met while dallying with one of his clients, stripper Candy Barr, had a better alibi: The night of the killing, he said, he had invited Joey Bishop to dinner with him at Rondelli's; would he have asked a guest along if he was planning on having somebody murdered?

Joey was called to testify. He told the jury that DeCarlo had, indeed, asked him to an Italian restaurant that night, but that he'd told the agent to call him just before their scheduled appointment because, as he explained, "I have a reputation for not keeping dinner engagements." When DeCarlo called, Bishop begged out, claiming he was exhausted from a long day golfing (he would play as much as forty-five holes in a row to allay loneliness); he invited DeCarlo to stop by the Cloister nightclub on Sunset Strip later on to catch his second show. Joey reserved a ringside table, but the guy never showed; when they ran into one another later in the evening, Joey asked what had happened. "Well," replied DeCarlo, "read the papers and you'll know why I didn't show up."

Cohen and company were acquitted, and LoCigno got the light sentence he'd originally been promised—one to ten years. Cohen would've wished him a hell of a lot worse: He never forgave his former soldier for implicating him. "LoCigno lived like a rat bastard and he died like a rat bastard," he groused. "Because he's dead doesn't make him any less of a son of a bitch."

He had nothing but kind memories, however, of Joey.

You and I will always be friends

Frank may not have been welcome at the White House, but Peter always was—and not only because he was the president's brother-in-law. Perfectly polished, cultured, dapper, with that fetching English accent, he was still the nation's idea of a sophisticate. Frank was the one who had the bad reputation in the papers; Peter, for all the salacious goings-on in his life, seemed almost as respectable as Jack.

Over the years since the inauguration, Peter's association with the Kennedys had become a point of interest for film producers. Earlier, his arena had gradually shrunk through the years from film to TV. But Jack's rise in power and his association with Frank had rescued him.

Throughout the early sixties, Peter was, moderately, in demand. Darryl Zanuck wanted him to play a war hero in *The Longest Day*; Otto Preminger wanted him to play an anti-Semitic English soldier in *Exodus* and a skirt-chasing senator in *Advise and Consent*. He knew that these roles were offered to him only nominally because of his talents—all three films would be helped by having some sort of unofficial liaison to the government—but he took the work, the first movie roles he had in almost a decade that hadn't fallen to him off of Frank's plate.

He tried to resent the public's awareness of his predicament as an appendage to powerful friends and in-laws: "People seem to forget," he told a reporter, "that I have been in this business for 20 years. I had a career before I ever met Pat Kennedy." But in the very next breath, he admitted that he was protesting too much: "If you could call it a career. . . ."

Jack, always intrigued by the business and gossip of Hollywood, was keenly aware of the rises and falls in Peter's career. The president had occasionally brushed off suggestions that he separate himself from Frank with the rejoinder that Frank was the only man in Hollywood giving Peter work; he agreed to allow his speechwriter, Arthur Schlesinger, write movie reviews "as long as you treat Peter Lawford with respect"; he once buttonholed Peter's manager, Milt Ebbins, at a White House photo session with "When are you gonna get Peter a job?"

Jack even tried to give Peter a job himself. Recalling the sound advice that Peter had offered before the debates with Richard Nixon, Jack asked Peter to critique his demeanor and appearance on TV regularly, proposing to use him as an unofficial adviser much as Dwight Eisenhower had Robert Montgomery. After one speech, Jack called Peter at the Desert Inn in Las Vegas and peppered him with questions about his makeup and delivery. Peter hadn't watched the speech, but he bluffed his way through the conversation. Sometime later, Jack asked Peter to evaluate the script of *PT 109*, the projected film about his naval heroics. Peter got drunk and fell asleep with the script only partially read. When he told Jack what had happened, the president smiled as if it were John-John talking and never asked his brother-in-law's help in politics or show business again.

Still, if Peter's only crime had been laziness or a failure to have been bitten by the political bug, the Kennedys might have found a way to live with him. What finally drove a wedge between the actor and his in-laws was the failure of his marriage. Pat had somehow managed, like her mother and sisters and sisters-in-law, to endure Peter's serial womanizing, and she matched her husband drink for drink and digging insult for digging insult; she even carried on affairs of her own. But what she couldn't stand was the increasing awareness of how weak-willed and spineless her husband was. She thought she had married a god; he turned out to be just another flawed mortal.

Peter disappointed his wife in almost everything. He had no interest in their children, he barely made a show of sexual fidelity, he wasn't as educated as he seemed or clever as he sounded, he didn't make a lot of money—nothing.

The last straw seemed to observers to be Peter's clumsy complicity in the decline and death of Marilyn Monroe. The Kennedys were properly aghast at the tragedy they'd inadvertently helped orchestrate, but no one in the family ever blamed Jack or Bobby for their roles in it. So, though he was merely doing for his brothers-in-law what they'd asked, Peter became the scapegoat for the incident.

"Everything he went out of his way to do for them, they held against him," remembered Peter's old MGM pal Jackie Cooper years later. "They didn't want him around. They cut him off. If he had been at Chappaquiddick he probably would've gotten blamed for that, too."

Frank, so much more attuned to the subtle flows of power, had tried years earlier to alert Peter that his position in the family was unstable. Way back during the weekend that Jack was inaugurated, the singer sent for Milt Ebbins and told him, "If Peter doesn't watch his ass, he's gonna lose his old lady. You'd better tell him to wise up and get his act together."

Ebbins replied that the message would mean more coming from somebody with more clout: "Frank, can't you help?"

"Shit, I'm not his keeper. You just tell him to watch himself or he's going to lose everything."

At the time, Pat and Peter were actually living in separate hotels in Washington and Peter was actively screwing around; he didn't even attend the inauguration ceremonies—he watched them on TV from his hotel room in a bathrobe.

By 1963, the couple's frequent estrangements had come to seem the norm. They decided they'd divorce, but, being Kennedys, they went to the White House to solicit Jack's counsel on the matter. It was an unprecedented request. Despite all the just cause over the years, no Kennedy had undergone so much as a legal separation; now Peter and Pat were asking for permission to do something that would surely be loud and controversial. Just having to seek Jack's counsel caused Peter to break down in tears in the Cabinet Room.

Jack reassured him. "Don't worry about it," he said. "If it's going to happen it's going to happen. Let me tell you something—it's not all your fault. I know Pat better than you do. You and I will always be friends, Peter. You're not going to lose me." He gave the couple his consent, opining that "it won't be such a big deal."

Milt Ebbins demurred: "If we announce this tomorrow, there will be three pictures on the front page of the *New York Times* the next morning: Peter's, Pat's—and yours."

Jack saw that he was right. He asked Pat and Peter to indulge him by keeping the facade of their marriage intact for two more years. If they could wait until after the 1964 election, he wouldn't stand in their way.

They agreed. Peter was now adrift from everyone that had ever tied him to respectability—his father, Louis Mayer, Frank, Pat.

Ebbins tried to keep him busy with work. The acting jobs

started to dry up again, but there was a production company, Chrislaw (named after Peter's son, Christopher), that had a hit TV series on its hands (*The Patty Duke Show*) and went into feature film production in 1963 with *Johnny Cool*, a story about a mob hit man starring *Ocean's Eleven* vet Henry Silva and featuring Sammy and Joey Bishop in small roles.

On his own, Peter continued to perform as a straight man for Jimmy Durante in the nightclub act that took him to New York, Lake Tahoe, and Vegas, where they were regulars at the Desert Inn. There, Peter indulged himself excessively. One hotel official, according to the FBI, declared that Peter had "run wild, had signed numerous charges that were not authorized, such as gifts, railway tickets, food, etc." They hadn't wanted Peter on the bill in the first place, and now they were stuck with the tab for his caprices. But without Frank to shield him from the powers that ran the city, Peter was called to reckoning: Failing to achieve satisfaction any other way, the Desert Inn sued him in May 1964 for $20,000.

They could get in line.

It always ended up as a threat

After the Palm Springs debacle, and with Sammy increasingly tied up in his million solo projects, Frank and Dean became more and more a two-act, the core of the Rat Pack and, often, all that was left of it.

They decided to make another picture together, but this time it was Dean who came up with the project. Maverick director Robert Aldrich, who, on the strength of such hits as *Vera Cruz, The Big Knife, Attack!,* and *Kiss Me Deadly,* had formed his own production company in 1960, had been floating a script around town for a big, comic western with Gina Lollobrigida and Anita Ekberg. In late 1962, Dean agreed to go partners on the film with Aldrich, and they shopped the script to such bankable actors as Jimmy Stewart and Robert Mitchum, hoping to land a name to costar with him. In March 1963, Frank read the script, and two weeks later he was in.

The picture, once known as *Two for Texas* but now called *Four for Texas,* would be a coproduction of Dean's, Frank's, and Aldrich's companies, along with Warner Bros. Dean would make $250,000 against 10 percent of the gross; Frank would make three times that, with the same percentage guaranteed. Shooting would commence on location in Red Rock Canyon near Mojave, California, just before Memorial Day and run through mid-August in Burbank. Lollobrigida was replaced by Ursula Andress—talent Dean and Frank hadn't grown bored with yet. Charles Bronson, Victor Buono, Arthur Godfrey, and the Three Stooges all had roles.

As the stars and coproducers, Dean and Frank loaded the picture with flunkies. Dean had a personal entourage of four, including Mack Gray, which cost a combined $1,100 a week; Frank's personal crew of eight, which included a hairpiece handler, raked in a total of $2,125 a week. (In the spirit of her bosses and costars, Ekberg racked up $479 in transportation overcharges when she insisted on a chauffeured Lincoln to take her shopping and visiting and to ferry her husband on errands.)

But if coproducer Aldrich was upset with his stars, he kept it to himself—until production started and Frank began to raise hell. Aldrich had sent Frank a completed script on the first of May, but Frank waited nearly four weeks to complain that the opening sequence, a chase-and-shoot number in which he and Dean survived a stagecoach holdup, was too elaborate. Aldrich, who was already up at the desert location, conceived of the scene as the high point of the film, but he made a bunch of cuts anyway. Not enough: Frank called him up to complain that the sequence was still too long and that he would be leaving the location after five days—despite being scheduled for ten—"whether the sequences were completed or not."

On Tuesday the twenty-eighth, Dean and Frank flew into Mojave by helicopter, watched their doubles rehearse a scene, dressed, and came back to the set where Aldrich discovered that they knew neither their lines nor the physical actions they were supposed to perform. Frank stared the director down and told him to cut two pages out of the scene. As Aldrich wrote to his lawyer, "Faced with the dilemma of whether to make this 'make or break declaration of difference between us' (since we had yet to make Shot One), I decided to avoid that kind of showdown and we proceeded with the day's work."

The rest of the day went productively—Aldrich had compressed the schedule to try and get Frank back to L.A. in five days, and he got twenty-four setups and four and a half pages shot. The next day, he had twenty-six setups in the can before lunch. Frank, satisfied that he could make this thing move as fast as he fancied, chose this moment to tell the director that he'd be leaving on Thursday, not Saturday. Aldrich was dumbfounded and said it couldn't be done.

"His reply," the director remembered, "was wordless but significant."

That night, Sinatra sent Howard W. Koch, producer for Essex Productions, over to Aldrich to reiterate the star's intention to leave the location the next day. "The manner in which Mr. Koch phrased these remarks was always most polite, proper and professional," Aldrich recalled, "but regardless of the phrasing, it always ended up as a threat and an ultimatum." Aldrich spent the night trying to rework his schedule to accommodate Frank, then told Koch in the morning that the changes would result in cost overruns and he wanted Essex to reimburse the production for the expenses. Koch agreed.

But Koch had no control over Frank's behavior. "During the day," Aldrich wrote, "there were many unfortunate and unnecessarily negative and derogatory remarks by Sinatra (but never to me) about the uselessness of the shots being made and that the crew was unpardonably slow. . . . We only made eighty-two setups in two and two-thirds days. . . . SLOW???"

Before the day was done, Aldrich told Frank that there'd be

a brief break, then another ninety minutes of work, and then he'd be all finished at the location. "That's fine," Frank said, and he wandered off in his car. Five minutes later, Koch approached Aldrich. "Frank says he's had it . . . he's tired, he's going home."

Once again, Aldrich protested. "Koch honorably and professionally replied that he completely understood this," he recalled, "but the situation [the control of Sinatra] was more than he could cope with or handle."

Aldrich struck the set and dismissed the crew even though there were hours of light left. He then ordered his assistant director to give Dean and Frank calls to appear ready to shoot the next morning, making Koch swear in front of witnesses that he'd see that Frank showed up. Aldrich then sent telegrams reiterating the call to Frank's homes in Beverly Hills and Palm Springs, his office in L.A., his agent's office, and his lawyer's office.

At 11:00 p.m., he got a telegram from Frank in response: "You're kidding." Frank never came back to Mojave.

"In closing," Aldrich wrote, "it should be noted that the impossible was almost accomplished. By concentrating on Sinatra we could have finished his originally scheduled 10 days work in three—a three that was telescoped at considerable sacrifice to both quality and performance from an already difficult five. And to what avail?"

Filming proceeded in Burbank without any further eruptions, though crew members routinely asked one another with trepidation, "How's Sinatra?" when they showed up for work.

And Dean, who was the soul of cooperation out in the desert, finally showed his own form of truculence when it came time to shoot promotional materials for the film, flat out refusing to do it. (He'd always been awful about such stuff: It had been a sore point between him and Jerry.)

Aldrich wrote in despair to Jack Warner's assistant Steve

Trilling: "Don't you think it's about time that you should make it your business to see that the stars of this picture perform in a professional business-like manner, or are you and/or Warners going to step back and sit back with your new deal and say 'that's Aldrich's problem'? . . . I don't see any constructive or intelligent (let alone responsible) behavior from you and/or Warners in disciplining anyone who can remotely shout back. . . . Since you appear to be so anxious to 'hold the line,' why not begin here?"

Trilling showed the letter to his boss, who suggested that it be filed in a folder marked "No Purpose Answering."

He's needed this for years

The Cal-Neva Lodge was the jewel of the north shore of Lake Tahoe from the time it opened in 1927, when Las Vegas was just a desiccating old railroad town hardly worth a stop on the drive between Salt Lake and L.A. The hotel was built by William Graham, a Reno political fixer with a conviction on his record in New York for shifty dealings with stolen bank bonds.

The architecture capitalized on the gorgeous setting between the icy lake and the forest-covered mountains— a real log exterior, stone vestibules and floors, a huge A-frame lobby studded with granite boulders, a massive stone fireplace, thick wooden ceiling beams. There were guest rooms in the main building, chalets for high rollers and celebrities out back. The big novelty was the way the hotel straddled the state line. The rooms and restaurant were in California, the casino was in Nevada; the border ran right through the massive fireplace and the big outdoor swimming pool. ("You could violate the Mann Act without even going outside," the joke went.)

The Cal-Neva thrived through Prohibition and the war, but the fifties weren't so kind. Heavy winter snowfall in the Sierra Nevada meant the place was only accessible during the warm months, and the rise of Las Vegas cut heavily into the business of even the toniest casinos in the Tahoe-Reno region. Elmer "Bones" Remmer, the San Francisco gangster who owned the place through the decade, hit a wall of tax troubles and passed the hotel over to his friend Bert "Wingy" Grober (the name referred to his having only one arm), who couldn't make any better a go of it.

Grober's knights in shining armor arrived at the dawn of the sixties: Frank and Dean, along with Frank's piano-playing business buddy, Hank Sanicola, and Skinny D'Amato, the gambler and pimp who ran the 500 Club in Atlantic City and had greased the wheels for Jack Kennedy's primary victory in West Virginia. The foursome offered to buy up most of Grober's interest in the casino for a mere $250,000: Frank would get 25 percent, Sanicola 16, D'Amato 13, and Dean 3. They would invest more than $2 million in a complete renovation of the premises, add an acoustically superior showroom, even spring for improvements to local roads to make the joint more accessible through the winter.

To pay for these upgrades, the new owners sought a $3-million loan from the Teamsters Central States Pension Fund, which had made such a specialty of investing in hot new Vegas properties. They felt reasonably assured of being approved because their entrée to that fountain of money was provided by a silent partner in their enterprise, Sam Giancana, who thought it a routine enough matter to ask Jimmy Hoffa's union to lend him $3 million. Giancana, though, was all kinds of hot on account of being investigated by the feds, and Hoffa turned him down. Giancana was livid: "Once I got $1,750,000 from him in two days," he told friends. "Now all this heat comes on and I can't even get a favor out of him now. I can't do nothing for myself. Ten years ago I can get all the fucking money I want from the guy and now they won't settle for anything!" The grubstake—$1.5 million—wound up coming instead from the Bank of Nevada.

Sinatra performed at the hotel that summer, inviting the cast of *The Misfits*, which was then filming near Reno, to be his guests; Marilyn Monroe and her husband, Arthur Miller, were among those who took him up on the offer. Joe Kennedy showed up as well—he held court at the hotel before the 1960 Democratic convention, sporting with women, huddling with gangsters, and brokering the deal through which Frank would take ownership of the place. With all the commotion, he must've felt like he already had.

"Dad liked Cal-Neva because it was unpretentious yet glamorous, homey yet exciting," remembered Nancy Sinatra. But he had ample reason to abhor it as well: It was one of the places he'd tried to off himself a decade earlier in despair over Ava's headstrong ways.

But those bleak days were forgotten now, blasted away by sunny dreams of his own casino, more intimate than the Sands and more his. The deal finally went through in the summer of 1962, albeit with the ownership equation slightly changed: Dean, for one, wanted no part of splitting money with Giancana, and D'Amato, who was brought West to keep an eye on the mob's cut, wasn't likely to be welcomed at the airport by Nevada licensing authorities. Instead, they'd set up a dummy corporation, Park Lake Enterprises, that would take possession of Cal-Neva for Frank, Sanicola, and Sanford Waterman, a bookmaker and casino manager who'd worked in Meyer Lansky's Havana joints. Under this new arrangement, Frank had a full 50 percent of the place.

On paper. For as Sam Giancana made it clear to Johnny Rosselli, at least that much of the hotel was his. "Who gives a fuck about Cal-Neva?" he laughed. "I'm gonna get my money out of there and I'm gonna wind up with half of the joint with no money." (It sounded like a sweet gig to Rosselli: "If you do that, please send me there, will you, to look out for you?")

The Cal-Neva reopened all gussied up on the last weekend of June 1962, a gala to which Frank flew planeloads of Hollywood friends. He, of course, was the main attraction, which didn't stop him from getting into an ugly beef. On the second night of the grand reopening, Frank traded blows in the hotel kitchen with a sheriff's deputy who'd recently married a waitress with whom Frank had a romantic history. The cop belted Frank so hard that he couldn't finish out the weekend's performances. He went into Reno and complained to the sheriff, who promptly suspended his man; two weeks later, the guy died in a mysterious automobile accident not far from the hotel.

Not long after that, a prostitution ring that was operating right out of the front desk was busted, and then somebody got shot on the front steps as he showed up for work.

And not long after *that*, Peter Lawford, who'd once been mentioned as a potential partner in the place before he was banished from Frank's society, showed up at the hotel with Marilyn Monroe.

Bad, bad idea: Pat and Peter had been desperately trying to disengage Marilyn from the accumulating stresses of her life and had hit upon a swank getaway as a solution. It only got worse: Marilyn spent the weekend drinking and popping pills; there were suggestions that she was forced into sex acts; and Joe DiMaggio, her still-jealous ex-husband, was seen roving the perimeter of the hotel, unwilling to actually come in and talk with her because he was feuding with Sinatra.

Eventually, Marilyn succumbed to everything going on around her and everything she'd poured inside herself; she passed out in her chalet, and only the fact that she'd kept her bedside telephone connected to the hotel switchboard so that she wouldn't feel alone saved her life. An alarmed operator, hearing the actress's labored breathing, alerted Peter and Pat, who burst into Marilyn's room, revived her with coffee and forced walking, then snuck her out of the place to the Reno airport, where Frank's private plane was waiting to get them the hell out of town. Camera buff Frank had shot a roll of pictures of Marilyn around the hotel that weekend; two weeks later, when she died, he burned them.

Dead cops, hookers, shootings, overdoses: Frank had bought the Cal-Neva because he thought the place exuded quietude and class; instead, in the first two months it had operated under his ownership, it had become Dodge Fucking City.

And the wildest was yet to come.

In July 1963, the feature act in the main showroom at the Cal-Neva was the McGuire Sisters, starring Sam Giancana's girlfriend Phyllis (not their actual billing). Ten days before they were to open at the Cal-Neva's Celebrity Room, Giancana and McGuire showed up at the hotel for some R&R. FBI agents watched him play golf with Sinatra, lounge by the famous interstate pool, drive one of the hotel's house cars, and dine in the restaurant.

On opening night of the engagement, Sam, the McGuires, and Victor LaCroix Collins, the trio's road manager, retired to Sam and Phyllis's chalet for a nightcap. Something unpleasant was in the air: Phyllis kept punching Collins in the arm every time she passed him, and he started dishing her singing voice. It got a little too physical, and he wound up dumping her on her ass, a playful gesture—spiced, perhaps, with too much booze and a little ill will—that got out of hand.

The sight of his woman being manhandled drove Giancana into a fury. He went after Collins with fists flying, slicing open his eyebrow with the large diamond ring he wore on his right hand. It became a melee, and Collins got the upper hand. The loud commotion drew headwaiter Eddie King into the room, then Frank and his valet, George Jacobs. They pried Collins off of Giancana, then held him like a punching bag while the mobster revenged himself with a salvo of uncontested blows.

Giancana left the hotel the next day, but word quickly leaked out that he had been there and had gotten into some kind of bang-up, and that was a damn bad break. Giancana, despite being the shadow owner of the Cal-Neva, was barred from so much as stepping a foot inside a Nevada casino. He was one of the original eleven men listed in the Black Book, the slender pamphlet issued by the state Gaming Commission which carried photos, descriptions, and aliases of men who were banned for life from all licensed premises in the state. By allowing Giancana in the Cal-Neva at all—much less for ten days and with prime privileges—Frank had severely compromised the hotel. And the ensuing fallout was the worst public relations fiasco he had ever suffered.

Within a few days, reports of the gangster's visit to the hotel started popping up in the Chicago papers, along with allegations that the state Gaming Commission was investigating a possible Black Book violation. The commissioners spoke with Victor LaCroix Collins to get an account of the fight, then tried to get in touch with Eddie King, only to discover that he'd unexpectedly disappeared to Palm Springs.

On August 3, Ed Olsen, a former Associated Press Reno bureau chief working as chairman of the Nevada Gaming Commission, reached Frank by phone at the Sands. Frank admitted having seen Giancana leave Phyllis McGuire's chalet one evening, but claimed that that was the extent of their interaction. He knew nothing about a fight: "If there was a rumble there while I was there, they must be keeping it awfully quiet." And while he agreed to avoid Giancana and other

Black Book figures while in Nevada, he reserved the right to consort with whomever he wanted anywhere else: "This is a way of life," he said, "and a man has to lead his own life."

The Gaming Commission continued its investigation throughout the month in relative quiet, but the *Las Vegas Sun* got wind of it just before Labor Day, and the matter exploded. Frank's lawyers and spokespeople immediately denied that Giancana had ever been to the Cal-Neva or been in touch with Frank, but Olsen, interviewed in the *Los Angeles Herald Examiner,* suggested that "certain discrepancies" had arisen in various accounts of just such a visit.

Frank didn't care for this last implication, and he asked his accountant, Newell Hancock, a former member of the Gaming Control Board, to invite Olsen to the Cal-Neva for dinner, a show, and a private meeting to clear the air. Olsen said that he didn't feel it would be appropriate for him to meet Sinatra at the hotel, and he suggested to Hancock that Frank come up to his office, which was deserted during the holiday weekend. Hancock explained that Frank wouldn't care for that, so they chose a neutral site—Hancock's Lake Tahoe home—and set an appointment.

A half hour later, Olsen's phone rang again, and a secretary asked him to hold for Mr. Sinatra.

Frank wanted to know why Olsen wouldn't come to the Cal-Neva, and the commissioner reiterated his belief that he shouldn't enter a hotel that was being investigated; he repeated the suggestion that Frank visit him in his office.

"You're acting like a fucking cop," Frank responded. "I just want to talk to you off the record."

Olsen tried to assure him that no reporters would know of his visit, and Frank interrupted him: "Listen, Ed, I haven't had to take this kind of shit from anybody in the country, and I'm not going to take it from you people." He repeated his invitation once again, this time including the commission's chief investigator, Charles La France: "I want you to come up here and have dinner with me . . . and bring that shit-heel friend, La France."

Olsen couldn't believe his ears, and he motioned to a couple of colleagues who were in the room with him to pick up phone extensions. They listened in as Frank continued: "It's you and your goddamn subpoenas which have caused all this trouble," he said.

Olsen said that the subpoenas were completely confidential and had not generated the press reports. "You're a goddamn liar," Frank retorted. "It's all over the papers."

"No, they're not."

"I'll bet you fifty thousand dollars."

"I haven't got fifty thousand dollars to bet."

"You're not in the same class with me."

"I certainly hope not."

That did it. "All right," Frank hollered, "I'm never coming to see you again. I came to see you in Las Vegas and if you had conducted this investigation like a gentleman and come up here to see my people instead of sending those goddamn subpoenas you would have gotten all the information you wanted."

Olsen reminded Frank that Eddie King had skipped out on one of the subpoenas and that Skinny D'Amato had outright refused to talk to investigators, adding that he wasn't satisfied that Frank had been entirely forthright, either.

"I'm never coming to see you again," Frank said.

"If I want to see you, I will send a subpoena," Olsen replied.

"You just try and find me. And if you do, you can look for a big, fat surprise—a big, fat, fucking surprise. You remember that. Now listen to me, Ed. . . . Don't fuck with me. Don't fuck with me. Just don't fuck with me."

Olsen couldn't believe his ears: "Are you threatening me?"

"No, just don't fuck with me, and you can tell that to your

fucking board and that fucking commission too."

Finally, Olsen suggested that if Frank didn't want to submit to the gaming authorities he simply get out of the gambling business in Nevada altogether.

"I might do just that," he replied, "and when I do, I'm going to tell the world what a bunch of fucking idiots run things in this state."

He then, in a knee-jerk resort to diplomacy, repeated his dinner invitation and got off the phone.

A few hours later, Newell Hancock reached Olsen at home and asked, in genuine innocence, if Frank had called the commissioner earlier. When Olsen rehearsed the conversation for him, Hancock groaned, "Well, I may have just blown a client."

Hancock was actually calling about something else that had happened that afternoon, a terrible coincidence that was guaranteed to exacerbate an already ugly situation. Following a schedule that had been set up months in advance, two Gaming Board agents had shown up at the Cal-Neva to monitor the evening count of the take from the casino's drop boxes: strictly standard stuff. They arrived, however, just after Sinatra's outburst to Olsen, making it look to Frank as if the commissioner was avenging himself with a pop investigation. When Skinny D'Amato told Frank that two inspectors were in the casino, he exploded, "Throw the dirty sons of bitches out of the house!"

It turned out that the agents were already leaving; they'd come late—the count had already begun—and they'd already arranged with casino manager Irving Pearleman to come back at 6:00 the next morning to observe the next count. Which is just what they did, and as they were getting ready to leave, satisfied that everything was kosher, they were startled by Skinny D'Amato, who stood between them and slipped hundred-dollar bills into the crooks of their arms—for the previous evening's inconvenience, he explained. Unbelievable: In the middle of this shitstorm, Skinny was openly greasing gaming officials.

Olsen was now determined. On September 11, he charged that Sinatra "associated and spoke with" Sam Giancana at the hotel and "did not request Sam Giancana to leave and made no effort to persuade him to depart." He threw in charges of threatening a state official, attempted bribery of gaming agents, and instructing hotel employees to resist subpoenas. Frank had two weeks to present a defense.

The case made headlines everywhere. Frank was the most popular entertainer in the country, with eight hit albums and three big movies in the last year and a half. The news that he was tied in with a mobster and had been abusive to a government official was irresistible. Even Jack Kennedy was intrigued: Passing through Nevada briefly to make a speech, he asked Governor Grant Sawyer, "What are you guys doing to my friend, Frank Sinatra?"

Frank managed to joke about the situation at, of all places, the United Nations, where he emceed a show for the General Assembly. Asking Secretary General U Thant if it would be okay if he smoked as he sang, he indulged in a bit of self-mocking stage patter. "It's essential to relax," he explained, "with the hot spots in the world . . . Vietnam . . . Congo . . . Lake Tahoe." He waited for the laugh to die, then asked, "Anybody wanna buy a used casino?"

When Frank's lawyers deposed Ed Olsen, learning just how much of Frank's testimony would be impeached by sworn statements from the likes of Victor LaCroix Collins and getting a look at the transcript of Frank's August 31 conversation with the gaming commissioner, they decided not to contest the charges at all. The deadline passed without Frank's offering any defense, and Frank's gaming license was revoked; he was given until the following January to divest himself of his interests in the Cal-Neva and the Sands.

Frank's office issued a statement, declaring that the singer had spent the previous six months preparing to separate himself from the gaming industry since "my investments and interests were too diversified." Describing himself as "surprised, hurt and angered" at the news of the Gaming Commission's desire to revoke his license, he said, "My immediate reaction was to contest such recommendation, although it was consistent with my future plans." The commissioners, in other words, were doing him a favor by showing him the door: He just wanted to do it in his own time.

In fact, Frank *had* been working to sell off some of his entertainment interests. During the summer, he'd begun talks with Warner Bros. about forging an alliance between his own film and record businesses and the larger company's. The deal called for Frank to sell Reprise to Warner Records for $3 million, then for one-third of the new Warner Reprise Records to be sold to Frank for $2 million, netting Sinatra a cool $1 million. (He carried a check for that sum around with him for a couple of days, showing it off to friends and crowing, "Now that's what I call pocket money!") At the same time, Frank's Artanis Productions film company would partner up with Warner Bros. Pictures on movie and TV projects, with Frank serving as a special consultant to Jack Warner. Finally, Frank managed to convince Warner to lease his interest in the Cal-Neva from him, separating himself from the property for good.

Frank was also pretty much separated for good from Sam Giancana, who watched helplessly from Chicago as Sinatra turned a bad situation awful and a gusher into a dry well. "Sam never could figure out why Frank would deliberately pick fights," recalled Phyllis McGuire. "He would always say to him, *'Piano, piano, piano.'* 'Take it easy, take it easy.' Sam never could get over the hotheaded way Frank acted."

Especially, apparently, when Sinatra was endangering not only his own investment but Giancana's. The gangster told associates that Frank's fuckup in Nevada cost him $465,000. "That bastard and his big mouth," Giancana snarled. "All he had to do was keep quiet, let the attorneys handle it, apologize, and get a thirty-to-sixty-day suspension. But no, Frank has to get on the phone with that damn big mouth of his and now we've lost the whole damn place."

You couldn't find anyone anywhere who thought Frank was in the right. The following November, Ed Olsen was at the Sands when Sammy spotted him and sauntered over.

"Oh, God," Olsen remembered thinking, "here comes a brawl for sure." Instead, Sammy took him quietly aside, "to tell me in many of the same four-letter words that Sinatra used what a great thing I had done."

Olsen thought Sammy must have been drunk, then, realizing that the singer had just finished his show and was stone-sober, he relaxed and let him continue: "That little son of a bitch," Sammy told the commissioner, who was now beaming. "He's needed this for years. I've been working with him for sixteen years and nobody's ever had the guts to stand up to him!"

Say goodbye

Marilyn.

Picky Peter wouldn't have her, but Frank did, and so did Jack, and maybe Bobby and maybe Mo, and Sammy and Dean didn't but wouldn't've said no.

Her body was a mecca, and they—mere mortals—drew toward it like wild-eyed hajis.

She instigated one of Frank's more sensational brushes with the law—the so-called Wrong Door Raid of 1954; she was linked in the gossip sheets with Sammy; she showed up ringside at the Sands; she visited the Cal-Neva at a time when Giancana was skulking around the joint; she was making a picture with Dean when she slipped into her final fatal spiral; she made her last phone call to Peter.

Flaubert would've based his entire career on her. Of all the women they ever used up and spat out, she was the only one powerful enough to defy them. It cost her, flying in their altitude: the anxiety, the doubt, the fear. But she was the credibly real thing: one of them. It frankly scared them. And whether they did her in out of indifference and neglect or out of cunning and deliberation, they made sure, in a way that their world condoned, that she'd be the last one that would get so close.

She was never truly *of* the Rat Pack, of course, but she blew through their world like an ill omen. Other women passed through as many of their hands, but none had her iconic power—a strapping American blonde dipped in sex—and none, of course, was to die so mysteriously, not even Judy Campbell, who ratted them all out and had reason to worry.

Alive, Marilyn was a walking embodiment of license and pleasure and surfeit and fun—as desirable and modish and swank as tail fins and sharkskin. Decades later, though, that body that had been the focus of so much lustful attention decomposed, and awful stories leaked out of it. She evolved into something sullied, a cesspool of rue and guilt and terrible secrets, a martyr to a culture that didn't have the courage to admit what it wanted from her.

The world would learn that she was a game piece, that powerful men conquered and colonized and twisted her, that she was an object to possess, a weapon to be deployed. America's greatest baseball player, its greatest playwright, its biggest stars, its most powerful men, the president himself: She had been a rite of passage, an initiation into a select pantheon.

But in accumulating lovers, in becoming a nexus of so much secrecy and power and license, she became a threat as much as a pleasure. By the summer of 1962, she was wet dynamite, capable of inflicting all kinds of damage if her chemistry wasn't just right: a recent bedmate of the president, the attorney general, and the nation's most popular singer; under surveillance by the FBI, the mob, and the Teamsters; strung out on drugs and rotten luck; with only Peter Lawford and a showbiz shrink to keep her steady.

That, clearly, wasn't enough. She could rip the world apart if she felt like it, and she was big enough to make it stick. She'd started to play dirty with her playmates just like they always had with her. She bugged her own house so that she could catch a Kennedy making promises or simply sporting himself. And she began talking about using the tapes.

Frank had gotten close to her not much earlier, and he had found it scary. She'd get boozed or doped up, she'd wander through the house naked and stumble into rooms where there was company, she'd neglect herself or shoot her mouth off about something he felt she knew nothing about. Yes, there was the sex, but Frank could have that anytime. He liked dames with class, and he was disappointed to the point of anger to find out that Marilyn didn't, in his book, have it.

But Peter, who'd known her forever, stayed beside her. For one thing, he was guilty at having nudged her into the whirlpool that was swallowing her up. For another, he empathized with her as a kind of dopey sex object caught in the machinations of the gods. He himself felt so wee and inadequate around Frank and Jack and their ilk that he could immediately identify with anyone else similarly bedazzled by the circumstance. In the whole world, she was the only person, it seemed, who needed him to be strong; he couldn't live up to it, but he tried, which is why he deserved her kind final words: "Say goodbye to yourself, because you're a nice guy."

Nice: not exactly a quality prized in these circles. With Marilyn gone, Peter became the last living vestige of the danger she presented. Frank was already through with him, and now Jack and Bobby, who'd always indulged in him like a harmless little vice, grew remote. The only one among them who tried to help her, he wound up taking the rap for the mess the rest had left behind.

They swept her under the rug: a freak accident. They lied even to themselves. Decades would pass before anyone could call them on it, and by then most everybody who might've known the truth was dead or determinedly silent.

Still, there had to have been a general shudder when the news of her death came. Whether they were complicit or not, whether they'd been with her or not, whether there was a conspiracy before or after, a murder or a cover-up, they were all implicitly to blame.

Marilyn had been the best of what they took such pains to make everyone believe mattered to them, and they'd trampled and discarded her and left her to the vultures.

She was the one true sign before Dallas that something was extremely rotten in their world.

"**H**e taught me everything I know. He's one of the reasons I became a star. He's always been one of my great friends."

That was Frank, describing his pal Gene Kelly, the guy who taught him how to dance, how to endure the longueurs of moviemaking, how to play to the motion picture camera, everything. They met in 1944 on *Anchors Away*. Kelly was a hot new star; Frank was just some crooner who'd arrived at the MGM lot after making a couple of low-budget films at RKO. They made three films together all told—*Take Me Out to the Ball Game* and *On the Town* followed in 1949—and Frank never tired of telling folks how Gene had taken him under his wing when he arrived at the world's premier movie studio.

"Because I didn't think I was as talented as some of the people who worked there, I went through terrible periods of depression and I'd get terribly embarrassed," he admitted years later. "It was Gene who saw me through."

In the summer of 1963, when he was looking for somebody to oversee production on a new Rat Pack movie, a musical gangster picture (in which they would play Chicago mobsters, yet!), Frank turned to Kelly, who'd been producing and directing for nearly a decade, with such films as *Singin' in the Rain* and *Invitation to the Dance* to his credit. This new film, with a period setting and several full-scale song-and-dance numbers, struck Frank as something for which Kelly was a perfect fit.

The movie was scheduled to go before the cameras on Halloween, but it started hitting snags before the cameras ever rolled. In September, Joey found himself thrown off the film. He'd been signed in June to a $75,000 contract, but after some sort of breach of etiquette, Frank showed him the door. Some said that Joey had been carping about the accommodations he was given when he played the Cal-Neva, which would've been especially ironic considering that Frank had given up ownership in the hotel by the time the film went before the cameras. Whatever happened, they weren't on speaking terms for about a year, and, with a few little exceptions—a mini-Summit at the Sands in 1966, a few TV spots, some benefit one-shots—they never really worked together again. His role wasn't even recast; it was simply written out of the picture.

Then, three weeks before the first day of filming, Kelly quit. At first, his exit from the film was explained to the press in gentle terms: "We didn't see eye-to-eye on some areas," he told *Variety*. "I thought it best to withdraw before I got too deep into production. We were wide enough apart I felt I should leave. There was no blowup."

But another story soon got around: Frank had called Kelly to complain that the picture had too much dancing in it and ordered him to cut three numbers out. Kelly didn't care for his former protégé's tone: "Why don't you stick to your acting and let me stick to my producing," he answered, and Frank cut his throat for him.

A week later, Kelly was back in New York after visiting the White House and was plainer about why he left the picture. "If you're the producer you're supposed to make the decisions," he told a reporter. "I wasn't making any decisions. I was taking orders." He didn't harbor any grudges against Frank or his cohorts: "Quietly, I like the boys, but friendship isn't always everything in this business."

He kept insisting that there were no hard feelings, but he sounded more defeated than that: "I'm going to take a few weeks off to think about this whole business of moviemaking," he mused. "There are times in this business when you have to sit by a quiet lake and think about life. Sometimes the business gets too deep under your skin." He was thinking, in fact, about returning to the theater: "The most appealing thing about Broadway is that it's a couple of thousand miles from Hollywood."

Meanwhile, in Hollywood, with Frank taking over the production reins himself, the new Rat Pack picture, *Robin and the Seven Hoods*, went into production as scheduled. It was an updating of the Robin Hood folktale, with Frank as a Chicago gangster in the Roaring Twenties named Robbo, Dean as gambling sidekick Little John, Sammy as his aide-de-camp, Will Scarlet, and Bing Crosby as a cheerfully corrupt orphanage administrator named Allen A. Dale (Richard Condon of *Manchurian Candidate* fame had worked on a script draft).

The title of the film had little to do with the actual number of men in Robbo's gang. Like the three other buddy films that Frank had made—*Ocean's Eleven, Sergeants Three, Four for Texas*—its real meaning lay in the number itself. And you didn't have to be a numerologist to figure it out, either: 11, 3, 4, 7: Frank was shooting craps with house money.

Schlockmeister Gordon Douglas, whose chief talent was the ability to schedule other work until noon, when Frank preferred to show up on the set, was the director. Character actors like Peter Falk and Victor Buono filled out the cast, which was also liberally sprinkled with old movie gangsters like Edward G. Robinson and Jack LaRue, a Frankenstein-faced B-movie bad guy whose name graced a Studio City pasta joint Frank favored.

After the tumultuous preproduction, work on the $3-million film went well. By the third week of November, the picture was a day ahead of schedule and clipping along nicely. On Friday the twenty-second, Frank was the only star on the call sheet; the crew was filming on the Warner Bros. lot.

The horrible news arrived from Dallas just before 11:00: Jack Kennedy'd had his brains splashed all over his wife's pink suit. Work stopped for a half hour—the famous "where were you when?" moment—and then they carried on. As soon as they were back on the soundstage, sixty-one-year-old Jack LaRue passed out. They revived him and shot nine more setups—a total of nineteen takes—before Frank went home at 2:50.

A full day's work: What the hell were they thinking?*

Frank was devastated: Frank who'd been a puppet and a bagman and a pimp, Frank who'd been part of the web connecting Jack with the people who might finally have ordered him dead. He took off for the Springs and spent the weekend in seclusion. He called the White House and spoke to Pat Lawford, but he wasn't asked to the funeral. "It just wasn't possible to invite him," Peter remembered. "He'd already been too much of an embarrassment to the family." He did what he could: He withdrew *The Manchurian Candidate* from circulation; a few months later, when he learned that Lee Harvey Oswald had been a fan of *Suddenly,* the 1954 picture in which he played an assassin, he withdrew that as well.

---

* There's an alternate version of the story. Sammy remembered showing up that morning to shoot at a cemetery, getting grief from Frank for being late, having lunch and drinks in a trailer with Dean, Frank, Bing, and Joey, then hearing about the assassination from his valet. But the production documents from the set that day didn't mention him or Dean or Bing (Joey, of course, wasn't even in the picture), and the call was for the lot, not a location, and it's unlikely that anybody had had lunch and drinks before 10:30 a.m. West Coast time, which was when the hit in Dallas took place. Years later, on the far side of drug and alcohol addictions, Sammy seemed to be the only person in America who *couldn't* remember where he was and what he was doing when the world blew apart that day.

Dean left no record of his reaction—he'd always managed to keep a distance between himself and the whole Camelot charade—but Peter was, once again, destroyed: Frank had rebuffed him, Marilyn had practically died in his hands, and now Jack.

Peter was in Tahoe performing with Jimmy Durante at Harrah's and carrying on, once again, in a manner that concerned his employers—drinking all day, partying all night, broads. When the news came just before noon, he'd only been asleep about three hours; he threw up all over the kitchen and fell in his own puke, wailing. He took Bill Harrah's private plane to Santa Monica airport and helicoptered to his beach house, where Pat sat in a state of catatonia.

Reporters were swarming all over the place; priests, nuns, and a psychiatrist were on hand; the living room was filled with stunned friends, including Judy Garland, who was drinking and weeping that she'd "never sing 'Over the Rainbow' to him again." Pat, sedated, fielded some of the blizzard of calls that came—including one from a family friend back East suggesting that Peter didn't belong at the funeral. She put her foot down: "I'm going back with my husband."

Throughout the following days, a stunned Peter watched uncomprehendingly as the Kennedys waked the slain president. He was in shock, couldn't eat, sleep, talk; they ate and drank and made jokes about their mourning attire, a boisterous Irish brood to the bitter end. Peter was appalled at such a display, but, really, he was no better: The night before the funeral, he snuck off to make hey-hey with a stewardess he'd met on the *Air Force One* press plane. The next day, he stood in black amid his weeping in-laws.

Afterward, the Kennedys repaired to Hyannis Port to spend a gloomy Thanksgiving. Peter knew better than to tag along. He returned to L.A., and then to Tahoe, where, to the sickened amazement of the world, he took the stage to joke and sing with Jimmy Durante. Offstage, he wept and wailed and drank himself to sleep; but every night he performed—a trouper, all of a sudden.

He had once been blessed with looks and mien and charm and, perhaps above all else, godlike timing.

Now he looked to the whole world like he was dancing on his brother-in-law's grave.

And just two weeks later, also in Tahoe, somebody kidnapped Frankie Jr.

He was out on the road with the Dorsey band wearing bow ties and singing his pop's old tunes: For some reason, he had chosen a suicidal career as his Old Man Manque.

Who could live up to it? Who would try? It was nuts.

Poor kid. He never really felt like he belonged anyhow: Frank favored the girls, everyone said. Somehow Junior had hit on music as the answer; Nelson Riddle, his dad's greatest arranger and a guy with a full house of kids of his own, noticed him moping in the corner: "Frankie's not an athlete like Dean Martin's kid; he's not a great student, he's not a comedian or a back-slapper. He's an introspective guy: Broods a lot."

Fun.

But *this:* Jack Kennedy just dead, Frank reeling in the desert trying to make sense of things, the whole nation sick to its stomach: *this . . .*

A few horrible days followed: Frank flying from the Springs to Reno then back to L.A., where the kidnappers jerked his chain in a hundred directions before picking up the money and letting the kid go.

The FBI had been all over the case from the start, thanks in part to Peter: As soon as Frank had gotten off the phone with the kidnappers the first time, he called Peter for help in reaching Bobby Kennedy.

It was a strange moment. They hadn't spoken in more than eighteen months, ever since Palm Springs, not even after Jack's murder.

"There was no hello, no apology, nothing like that," Peter remembered. "He just said for me to call Bobby and get the FBI on the case and get back to him in Reno. I called the attorney general right away and he told me to tell Frank that they were doing everything they possibly could. . . . Bobby said, 'I know how Frank feels about me, but please tell him that everything is being done and we'll get his boy back as soon as possible.' Bobby called Frank the next day, but I gave him Bobby's message that night and he listened. I think he said thank you before hanging up, but that was the last time we ever spoke to each other."

Peter kept abreast of the case on his own over the next few days, placing several calls to FBI offices in New York ("He appeared to have been drinking," read one agent's account of a conversation with him); he made such a nuisance of himself that he had to be scolded into quiet. A ranking official told the New York supervisor to "tell Lawford very firmly that while we are investigating, there was no information that could be furnished to him, so as to discourage any further inquiries from him."

The feds monitored the money drop and quickly got their hands on three guys. One had gone to school with Nancy Jr. They were put on trial in the spring, and they came up with a despicable defense, claiming that they hadn't really kidnapped Frankie at all but were merely part of an elaborate publicity scheme the youngster had cooked up to give his singing career a boost.

The judge, disgusted at this line of argument, instructed the jury to ignore it; within a few hours, they returned three convictions. Two were given life terms; the other seventy-five years. A few years later, from prison, they made headlines trying to peddle a screenplay about the case, still floating the utterly baseless canard that Frankie had masterminded the whole affair.

The innuendo stuck for years: Comics joked about it; it became confused in the public mind with the real facts of the case. The trauma that should have cemented the bond between the two Frank Sinatras wound up weakening it instead.

Two years later, when the whole world celebrated Frank's fiftieth birthday, Frankie skipped the party, leaving his dad sobbing. The following spring, when Frank got married for the third time, not only was Frankie not invited, but he first heard the news from a reporter. "I think you got the wrong party, pal," he declared. "I don't believe it, I just don't believe it."

He took the stage that night and, before launching into the tribute-to-Frank portion of the show, announced, "I'm going to devote exactly five minutes to my father because, as he once confided in a moment of weakness, that is exactly how much time he devoted to me."

part 4

I've got five good years left

This was what it had come to: insanity, violence, kids disgusted with their parents, and nobody wanting to see them: *Four for Texas* opened around Christmas and died.

What the hell had happened?

In November, Jack was president and they were making their little Robin Hood movie, another crass, brassy lark.

In August, the movie came out: Jack was dead, and this bunch of kids from England with funny suits and haircuts had grabbed up five number one singles—more than Frank, Dean, and Sammy had ever had in their lives *combined*. Dean knocked 'em off the charts that month with "Everybody Loves Somebody," but that was just one last punch from a heavyweight champ who was most definitely going down: They were *over*.

All those years spent climbing a mountain, who's gonna tell you that you're gonna hit a sheer cliff and fall?

There'd been chinks and fractures and staggers and stumbles before, of course, but the scale of this: They would never, ever, *ever* get back on their feet.

Oh, it was still possible in the spring of '64 to pretend things hadn't changed. Frank and Dean showed up on a Bing Crosby TV special, then the three of them went into the studio to record the sound track to *Robin and the Seven Hoods*. Effortless stuff: three gods with more than a century in the game between them.

Yet there were intimations in the air, and Frank, being as he liked to be on top of the flagpole, felt them more profoundly than anyone. This wasn't like back when he fell, the time with Ava and Mitch Miller and his voice going south on him. This time, he stayed right where he was—right on the summit— and the world receded from him. He stayed big; the pictures got small.

For another three or four years, Sammy could still galvanize an audience and lead a people, Dean could still sell records and movie tickets and TV advertising (he'd even get a golf tournament named for him), Joey could still be considered marketable enough to hang a talk show from, even Peter could still get jobs. Frank was king, there was no question; he would *always* be king. But how strangely grew the realm.

In May 1964, he was in Kauai to direct a movie. One day off, he was wading in the ocean with the producer's wife when a riptide pulled them a couple hundred yards out. Gulping water instead of oxygen, he was too blinded to see when fullback-sized actor Brad Dexter fought the heaving surf to reach them.

Frank was sobbing: "I'm finished. It's all over, over."

Far off on the beach, rescuers were assembling with surfboards and tow ropes. Dexter grabbed ahold of the woman and dragged her over to Frank, who was still blubbering.

"Please take care of my kids. I'm going to die."

Dexter struggled to get Frank to help himself.

"I tried to get him angry enough to start fighting back by calling him a fucking lily-livered coward," he remembered. "A spineless, gutless shit. But he didn't react."

The woman was no better. Dexter slapped their faces, heaved them up into the air to breathe, held them under his arms while he fought to tread water.

The surfboards finally arrived, and Frank and the woman were ferried back to shore strapped to them; Dexter floated in on his own—in more ways than one.

"My family thanks you," he quixotically told Dexter—the only thanks the actor ever got directly from him.

"I just got a little water on my bird," Frank joked afterward.

For a while, Dexter was immediate family, another Hank Sanicola or Jilly Rizzo big enough to toss some muscle at anyone asking for it, but more pal than bodyguard. He was given a job in Frank's production company; he got parts in a few films; he was lavished upon when Frank was in lavishing moods.

But there was always a faraway part to it, too, a coolness that Dexter always blamed on that day in Kauai. "My rescue efforts probably severed the friendship right then and there by depriving him of the big-benefactor role," he reflected. "Frank would have much preferred performing the grand dramatic gesture himself and saved my life so that I would be the one who owed him."

It could've been that. But it could also've been that Frank was just feeling the weight of his days. He was staring down fifty, and even though he was one of the great middleweights of his era, he was feeling sated. He wasn't accumulating people the way he did five, ten years before; there would be no more clans. He would work with Dean and Sammy, he would still make movies and records and tour and do TV shows, but he was starting to look inward, thinking about that half-century he'd owned. His tank was full—overflowing—and he was willing to let some of it dribble away, to let his spirit slow down to a pace like the rest of the world's.

Little by little, anyhow. He still swung, he still tore up joints and banged broads and filled Vegas with high rollers and made a mint. It wasn't like it was a few years earlier, what with Jack and Marilyn now dead and him not owning the same pieces of the action, but he could still wail.

He played dates with Count Basie, the rockingest big band of them all, and made marvelous, sexy, modern-sounding records with Quincy Jones and Antonio Carlos Jobim (this latter collaboration produced, in 1967, *Francis Albert Sinatra and Antonio Carlos Jobim,* an absolute landmark record, as cool and sexy and dreamy and beautiful as anything he'd ever cut—and as important an LP of its type as anything the Beatles or Bob Dylan was doing at the time). He sang starkly and feelingly about his age—"It Was a Very Good Year," "My Way"—but he could still make you stand up on your chair and shout along with him: "The Summer Wind," "That's Life." So what if he gave up trying in his movies and never could figure out TV? When he had a good song and a good band, nothing compared. In his third decade as a pop star he was still the all-time Best of Breed.

Throughout 1965, in fact, that was the big theme: the View from the Top at Fifty. He cut a double album extolling himself—*A Man and His Music*—and starred in a hit TV special to promote it. *Life* and *Billboard* devoted special issues to him; CBS did a much-anticipated prime-time hour about him. His records didn't have anything like the commercial impact that the Beatles were having, but he could still command all showbiz with a gesture.

And, weirdly, he had his eye on a new bride. He'd been with the little *mammarella* from the neighborhood, and he'd been with the Queen Bitch Sex Goddess. Now he was courting a nineteen-year-old flower child who starred in a soap opera and didn't quite weigh one hundred pounds. Frank Sinatra and Mia Farrow: The world stared in slack-jawed wonder.

They didn't really know who Mia was—Maureen O'Sullivan's kid, right?, and she had that part on *Peyton Place*. But look at her: no tits, no ass, no *hair*, for chrissakes. Frank had daughters older than this broad and better looking. What the hell was it all about?

From her point of view, it was uncomfortably clear. Her dad had been movie director John Farrow, a drinker and skirt-chaser much like Frank; the two men even wore the same cologne ("I can say it now," she wrote, reflecting on Frank, "they had the same identical smell"). Frank was still Swinger Number One on Planet Earth, and he wooed her with a combination of extravagance and tenderness, letting her in on his childhood hurt.

What Frank got out of the relationship, who could say? Mia's mom saw her daughter's frailness as a cause: "Men had an instinctive desire to protect Mia. That's the secret." And Frank was certainly a great one for finding people to protect. But that didn't mean he had to get serious.

Maybe it was simply that he was spending so much time with his own kids that he was beginning to appreciate the scene. Frankie—poor Frankie—was still playing lounges and everyone was still encouraging to him, but out of sight of him, they were a little sad, and he knew it—he *had* to know it. Yet he kept on at it, walking through his career like it was his doom.

Nancy had followed Dad, too, after divorcing her pop star husband, but Nancy was a kind of sensation. She sang these terrible songs and put on short shorts and vinyl boots and go-go-danced and was enthusiastic as hell—maybe too much. Whatever: She sold records and tickets—a good earner for Reprise. She and Frank cut a number together, and damned if he didn't get his first-ever gold record with it—"Somethin'

Stupid," a bossa nova pillow-talk thing that the wags around town called "The Incest Song."

Frank showed up on TV with the kids, onstage with them, in movies (poor Frankie Jr. showed up and smiled, despite himself). Their friends, their scene: It was a gas, a big turn-on. Over in England, Sammy and Peter were swinging with wild young chicks. Frank did too.

But marriage? Was he honestly talking marriage?

Throughout 1965, gossip columns went nuts with this story, and the love birds did nothing to squelch it. Their romantic cruise through New England—chaperoned by Roz Russell and Claudette Colbert and their husbands—made headlines, especially after they dropped in on the addled Old Joe Kennedy and then lost a deckhand in a freak drowning. They returned home, away from the glare of reporters, playing house—doing crossword puzzles, playing with kittens and puppies, confounding the world with their closeness.

Then she started to drift from him, to spend time with someone closer to her own age. Frank was stunned by the idea that she might be leaving him; he got serious.

"What the hell?" he told Brad Dexter. "Let's say I've got five good years left. Why don't I enjoy them?"

Mia returned home and Frank proposed. Very quickly, with neither of their families represented, they married—and Mia was in for some very weird shit.

Proximity to Frank had made her famous, so she was able to jump from TV to movies. Maybe too fast: Frank hadn't liked following Ava around the world when she had work and he didn't, but he wanted the new Mrs. Sinatra to do that for him. She wanted to be in movies? She could be in *his* movies. They would fight over her projects for the whole of their time together.

Eventually, they divorced over her choice to make *Rosemary's Baby* in California rather than act with him in *The*

Detective in New York. Without any real warning, rather like the way in which they were married, Frank had his lawyer serve her with papers on her set. She sold off all the jewelry he'd ever given her and gave away the proceeds, then ran off to India to join the Maharishi Mahesh Yogi's ashram with her sister, Prudence, and, presently, the Beatles. She mourned her failed marriage for some time, but in ways that revealed what a strange union it had been from the start: "It was a little bit," she said, "like an adoption that I had somehow messed up."

And Frank?

Like it never happened . . .

One of the curious corollaries to the ten-year difference in age between Sammy and Frank was that Sammy was dragged through Frank's middle-age angst when he himself was only in his thirties.

Frank had assembled the Rat Pack as a stay against his own mortality, as a reminder to himself and the world that no one was bigger, no one would *ever* be bigger, death and age be damned. Sammy was just—gratefully—along for the wild ride; it wasn't until *after* the Rat Pack began to dissolve that he headed toward his own crises of aging—and by then he'd grown so jaded and fractured and dizzy from overexposure to Frank's world that he nearly destroyed himself. Frank's little party gave him a hangover from which he never recovered.

Take marriage: When Sammy married May Britt, he was the same age as Frank when he and Ava wed—that same ten-year gap, even though Frank's ill-starred union seemed to have occurred ages, epochs earlier. Frank was alone in the world then, his talent tattered, his public image tarnished, his emotions unmoored, his mentors scattered and dead; he went through the trauma of Ava alone, with barely any chums to encourage him along as he stumbled.

But Sammy and May were at the center of things, even if, to accommodate the Kennedys and Frank's political ambitions, they stepped quietly out of the spotlight. When Sammy got hitched (that first sham marriage of convenience can't be counted), Frank orchestrated it as much as he did any event in his own life. It was Frank, recall, not May, to whom Sammy first announced that he was delaying the wedding to quell the Kennedys' anxieties.

It was no wonder, then, May didn't care too much for Frank and his hurtful brand of friendship. She was willing to give up everything she'd ever worked for for her husband, but when she looked for equity from him, she always found him constantly at the ready for Frank's summons to party, to work, or simply to stay up till all hours engaged in pointless talk over whiskey bottles and ashtrays. She became openly surprised whenever Sammy was willing to turn in after only three or four hours of schmoozing with Frank. Once at the Fontainebleau, in the elevator coming back from one of Sinatra's soirees, she turned warmly to Sammy and said, "I never thought you'd leave a party at Frank's so soon"—it was 4:00 a.m.

That was the exception, though. More common were times like when she refused to visit the set of *Robin and the Seven Hoods* because she ws so tired of seeing her man belittled by Frank, even in jest. "The way he treats you," she explained, "the jokes, the way you kowtow to him. . . . I don't mind him being 'Sinatra.' But I can't take it when he treats you like 'the kid.' You're a grown man."

Sammy knew that she was right, but he also knew that he was complicit in Frank's behavior. Later that day, when he arrived late at the set to a particularly pungent joke from Frank, he conceded to himself that he was glad she wasn't there.

During some of these rueful periods, Sammy struggled to

devote himself to May and their three children (a natural daughter and two adopted sons). But bachelor Uncle Frank was always dropping in, giving orders, making Sammy snap to, driving a wedge between the normal family life that, somewhere inside, Sammy wanted and the swinging Frankhood that signaled to him that he'd finally made it in the world.

When Sammy was starring in a revival of *Golden Boy* on Broadway and trying desperately to keep his marriage and career afloat at once, Frank breezed into town and ordered him to Jilly's for drinks, Chinese food, and schmoozing—on a night he'd set aside for an intimate dinner with May. He obeyed Frank, dragging May along.

A couple years later, after they'd separated, Sammy promised to take the kids to a game at Dodger Stadium. The inevitable call came from Frank and, poof: Sammy was in Palm Springs. Come Sunday, he woke up around two, bathed in his wonted brew of hot water and three different colognes (Lactopine, Hermes, and Au Savage), strolled into the living room, grabbed a drink, and sat down to watch TV. It was the ballgame. The camera panned over the crowd, and he saw his kids: "They were having a good time. And I was where I should be. But I wasn't much of a father. No buts—fuck it."

Sammy had wanted a houseful of babies—in the abstract, anyhow—but he didn't, really, it seemed, want actual children. He couldn't make time for them, couldn't figure out what to do with them. He didn't like the zoo, he put the kibosh on picnics and camping trips, he even skipped the *shabbat* dinners that May put on so as to raise the children in their father's adopted religion. She finally confronted him with the most simple of requests: "Mark would love to have a catch with you right here in our backyard." He balked: "Then somebody will have to teach me how to have a catch. I never played ball. When I was Mark's age I was sitting around green rooms playing pinochle."

He made a few stabs at domesticity. For a while, when *Golden Boy* was still playing, he turned down new job opportunities and requests to do benefits; he even tried to teach his preschool kids to play Monopoly. But he was afraid to desert the swinger image that had become so linked with his success and stardom.

May loved her family, but she couldn't stand being made to feel a prop in Sammy's whirlwind one-man-show of a life. She didn't like the big Fifth Avenue town house he'd chosen for their New York home after she'd found a smaller, more family-friendly place; she didn't like to put on the dog and then hang out in his dressing room schmoozing before and after the show; she didn't like posing for magazine layouts touting Sammy's happy homelife; she didn't like Sammy's gaudy spending habits (his personalized Abercrombie & Fitch bowling ball, for instance, did *not* go over with the missus).

One night the whole mismatched relationship fell into uncomfortable focus for both of them. He'd invited Judy Garland and little Liza by the house for dinner; Leonard Bernstein, Betty Comden, Adolf Green, and Jule Styne were there: strictly A-list stuff. Laughs, drinks, food, and everybody singing and doing shtick around the piano. Sammy was lit up like a little Christmas tree.

"Y'know what I was thinking?" he asked May. "Why don't we do a weekly 'Sunday at Sammy's'?"

"Why don't we talk about that?" she shot back.

Later on she gave it to him straight: "Sammy, I love you but I hate our life."

The feeling was, sickeningly, mutual. May didn't want to share him with the world of glitter and glitz. Sammy grew anxious as he felt his image recede from Swinger Par Excellence to Homebody. They had misread one another, or simply been wrong in thinking that their love could fill the spaces described by their differences.

"Whatever happened to the Mary Movie Star that I married?" he asked sadly.

"I'd rather be plain Mrs. Sharlie Brown."

Sammy knew that there was no resolving it. He could submit to his marriage and hate himself, or he could turn back to his career with characteristic vigor and fulfill, as he saw it, his destiny. It wasn't really a choice; he set his agents and managers into motion, and within a few weeks, while still on Broadway, he was taping a TV series, filming a movie, and doing so many benefits that he lost count—all, virtually, at once.

And May took the kids to Los Angeles. The divorce became final in 1968.

He became a crazy man—working, partying, spending, moving, *being* like nobody ever had. Two years starring in a hit Broadway show, *plus* specials on ABC, *plus* an NBC series (for which he was so overextended that the first three of what turned out to be only fifteen or so episodes were hosted by Johnny Carson, Jerry Lewis, and that paragon of variety entertainment, Sean Connery), *plus* an original cast recording, *plus* LPs of his own on Reprise, *plus* a best-selling autobiography dictated to journalist pals Jane and Burt Boyar, *plus* an endless string of benefits (some truly exploitative of his good-heartedness). Exhausting: He suffered a nervous collapse in 1964 but treated it like a mere pit stop and cranked right back up soon again.

He knew, somewhere, how far gone he was: He produced and starred in a strangely autobiographical movie, *A Man Called Adam*, that was both lurid confessional and Rat Pack reunion. The costars included Peter, Cicely Tyson, Louis Armstrong, Mel Torme, Frank Sinatra Jr., and his own mom, Elvera. Sammy played a jazz trumpeter plagued with guilt after killing his wife and kids in a car wreck (!). After a botched romance with a civil rights activist (!), he joins in a wild jam session with Satchmo and dies right onstage (!): *All That Jazz*, of *The Champion* by *Young Man with a Horn*. (Frankie Jr., ever the masochist, reprised his dad's most famous part. A member of Sammy's band, he was beaten as a nigger-lover by racist whites, dying, a la Maggio, in their arms.)

Money was rolling in—$2 million in 1966 alone—but it was rolling out just as fast. Despite having worked as a single for nearly a decade, he still split his dough three ways with Old Sam and Will Mastin. And he was still spending like a kid in a candy store: the fifteen-room house in Hollywood that May hated but he just had to have; dozens of hand-tailored suits and pairs of shoes; a $25,000 customized navy-blue Cadillac limo; collections of canes, cameras and photographic equipment, tape recorders; huge cut-glass bowls filled daily with packs of cigarettes; a staff of thirty; a grand or two a week in gambling money. He reckoned he needed to make $17,000 a week just to break even, but he didn't really know— and he didn't care.

"I still live way beyond my means, I know that," he told an interviewer, but that wasn't going to stop him. "It's my *pleasure*. I love it, and I earn it, and nobody gives it to me, and nobody works any harder for his than I work for mine. That goes for a riveter on a bridge, for a ditchdigger: don't *nobody* work no harder than me, no matter what he works at. I'm out there sweating blood. So if I feel like having me a little Rolls Royce, I buy one."

When he finally let *Golden Boy* die—"It became too hard to perform, and finally I got bored with it"—he couldn't stand the quiet. He hit the Sands for the first time in two years and then went out on the road for a gargantuan solo tour—a big hit, sold out wherever it went.

And since he was traveling—what the hell—Europe and a

whole wild new way to party. In Paris he had a passionate, drunken affair with actress Romy Schneider, a liaison promoted and mentored by Porfirio Rubirosa, Frank and Peter's old pal from the Kennedy days. In London, he hung with the Rolling Stones, Jimi Hendrix, Cass Elliot; he smoked dope, dropped acid, snorted cocaine; he wore Nehru jackets, paisley shirts, beads; he covered numbers by Jimmy Webb and Blood, Sweat and Tears: a life out of Petronius with a score by Lennon and McCartney.

"Every day was like going into Tiffany's or Cartier's," he remembered. "It was 'What's gonna happen today that's new and glittery and shiny and bubbly?'"

In 1967, he and Peter made a Swinging London comedy together, *Salt and Pepper*. They played nightclub owners caught up in a James Bond-style goof, with murder and submarines and Nietzschean madmen and hot chicks. It made money for them both (they executive-produced), so they ordered up a sequel and asked Jerry Lewis, of all people, to direct it—to predictably awful results.

While working on these films, Sammy partied harder than anyone ever had during the making of *Ocean's Eleven:* orgies with who knew who, a little dilettantish Satanism, drugs with Roman Polanski and Sharon Tate. "I was ready to accept the wildness, the rolling in the gutter, and having to get up the next morning and wash myself clean."

It was all as much an escape from the world as his titanic stage performances ever were, but it had a more insidious edge than before. It used to be that he would push himself to knock the racism and doubt out of the audience, to compel it to love him; now it was him running from himself, him dousing his mind, him "wanting to see how far the rubber band could stretch, how much I could tempt fate, how close to the edge I could go and still come back."

One night he got ripped on pot brownies, walked onstage,

did a single song, said "Thank you and good night," and walked off. He thought he'd done a whole show: Dean's old bit—"How did all these people get in my room?"—in reverse.

If his head hadn't been attached to him, it would have spun off into space.

I don't know what
hit me

Joey may have gotten the boot from *Robin and the Seven Hoods*, but the Summit had launched him, it seemed, out of the clubs, and he was able to ride with that for a couple years.

So much as he wanted to, anyway.

It was that attitude thing again: He'd be granted some golden chance, and he'd seem reluctant to take it; he'd have fortune at his feet, and he'd be chary of bending over to pick it up.

NBC gave him a sitcom in 1961, but he approached it with that characteristic mixture of wariness, indifference, micromanagement, even hostility.

"They think they bought a following," he shrugged going into it. As far as pretensions to art, he sounded like his old man talking about the bike shop: "I figured over a period of time it would be good income for my family. I'm not trying to conquer worlds."

He was cast as a P.R. agent—an effort to cash in on his renowned proximity to more famous fellows—and he had an officeful of fictional wiseacre colleagues and a make-believe family who were always looking for something from him. Danny Thomas was the producer; his daughter, Marlo, played Joey's kid sister.

Throughout the publicity drive leading up to the premiere, Joey seemed ginger, cautious. He was right: The show debuted to devastating reviews. He had always been a critics' darling. Not anymore.

"Joey was like a man in shell shock," recalled Joe Flynn, who'd been cast as the star's brother-in-law. "He was the press's darling and he'd never been attacked before. He began taking the script home at night to 'fix it.' I remember once he was supposed to tell Madge Blake to 'Shut up!' He changed it to 'Mom, please!' That's how desperately he wanted to be loved. Then when he began to explain to me what a joke was I knew we were in trouble."

Like Frank, he started showing a temper around the studio: "When he first came around and hollered, we got scared and resentful," said a crew member. "Now we know that when he hollers, five minutes later he won't be hollering, so we let him holler."

Soon enough, wholesale tinkering: Characters were jettisoned, writers, the director; Joey's character went from an L.A. P.R. man to a New York talk show host. Danny Thomas couldn't take the aggravation anymore so he quit overseeing it—only to discover that there wasn't exactly a line of guys waiting to take over the job: "I guess I'll have to get my brother-in-law to produce this show," he sighed.

Joey found somebody to take on the assignment—Eddie Rio, an old vaudeville buddy who'd been driving a truck during a protracted career lull. He also sent to Florida for his brother Freddie, who was hired on as dialogue coach direct from a stint as a Miami Beach headwaiter. Other ghosts from the past appeared on-camera: his former Bishop Trio cohort Rummy Bishop and his older brother, Morris Gottlieb, a handbag salesman, who turned up on the show one night playing the mandolin and doing an imitation tap dance with his teeth.

No one who watched exactly forgot the Summit; eventually, NBC gave up on the show and it switched over to CBS.

Absent Frank's company, Joey drifted listlessly along. He could still draw in nightclubs—Vegas, Miami, Chicago, New York, L.A.—but never with anything like the old sizzle. He formed an entourage of his own hangers-on, and he bade them surround him in an effort to cheer himself up, but he was too much the loner to pull it off. "He hardly ever talked to us," whined one of his lackeys.

In the spring of '65, the plug was finally pulled on the show. "I feel like someone who has been in an auto accident," he told a reporter. "And I don't know what the hell happened, except that I'm bruised. I don't know what hit me."

He finally reconciled with Frank. After that near-drowning in Hawaii, he sent him a telegram reading, "You must have forgotten who you were. You could have walked on the water"; it went over well. In April '66, he was back at the Sands with Dean and Frank for a mini-Summit reunion. At around the same time, he made a doofus western with Dean, *Texas Across the River*; stone-face Joey played an Indian—an idea funnier in concept than execution.

It was his last real Rat Pack gig.

Too bad, too, because he missed a doozy. In June of '65, Frank had summoned Dean and Sammy to St. Louis to play a benefit for a favorite charity of his (and of his pals over at the Teamsters), Dismas House, the halfway house for ex-cons founded by Father Dismas Clark, the inspiration for the gritty little exploitation film of 1961, *The Hoodlum Priest*. The novelty would be that they'd broadcast the thing—via closed circuit—

to movie houses in New York and L.A. so as to augment the money raised in St. Louis.

Joey had been invited too, but he was replaced by Johnny Carson after he hurt his back: "He slipped a disc," Carson quipped, "backing out of Frank's presence."

The show was yet another Summit reprise, the old format cold, from Dean's "When you're drinkin' . . ." through the ensemble finale of "The Birth of the Blues," with only the novelty of a different emcee up there to keep anyone onstage awake.

The broadcast was filled out with performances by Trini Lopez, Kaye Stevens, and the Step Brothers, a tap dance act that had once upon a time towered over the Will Mastin Trio. The Count Basie orchestra, with which Frank was making records and playing club dates at the time, provided the music. (At show's end, Father Clark, bestowing tokens of Dismas House's esteem on the performers, mistook the rotund Mr. Basie for a Step Brother.)

The performance became famous three decades later when a kinescope of it was discovered in a closet in St. Louis; it was shown to great huzzah at museums on both coasts.

But it was actually kind of sad. Compared to a show taped surreptitiously at the Sands three years earlier, or to the unreleased Villa Venice recordings, there's something perfunctory about it, something tepid and canned and routine.

Maybe it was the presence of Carson—that avatar of late-night, middlebrow Coziness Unto Sleep.

Maybe they were on their best behavior in front of the good father.

Or maybe they had simply stopped being dangerous and dynamic and thrilling.

It was perfect that no real recording of the Summit ever surfaced, after all: What they did, exactly, was never really the point of who they were or what they meant. They'd been a majestic triumph of style and attitude over content. And now that they'd stopped really mattering . . .

1965: *Marriage on the Rocks:* the last Rat Pack movie and a damned ugly way to go.

Frank is a straitlaced guy with two teenage kids (one played by his own daughter, Nancy) and a wife (Deborah Kerr) who's thinking about divorce. Through inane comic mix-ups, the couple winds up in Tijuana and she accidentally gets her wish: The marriage is off. Before they can tie the knot again, Frank hies home and asks his pal (Dean) to go back and fetch the missus. Then *another* string of idiotic coincidences results in her marrying *him*. Meanwhile, Frank is getting into the groove of the single life and enjoying it; he even frugs in a go-go cage. What larks!

With material like this—better suited to Rock Hudson or Dick Van Dyke—it was clearly all over. There had been something dangerous and sexy and rebellious in *Ocean's Eleven,* even though it wasn't much of a movie, even though the rebels were all millionaires. But this—this was beneath everyone. And nobody paid money to see it.

Dean, frankly, didn't need it. He was more popular on his own in movies than ever before—he'd just started making some campy action movies about a mock James Bond named Matt Helm—and he'd been given his own variety hour on NBC. *The Dean Martin Show* debuted in September 1965, the very same day that *Marriage on the Rocks* slunk into theaters. The first episode featured Bob Newhart, Diahann Carroll, Joey Heatherton, and, surprise, surprise, Frank, who stomped all over the host's rendition of his monster hit "Everybody

Loves Somebody"—which Dean had already mangled during the show's opening.

For the next decade, Thursday night at ten belonged to Dean—to his schmoozing with pianist Ken Lane; to his bevies of dancing girls, the Golddiggers and the Ding-a-Ling Sisters; to the little bar on the side of the set and the firehouse pole that he would slide down to make his entrance and the swinging doors through which celebrities sauntered to make "surprise" appearances.

He came through the tube easy, laid-back and nonabrasive in a medium that was better to Johnny Carson than to Jerry Lewis, to Andy Williams than to Frank.

And it was no act. The way he worked it with producer-director Greg Garrison, Dean did the whole thing in a single day: no meetings with writers, no casting sessions, no extra rehearsals, nothing. "I don't even breathe hard," he said. "I go to the studio at one on Sunday afternoon and I'm out of there by nine. That's all there is to it."

Sometimes it looked like there was a bigger hand than even Frank's directing them all.

In the summer of 1948, Martin and Lewis made their Hollywood debut at Slapsie Maxie's, a Wilshire Boulevard nightspot named after the punchy-old-pug-turned-minor-celebrity Maxie Rosenbloom; the real owners were clothiers Sy and Charlie DeVore and, behind them, Mickey Cohen. Dean and Jerry were riding high from their debut at the Copacabana, and they were thrilled to discover that the house band at Slapsie Maxie's—the Dick Stabile orchestra—had a similar energy to their own. They were a sock sensation, blew everyone away, became movie stars overnight. Among their admirers—Slapsie Maxie's bartender, an aspiring young comic so enamored of Dean's presence and personality that he started a comedy act just like it. And why not? He had the perfect name, after all: Dick Martin.

In 1952, Martin teamed up with Dan Rowan, another young comic, to form a kind of swingy George and Gracie act: two hedonistic sharpies, one (Rowan) cool and smart, the other (Martin) cool and dumb. They debuted at Hymie's Bar-B-Que in Albuquerque and made a total of six grand the first year, but soon they caught Walter Winchell's eye, and he promoted them in his column and broadcasts throughout the decade. People liked them; they rose.

In 1960, Rowan and Martin were playing the Riviera Hotel on the bill with the McGuire Sisters when Sam Giancana had Rowan's room bugged. That was the farce that began with Giancana jealous of Rowan's proximity to Phyllis McGuire and ended with Sinatra snubbed by Jack Kennedy in Palm Springs, the crazy little flitter of a butterfly's wing that set into effect the cosmic catastrophe that put the kibosh on Frank's Rat Pack party.

In 1966, Rowan and Martin had a summer replacement show on NBC in the slot that Dean Martin's hit show occupied throughout the rest of the year. It was called *The Dean Martin Summer Show,* even though Dean never appeared on it. It hit, and it gave birth to a full-fledged Rowan and Martin series a year and a half later.

In 1970, Peter, still in his Swinging London phase and well on his way to becoming a desiccated zombie, showed up at a TV studio for his semiregular gig on *Rowan and Martin's Laugh-In,* the hip, smash TV show that was peppered with, among myriad delights, cameos of well-known stars doing little unbilled bits of shtick. (Sammy made such a hit with "Here come da judge" that Bobby Kennedy once quoted it back at him.) Peter had been on the show once or twice a season since 1968, grooving at a party in one of the show's regular sequences and squirting out swingy one-liners. At one taping, he noticed a pretty young dancer. They met, they partied, they got married. She was twenty-one; he was forty-eight. Peter knew her dad: Dan Rowan.

And one of her bridesmaids at the denim-and-flowers Puerto Vallarta wedding ceremony: Toni Stabile, niece of Dick Stabile, the bandleader from that long-ago Slapsie Maxie's engagement at which the groom's old Rat Pack buddy Dean so impressed the bride's dad's future partner Dick.

Wild.

Sammy's phone rang, waking him from the fog: Bobby Kennedy was going to run for president; could he help?

Bobby: the good one, who fought to keep him invited to the inauguration, who listened when he spoke, who wasn't impressed with celebrities.

Sammy had worked for Bobby in 1964 when he was running for the Senate from New York. The most famous black Jew in the world, he was uniquely qualified to introduce him at rallies in both the Garment District and Harlem. Now, with Frank still forgiving nobody for Palm Springs, with Peter utterly on the outs with his ex-in-laws, with Dean *still* not giving a shit and nobody caring who Joey voted for, Sammy was the only warrior still in the arena, the Last Rat Packer for Kennedy.

He visited Bobby and Ethel in Virginia: Of course, he'd help.

He was in London that spring of '68. First came the morning his valet woke him, weeping, with the news about Dr. King. Then that other morning: Peter with the news about Bobby.

If he was going crazy, he wasn't alone in the world.

Racial politics got militant all of a sudden, it seemed to Sammy.

Or was it—as the radicals who viewed him with naked suspicion said—that he was too distracted by his own place in the white world to notice?

He tried to talk to kids; they scoffed him. He gave money to radical black organizations; *they* scoffed him. He had sit-downs with hard-core guys; he supported Bobby Seale for mayor; he wore a "Free Angela" button, dashikis, and, finally, a natural haircut—no more greasy whiteboy stuff.

It made black *and* white audiences uncomfortable: If he was *down*, why was his stuff so white? If he wasn't trying to *scare* people, why was he doing all this weird stuff? Black kids seemed to want nothing to do with him, to *loathe* him. He felt their disdain like a slap—a pioneer passed over by people who followed the trail he'd blazed, and forced to endure their catcalls and jibes.

There was a new lady, Altovise Gore, a leggy dancer from the London production of *Golden Boy.* She toured with Sammy as part of his act for a while (he had this notion, he said, of building up his reputation as a swinger, he said, by getting a bunch of gorgeous girls to fawn and fight over him onstage, strictly as a commercial move, he said). A year or two later, he asked her out on a Bahamian cruise with the Quincy Joneses and the Sidney Poitiers, and suddenly they got serious about spending all their time together.

It was good for him: a tall, outgoing Nefertiti whose showbiz ambitions went hand in hand with his, a girl who swung and partied and wasn't gonna start in with the baby food. One day in Philadelphia, after he'd taped *The Mike Douglas Show* and it was too rainy to golf, they got married.

Soon after, Altovise made her Hollywood social debut at a dinner party hosted by Jack Benny and Mary Livingstone: She and Sammy wore matching tuxedo hot pants custom-made by Sy DeVore. Milton Berle answered the doorbell when they arrived and his cigar nearly fell out of his mouth: "How does an old Jew like you get such a gorgeous young wife?"

Strange bedfellows. Another call: Would Sammy like to meet President Nixon, join a commission looking into economic opportunities for blacks? It was more than Jack Kennedy had ever asked of him—even just the visit to the White House would be a first.

He asked around—Jesse Jackson, the SCLC, the Urban League, the NAACP: Everyone said do it. He flew to Washington, visited the Kennedys' graves, then went to meet the man he'd postponed his own wedding to defeat back in 1960.

During the coming years, Sammy went to Vietnam at Nixon's request, he spoke to urban groups, he was chauffeured by *Air Force One* to attend Mahalia Jackson's funeral, and he got some quid pro quo when Nixon addressed certain black organizations for the first time at his request. Nixon used him, of course, but no more so than the Kennedys had a decade earlier—and a damn sight more equitably, to be honest.

Sammy was right to feel proud, even if, typically, it overwhelmed him: During the 1972 Republican National Convention in Miami, he performed at a big outdoor concert near the convention hall; when Nixon came up onstage to say a few words to the crowd, ebullient little Sammy engulfed him in the Hug Heard Round the World.

Blacks attacked him, editorialized against him, shunned him to his face in the very Sands casino that he had fought to open to them. The good lefty Democrats in Hollywood didn't know *what* they were looking at, but they shunned it, anyway: Sidney and Harry wouldn't even return Sammy's calls. Of the old gang, only Shirley MacLaine even bothered to ask what it all meant. He had never, ever, been able to please *everybody*, but the anger he felt now made him weep.

That same year, he bought 8 percent of the Tropicana for $720,000, becoming the first black man to own a portion of a Las Vegas Strip hotel. A few months later, he entertained at a state dinner and spent the night at the White House.

It was 1973; he was forty-seven. He owned a piece of a casino and he broke bread with the president.

Just like Frank.

Dean, on the other hand, never tried to be like anyone. Compared to Frank, whose every showbiz moment seemed some epochal assault on Olympus itself, Dean's lackadaisical mien was soothing; as their audience aged, he was much easier to swallow than the gaudy shit Sammy and Peter were into or Frank's ugly temper. Through the late sixties, his TV show grew so big that within two years NBC offered him a three-year extension at $283,000 a week—$34 million in total. He was worth every penny: The show was in the Nielsen top fifteen all three of those years.

He kept making movies—three Matt Helm pictures in all, plus a never-ending stream of awful westerns (he always loved westerns) and *Airport*. He spent the money on land all over Southern California: acreage, rental properties, office parks; he even tried to launch a country club in Beverly Hills. Frank's wealth may have seemed greater, but that was because he flaunted it; Dean was reckoned by many in town to be among the richest men in Hollywood.

Rich enough to tell Frank *no*.

In 1968, after Frank began a blood feud with the Sands and bolted to Caesar's Palace, Dean extended his deal with his longtime Vegas home; later, still ignoring Frank's summons, he moved up the road to the Riviera, where he was made part owner (ten points for eighty grand) and given his own private barroom, Dino's Den.

For several years, he'd outsold Frank at record stores on Frank's own label; now his was the highest-priced show on the Strip: $15.50, four bits more than Frank's.

But he acted like he was above it all—or not so much above it as apart. He'd always been reserved, even withdrawn, but he could always snap right out of it and join in the squirt gun fights, the carrying-on, the parties. In his fifties, though, he seemed more content to sit and let it come to him, and the hell with it if it didn't. He did what he pleased, swearing in Italian on network television, singing only three songs all the way through during a show in Vegas, walking off movie sets because he felt like an ass playing cowboy at his age.

His remove from the world became noticeable, making him something of a laughingstock to people who hadn't already tired of his booze-and-sex shtick. The TV audience began to dwindle; the movie offers came less frequently. He didn't care.

In December 1969, he had been running around so openly with some beauty pageant queen from Virginia that Jeannie, the beauty pageant queen he'd married nearly two decades before, couldn't stand the shame; she tossed him out and they began a lengthy, final separation that Dean would make permanent by filing for divorce on Valentine's Day, two years late ("I know it's the gentlemanly thing to let the wife file," he quipped, "but everybody knows I'm no gentleman").

Another end came in September 1970: NBC, declaring to the world that the Rat Pack days were dead and gone, removed the bar from the set of *The Dean Martin Show*.

'Scuse me while I
disappear

Only Frank, it seemed, was still filled with the piss and swagger of the Summit.

It even got physical. Sure, there'd always been fists flying whenever he was around, but things were taking on an uglier tenor than ever before. A businessman who asked Frank and Dean to keep the racket down at the Polo Lounge wound up with his head smashed in with a telephone; comedians like Jackie Mason and Sheckey Greene who did bits about Frank got shot at, harassed on the phone, beaten up, hospitalized.

"The air was volatile and violent around him all the time," Greene remembered. "We played the same audience every night, and when I was onstage, there was nothing but laughter. Yet when Frank came out, that same audience erupted and people started fighting, drawing guns, and swearing to kill one another."

Maybe they were just feeding off of Frank's disgust with things around him. He opened at the Sands in November 1966—the first gig of his Mia ever saw in Las Vegas—and launched into a bizarre monologue about the Watts riots and his marriage ("I finally found a broad I can cheat on"). It was tone-deaf, tasteless, shaming: He was out of it, and he was pissed off that he was out of it.

The world—*his* world—was changing right underneath his feet. A few weeks after Frank creeped out that opening night audience, Howard Hughes arrived in Las Vegas with $500 million to burn and started buying up hotels like he was shopping for souvenirs: in April, the Desert Inn; in June, the Frontier; and in July, the Sands—still the sanctum sanctorum of all that was swank in the city. Hughes had slunk around the casinos for years—keeping suites and tables constantly reserved whether he was in town or not—but now he had set himself up as King of the Strip.

This didn't sit well with Frank. Not only had he been number one man in Vegas for the past decade, but he had a personal animus against Hughes, who, before he got freaky, had chased a lot of the same Hollywood talent: Lana Turner, Ava Gardner, Marilyn Maxwell. Frank might've found a way to bury the hatchet if Hughes'd been willing to buy out his still-floundering stake in the Cal-Neva, but the billionaire turned him down cold and Frank seethed.

Through the summer, Frank began looking around for another deal, and his eye alit on the gaudiest sight on the Strip: Jay Sarno's brand-new Caesar's Palace, just across the street from the Sands. In private, though not so quietly that press reports didn't bubble up, Frank began negotiating a monster deal that would rid him of the Cal-Neva and guarantee him fortunes for his appearances.

In September, he was scheduled to play four weeks at the Sands, and all the little bitternesses, tensions, and animosities building up inside him hit the fan. First he called off his Labor Day shows—throwing a damp towel on the Sands's traditional highest-grossing weekend of the year. He said he had strep throat; Sammy and Dean filled in, then, as the hiatus dragged on, so did Nancy Ames and Frank D'Rone.

After huddling in Palm Springs with a pair of Caesar's executives, Frank returned to the Sands in an awful fettle. He was drinking and snarling and gambling heavily—and, as per his longtime practice, pocketing chips when he won and signing big markers when he lost. The Hughes people in the casino didn't like it. They were aware that Frank might be leaving the Sands permanently at any time, and they didn't relish the thought of him doing so with their cash in his pocket.

On Thursday night, Frank finished his show, then walked into the casino with several Apollo astronauts who'd been in the audience; they went up to a baccarat table and Frank asked for credit; General Edward Nigro, Hughes's new hotel manager, had already passed down the word that Frank wasn't to be allowed to run up any more tabs; the casino manager told Frank he couldn't do anything for him.

Frank tried to save face in front of the astronauts by joking that Hughes, for all he'd spent to buy the hotel, was just as much a tightwad as the old owners. But inside he was on fire.

He performed the next night, but he bailed on Saturday's shows, forcing Jack Entratter to pull Frankie Avalon out of thin air as a substitute. Frank was still in town, though—still at the Sands, in fact, in his private suite. But he was so close to signing with Caesar's that he didn't give a damn about his old stomping grounds anymore.

In the wee hours of Sunday morning, he went nuts. In full view of Mia and dozens of hotel employees, he threw a tantrum, destroying the furnishings in his suite, lashing out at the pit bosses who'd denied him credit ("I'm gonna break both your legs!"), and driving a baggage cart through a plate-glass window. "I built this hotel from a sand pile," he shouted to stunned onlookers, "and before I'm through that's what it'll be again!" Then, before anyone could confront him, he disappeared, flying to Palm Springs.

Later in the day, he signed his deal with Caesar's, and he celebrated by returning to Vegas to drink and gamble in his new playground. His mood, however, was anything but gay: "He was on a tear," said a Caesar's executive. "He spent some time gambling here, and I knew he was very unhappy with the way things were going at the Sands."

In the wee hours of Monday morning, Act Two: He wandered back across the street to the Sands and raised merry hell. He strode up to the bell desk and demanded to see casino manager Carl Cohen. Told that Cohen wasn't available, Frank grabbed a house phone and made the same demand of an operator, who, terrified, passed the call to her boss, who rang Cohen's room only to get no answer.

Frank next demanded to speak with Entratter, who, he was told, had asked not to be disturbed. He went apeshit: "You had better get him and tell him I will tear up this goddamn fucking place!" He turned to a nearby security guard and demanded to be shown the switchboard, but the guard held his ground. "You're pretty tough with a gun, aren't you? "Frank sputtered. "Well, I'll take that gun and shove it up your ass!"

The employees, many of whom were fond of Frank, were stunned. "You would have had to see Sinatra to believe it," said one. "He went to the second floor of the hotel, went into the room where the switchboard is, and yanked all the telephone jacks out."

Finally, Frank got through to Cohen, who agreed to talk with him. At 5:45 a.m., Cohen rose, dressed, and dragged himself down to the hotel restaurant for coffee and something to eat before dealing with the situation. ("When Carl is mad," his brother always said, "he eats with both hands and he don't give a shit about nothing.")

Frank found him at a table and walked up to him, demanding to know why his credit wasn't good in the casino.

"I don't own the hotel any more," Cohen told him.

"What are you so nervous about?" Frank asked.

"You just got me out of bed."

Frank had gotten what he wanted, he had Cohen right there looking at him, but he seemed not to know what to do next. "What are you so nervous about?" he repeated.

Cohen had had enough. "I'm not gonna listen to this bullshit."

He made like he was getting ready to leave.

Frank grabbed hold of the table with Cohen's breakfast on it and tossed it over before Cohen could get out of his chair. A pot of hot coffee scalded Cohen's groin and abdomen. In a flash, he put his 250 pounds behind a right to Frank's face, splitting his lips and knocking out two front teeth.

Frank put a hand up to his mouth. Blood flowed between his fingers. "You broke my teeth," he shouted. "I'll kill you, you motherfucker son of a bitch."

Jilly Rizzo, who had followed Frank around the hotel for both of his late-night rampages, reached into his jacket—who knew what for—but a bald, hulking security guard stepped right up behind him and told him not to make a move.

Cohen stood defiantly in front of Frank, who reached for a chair and swung it, missing Cohen but cracking the head of a second security man who'd arrived on the scene and would require stitches for his trouble. With blood still gushing from his mouth, Frank bolted through the revolving doors and out of the Sands forever, Jilly rushing obsequiously behind him yipping, "Wait, Frank, wait!"

Frank hightailed it to L.A. and had his dentist flown in from Connecticut to replace the caps Cohen had dislodged. As he sat being worked on in a borrowed dental suite, Frank received, legend had it, an urgent call; it was the powers back East who had sold the hotel to Hughes, men who valued Cohen's decades of work and knew Frank was a hothead pain in the ass. They told him, in so many words, not to retaliate against Cohen in any way. Then they called Cohen to apologize for the incident and to assure him, as Cohen's brother later recalled, "that if Frank lays a finger on you or even tries to shake your hand, he's gone."

The story hit the papers in dribs and drabs over the following days, along with Caesar's announcement of Frank's new deal. At first, all Frank's people had to say about the fight was that it was "a figment of someone's imagination," but reporters turned up a good dozen credible people who'd seen it all, so they backpedaled: "We can't deny any of what happened in Las Vegas. There were too many witnesses. I have to assume it's all true. We can't even deny that his teeth were knocked out." (In private, Frank admitted to Kirk Douglas that Cohen had bested him: "Kirk, I learned one thing. Never fight a Jew in the desert.")

All Cohen would say was "He's through." But he could've given speeches in the streets if he wanted to: He'd become an overnight folk hero to thousands of Las Vegans. The Sands was besieged by well-wishers and congratulators, as in this memo from a switchboard operator: "At approximately 8:00 p.m. on September 12, 1967, we received a call from a Mrs. MacBeth who wanted to donate $100 to Mr. Carl Cohen's fund. We informed her that we had no such fund and she went on to say that she had read about the incident concerning Mr. Cohen and Mr. Sinatra and as she was 70 years old she was glad she had lived to see it happen. She advised that if Mr. Cohen could use the money in any way she would be glad to donate it to him."

Two months later, when civic elections were held, mocking posters appeared around town showing Frank with his front teeth blackened out. They read, "Carl Cohen for mayor."

Frank tried to make Caesar's Palace like the old days, but he was unable to deliver his chums: Sammy stayed on at the

Sands; Dean finished the final year on his contract there, then moved up the road to the Riviera.

And Frank created ugly scenes at his new joint. Refused credit at Caesar's by casino manager Sanford Waterman, one of his partners from the Cal-Neva days, Frank came on so menacingly that the old man pulled a pistol on him in front of a crowd of onlookers. After the situation was defused, Frank walked out of the joint and vowed never to return to Nevada again; he didn't play the Strip for four years.

It was the damn times. He got more and more desperate to catch a whiff of something young and fresh. He cut an entire album of Rod McKuen songs, and he wore Nehru jackets and love beads and probably smoked a little grass.

He looked like an idiot.

And he didn't need it.

In 1970, he was fifty-five, and he had completely lost contact with his past: He came out for Ronnie Reagan for governor of California.

"It's a shock," said Joey.

"It figures," said Peter.

The next year, he announced his retirement. He'd spent a half-decade chasing something that seemed not to want him anymore; the hell with it.

He gave a lovely final performance at a benefit in L.A., closing with "Angel Eyes" and its haunting final line: "'Scuse me while I disappear."

It was beautiful and poignant—a great showbiz moment and a great piece of musical acting.

But to a nation that had, for the most part, turned away from him, it looked kind of like a white flag.

*

There were other ways to fade.

Take Joey.

In April 1967, he debuted as host of his own late-night talk show on ABC. He was gonna topple Johnny Carson, they said; they put $4 million into it. Regis Philbin was his sidekick, there were dancers and two wiseacres who sent up the news.

Opening night, he had Governor Reagan, who arrived late, Danny Thomas, who preached at the crowd, and Debbie Reynolds, who demonstrated how to smother a fire on a living person by tackling Philbin: crash-and-burn.

The thing limped along for two years, then he quit. ABC replaced him with Dick Cavett.

The rest was a slow diminution.

He was only fifty or so, but he was out of tricks. He became a semiregular on talk shows, quiz shows, bad multicharacter TV series. He mopped up for Mickey Rooney on Broadway in *Sugar Babies*, back in burlesque after all those years. He sat in frequently for Johnny on *The Tonight Show*—177 times over the years, more than anyone else; he was always welcome for short runs.

He moved out of Hollywood, south to Orange County, golfing, fishing, cruising in a series of boats named after his long-ago catchphrase: *Son of a Gun, Son of a Gun II,* etc.

He always had a tan, he occasionally showed up in a movie or on TV talking about the golden days with Frank and Dean and Sammy and Peter. He wrote letters to editors correcting stories they ran about the Summit and reminding the world that he was there.

"I'm writing my own book," he liked to joke, " 'I Was a Mouse in the Rat Pack.' "

He had been.

In November 1984, Peter, who'd been in and out of the hospital and a rehab clinic, had dinner with his old MGM pal Liz Taylor. She had tossed him a career bone—a few days' work on a TV movie she was making about Louella Parsons and Hedda Hopper: Decrepit Peter would play a shifty agent.

Over dinner, Peter teased Taylor about her loudly trumpeted sobriety, a means, perhaps, of covering up his fear of screwing up the job. Which he did anyhow, showing up in a weird fog, gray, mumbling, hazy. He finally passed out and got the axe.

Nothing had been right for him since Frank, Marilyn, and Jack.

After Dallas, Pat and Peter waited a decorous two years before driving a stake through their marriage. In late 1965, she went off to a high-class divorce ranch in Sun Valley, spent six weeks to establish residency, showed up in court for a single afternoon, and was rid of him.

A few months later, he pissed her off for well and good by taking a trip to Hawaii with two of her kids and Jackie Kennedy and hers; it looked to all the world like he was jumping his ex-sister-in-law's bones. Then he committed hara-kiri in front of the whole family by bringing some pickup in a black micro-skirt to Bobby's funeral; it might as well have been his own.

He didn't care. He drank even when he was in the hospital to be treated for drinking. He got deep into drugs—pot, pills, cocaine (he gave some to his son once as a birthday present)—and he started liking his sex more squalid: bondage, frottage, kinky role-playing, even a little pain: slaps to the face, razors to his nipples, hair-raising stuff. Eventually, he resorted to an Acujack, a kind of male vibrator that he would use for hours trying to achieve a pathetic little orgasm; his fourth and final wife (there was another one in there for a few months) left him out of disgust with the pastime.

He had long suspected that Frank had tried to blackball

him in the business, but the truth was he'd killed his own career himself. One producer confessed, "A lot of us hate Sinatra's arrogance. If that son of a bitch ever tried to keep anyone from working, I'd have hired that actor for that reason alone."

It was Peter's own squalor that did him in. He was lucky to get a film a year, and then it got worse: game shows, *Fantasy Island*, "nostalgia cruises" where he was forced to mingle with clutching, aging fans.

Even when he'd forgotten all his wives and was too embarrassed by his state to see his kids, he still missed palling around with Frank. "I tried several times to apologize for whatever it was that I had done," he moaned. "He wouldn't take my phone calls and wouldn't answer my letters. Wherever I saw him at a party or in a restaurant, he just cut me dead. Looked right through me with those cold blue eyes like I didn't exist. Friends of mine went to him to patch things up, but he'd always say, 'That fucking Englishman is a bum.' " In the late seventies, certain that enough time had passed, Peter flew to Vegas to catch Frank at Caesar's Palace; after he'd been seated for a while, a couple of goons showed up at the table to tell him that Frank insisted that he leave or there would be no show.

He stopped taking care of himself—shaving, bathing, changing clothes or bed linen. He'd once been so beautiful, so debonair; now he lived amid rented furniture in an apartment strewn with cat shit.

Friends tried to get him into rehab. They flew him out to Palm Springs—his Golgotha—and then took a rental car to the Betty Ford Clinic in Rancho Mirage. Peter wanted to know where they were taking him. "Betty Ford's," his wife said. "That's wonderful," he replied, thinking he was off on a social jaunt. "I've always liked Betty." The detox in the desert looked briefly like his salvation, but he undermined it, hiring a helicopter to meet him out in the desert with shipments of cocaine, then using his exercise time to walk out, meet the pilot, and get high.

Then dinner at Liz's—his last party—and the disaster on the movie set. The day after he collapsed, he was back in the hospital. His liver and kidneys had virtually shut down; he turned yellow; he slipped in and out of comas.

On December 23, 1984, he drank champagne and laughed. The next day, he went into spasm, blood spurting from his mouth, nose, and ears. That was it.

Four years later, the mortuary still hadn't been paid for his cremation or the cemetery for upkeep of his crypt. His widow declared indigence and blamed his kids, claiming they'd abandoned him in life and now in death. They offered to pay the bills if they were granted control over their father's remains; the widow refused, then accepted a payment from the *National Enquirer* for exclusive rights to cover the removal of Peter's ashes from his tomb and the scattering of them in the Pacific.

He was always being tossed by the waves.

Johnny Rosselli also wound up in the water.

He had kept scamming the world after Operation Mongoose went belly-up. Frank and Dean sponsored him into the Friars Club, and he spent a few years in the can after being caught rigging a high-stakes gin game there.

Soon after he got out, all the shit about Jack Kennedy and Judy Campbell and Sam Giancana and Havana and Dallas and all that started hitting the papers. Rosselli got called in to Congress to testify in closed session: *three* times. That was too many, even for a loyal guy like that.

They found him in an oil drum in Dumfoundling Bay near Miami, chopped up, done.

*

And Giancana they found in his own basement, his head full of .22 slugs, sausage and beans still frying on the stove where the killer got him.

He had maybe fallen worst of all, and he'd asked for it. He wanted to show the feds what a big deal he was, so they hounded him out of business. In the summer of 1963, just before Cal-Neva, they lockstepped him, walking a pace or two behind him wherever he went—airports, restaurants, office buildings, bars, men's rooms, everywhere. (Poor Mo was shy at urinals; he never could get the hang of relieving himself with an FBI agent lurking right beside him.)

They followed him onto golf courses and played in four-somes right behind him; the mighty Bill Roemer delighted in yelling "Fore!" just as Giancana hit the top of his backswing or in hitting his ball onto the green while the mobster was settling in over his putts.

The pressure of twenty-four-hour tails practically in his pants drove Giancana crazy. He tried all his driving tricks, all the ruses he could think of, and they'd still be there, waiting for him or beside him, watching, saying nothing.

The feds were emboldened. They followed him into the Armory Lounge, his clubhouse and office, and sat there sipping beer and enduring the grumbled jibes of a dozen or so of his mob cohorts.

When they left to resume their surveillance from their cars, they were followed by Giancana's lieutenant, Chuckie English.

"Sam wants to give you a message."

"What's the message?"

"He says if Kennedy wants to talk to him, he knows who to go through."

"Sounds like he's talking about Frank Sinatra."

"You said it."

Word about Frank's estrangement from the White House hadn't, apparently, spread to Chicago; he certainly wasn't bragging about it, and the Kennedys couldn't tell the world about the sordid reasons they'd given Frank the high hat. So everyone in town thought that Frank was still the conduit between the president and the Outfit. And when word got around that Giancana had revealed as much to the FBI, his colleagues were aghast.

Outfit underboss Strongy Ferraro visited political fixer Murray Humphries's apartment, which had been bugged since before it was even built, to talk it over.

Humphries hit the ceiling: "For Christ sakes, that's a cardinal rule! You don't give up a legit guy! He tells Roemer that Sinatra is our guy to Kennedy?"

"More or less, for Christ sakes," Ferraro replied. "I'm so fucking mad I could jump out your fucking window!"

They eased Sam out.

He hid for nearly a decade in Mexico, bribing the authorities for a shot at peace and quiet. Eventually, someone there turned on him: Government agents rousted him in the middle of the night, then hustled him off to the Texas border, still in his pajamas.

Soon after, the same congressmen who'd been talking with Rosselli subpoenaed him. Then somebody sent the guy with the .22 to make sure he had no more secrets to leak.

And Frank was still playing around with gangsters.

In 1976, he debuted at the Westchester Premier Theater, a Gambino family operation built on a landfill in Tarrytown, New York. The next year, with the theater—which had been built almost solely for the skimming possibilities it presented—on the verge of going bust, he returned, this time with Dean. No one thought the thing could be saved. It was built with the proceeds of a rickety stock scheme; its managers paid Vegas-sized salaries to entertainers without the prospect of turning gambling profits on showgoers; its parking lot, built over a marsh, filled with water whenever it rained. But Frank and Dean could help with one final score before bankruptcy—a Villa Venice-type last hurrah.

They arrived in May for a twelve-night run at a cost of $400,000 each. Dean had a nineteen-year-old girlfriend in tow; Frank had his new bride of eleven months, Barbara.

As soon as they hit town, Frank began telling the wise guys that he was worried about Dean: "You've got to get him out of his fucking shell," he told Gambino soldier Gregory DePalma, who ran the theater's concession and security operations.

But getting a sign of life out of Dean, whose boozing had evolved from stage joke to the real thing and had been supplemented with a Percodan addiction, was no easy chore. "I'm supposed to play golf tomorrow with Dean Martin," DePalma bragged on an FBI wiretap. "But he's drunk as a fucking log. He wanted to play today. He can't. So he wanted to play the other day, forget about it."

DePalma had a theory: "The broad. He's flipped out over the broad. He's gone, this guy. He's fucking gone. He came into the dressing room, he says, 'Hey, Greg, what's the password?' I says, 'What password?' He says, 'Don't you know the password?' I says, 'No.' He says, 'It's swordfish tonight.' This is a sick fuck."

When they finally did get Dean out onto the course, disaster: "This guy's on pills. Forget about it. He's got the shakes. His fucking head's gone. He played horrible. . . . He hit a fucking house."

DePalma and Frank both tsked at Dean's errant shot.

But Dean said nothing.

He never did care what mobsters thought of him.

I wanna go home

It was 1987, autumn; you could feel winter coming on—and the big winter they would all have to face. Dean and Frank were in their seventies; nimble little Sammy, a decade younger, had just had hip surgery.

Earlier that year, Dean Jr., the golden son whom Dean always loved, was killed when his Air National Guard F4-C Phantom smashed into Mount San Gorgonio near Palm Springs. (Just as Dean and Frank had become inseparable as performers in the public eye, so did this tragedy mark another curious connection between them: Frank's mom, Dolly, had died in a plane crash on the very same mountain ten years earlier.)

Even before his boy had died, Dean had been receding from work, friends, life itself, but in a genial way that people recognized as part of his lifelong desire for peace and quiet. After the crash, however, his introversion became more pronounced and had more of a tragic tinge to it; people worried.

Frank had him and Sammy out to the Springs for a weekend, and Sammy—always ready to turn a moment's pleasure into a show—thought it would be great if the three of them could work together again, maybe on the Strip. They'd

done little benefit appearances together in recent years—
fifteen-minute spots for black tie charity affairs—but he was
talking about a real gig, like back in the day.

"Why don't we find a good bar instead?" Dean asked.

But Frank liked the sound of it: a customized train, a tour
of the hinterlands: Houston, Pittsburgh, Detroit, Oakland . . .
He and Sammy talked about it like some fabulous dream.

A few days later, Frank was still thinking seriously about it:
"Smokey, let's do it," he told Sammy. "I think it would be
great for Dean. Get him out. For that alone it would be worth
doing."

Sammy didn't need convincing. He and Frank had been
estranged for several years because of everything that Frank
had heard about Sammy and drugs. (When they finally
reconciled, just-say-no Frank kept Sammy out all night at a
bar in Vegas.) Now that he'd been sober for nearly three years,
Sammy was eager to take on big things—and the big money
that went with them.

Dean, though, would be a hard sell. He'd virtually stopped
working even before the plane crash. He hardly played
Vegas anymore, and whenever he did perform anywhere, he
preferred single-night performances to extended runs; his
agent had been telling people point-blank, "He doesn't need a
job." He had last recorded in 1983, the same year that he,
Sammy, Frank, and Shirley MacLaine made *The Cannonball
Run II*, easily one of the worst films of the decade, a bomb so
awful that the producers opened it in Japan and didn't bring
it to America until six months had passed; it would be Dean's
last film.

Still, Frank had a way of convincing people. He had Dean
and Sammy over for dinner and laid out a plan: forty dates in
thirty cities, with the tour broken into spring and fall portions;
a full orchestra and tech crew; two private planes for the stars
(Frank had his own, they'd rent one for Sammy and Dean);

they'd play big auditoriums, just like rock stars—fifteen, twenty thousand seats.

Dean still wasn't enthusiastic: "Do you think we can draw that much?" He hated the road, he didn't need the money; it struck him as pointless.

"Dean didn't really want to do it," Sammy admitted, "but we were all aware that much of the allure was the return of the Rat Pack thirty years later and he didn't want to let us down."

In December, they told the world their plans. At a noon press conference at Chasen's, they kicked off what they called the "Together Again Tour," sponsored by American Express and Home Box Office. Wearing tuxedos and smoking, they fielded questions and, naturally, slipped into familiar roles— Sammy the eager kid, Frank the *padrone*, Dean the wiseass in the back row.

"Is there any way we can call this off?" he shouted out early on, and, later, asked how he felt about the tour, he responded in a mumble, "We're happy to be doing this thing. What the hell."

They joked about cigarettes, about Michael Jackson, about booze. The show would be spontaneous, they said, like the Summit had been. Scripts bored them. "That's like doin' a Broadway play," Dean said. "Which I hate."

A reporter asked a question with the words "Rat Pack" in it. Frank, who had politely deflected a question about Kitty Kelley earlier, sneered about "that stupid phrase"; the official publicity for the tour never used it.

They rehearsed a few times, first at Sammy's house, then on a rented stage in Hollywood. In March, they opened before 14,500 people in a sold-out Oakland Coliseum. Before the show, Dean asked aloud, of no one in particular, "Will someone tell me why we're here?" Then he took the stage.

The same old stuff: "When you're drinkin' . . ."; "Each time you drink it rains bourbon from heaven. . . ." Other words he just plain forgot.

He was having trouble with his voice, or, rather, he wasn't really using it; he mumbled into the mike. People shouted out to him, "We can't hear you!"

"I wanna go home," he said, and he wasn't kidding.

He drank his drink, he smoked, he looked out at the audience—the biggest he'd played to since Martin and Lewis headlined the Texas State Fair—and he knew deep inside that he didn't care: He flicked a lit cigarette at them.

Sammy was on next, then there was an intermission, then Frank, then all three of them at once for jokes and goofs and a medley.

Dean kept looking at his watch; Sammy sang "Hava Nagila"; they closed with the "Fugue for Tinhorns" from *Guys and Dolls:* "the oldest established permanent floating crap game." They weren't kidding.

Backstage, Frank made it clear that he was ticked off at Dean's surly behavior, but he'd get no satisfaction. Within the week, they were in Chicago and Dean was at it again. Frank didn't like the hotel accommodations waiting for them and ordered Dean and Sammy to pack up and go somewhere else with him; Dean didn't budge. Frank complained to Dean's agent that he wasn't really singing or trying hard enough. "I can't take this," Dean said, "I'm getting out of here."

He chartered a plane to L.A. and made a show of checking into the hospital for what they said were kidney problems. Frank and Sammy went on to Minnesota without him, then put the tour on hiatus. They reopened it in New York with Liza Minnelli in Dean's place; nobody was calling it the "Rat Pack Tour" anymore.

And Dean barely waited a decent interval before opening by himself at Bally's on the Strip, all better.

Sands
A PLACE
IN THE SUN

FRANK SINATRA
DEAN MARTIN
SAMMY DAVIS JR.
PETER LAWFORD
JOEY BISHOP

part **5**

Not a moment too soon

Blink, and it was the spring of 1990, and Vegas was another world.

In that thirty-year-old photo of Frank and Dean and Sammy and Peter and Joey standing in front of Jack Entratter's marquee, there had been an endless horizon and a crystalline sky; cars could park right there on the road in front of the casino; beyond the handful of trees: nothing.

But those days were over. The beautiful old sign was gone— no room for it beside the new tower that was erected just before Howard Hughes bought the hotel. And the brilliant sky, once dotted only by lampposts, was blocked out by concrete slabs—gigantic new hotels owned not by shady guys and their slightly less shady front men but big corporations, bigger even than Hughes.

The Strip was more choked with commerce and traffic than any suburban shopping district; even downtown had been gussied up. Vegas was legit, corporate, and booming; any sense that it had once been an adult playground was strictly nostalgia.

Theme parks: That's what these new joints were. Across the street from the Sands, where there'd once been little motor courts, there was a casino with a volcano out front, spewing fire all night long for the out-of-state yokels to gape at with their kids.

The old guys wouldn't have believed it: "If you told the old bosses you wanted to put a fucking volcano in front of their joint they woulda thrown you out on your ass," an old casino hand surmised. "They're probably dropping dead all over again in their graves."

But guys like that were finished. For new Vegas to even think of looking back, it had to be some kind of special occasion.

Like May 18.

That night, after dark, the lights on all the Strip's marquees were ceremoniously dimmed for ten minutes, the first time since Jack Kennedy was killed.

This time it was Sammy who was dead—and the town that he had helped build and integrate squelched its glittery facade to mark the passing of one of the most glittering spectacles it had ever seen.

Throat cancer: all those cigarettes.

A grueling year: chemo, radiation, pain, weight loss, grief.

He was down to maybe ninety pounds at the end.

A big, public funeral, the type they used to have in Hollywood in the old days. Frank and Dean were honorary pallbearers; Jesse Jackson spoke; "I Gotta Be Me" on the P.A.; Altovise, the widow, wore white; he was buried alongside his dad and Will Mastin in the Hollywood Hills.

He had never really gained the absolute control he'd hoped to have, never quite sat comfortably atop that mountain that he'd built himself. Styles changed even faster than he could adapt to them; markets dried up; the IRS hounded him, even after he was gone. He had become a beloved figure, yes, but a mocked one as well: Showbiz turned out en masse to celebrate his career on TV (Sammy, obviously ailing, danced with stunning verve alongside Gregory Hines—an old Moulin Rouge performer!—who humbly kissed the master's shoes), but lots of bad comics made hay imitating his obsequious talk show mien, hepcat lingo, the infernal monster hit "Candy Man." As widely as his stunning achievements were recognized, he became a shorthand punch line for all that was tacky and passé in showbiz, he who had once been the living embodiment of hipness and the Now.

Still, he'd been blessed. All the things he had against him, all the barricades in front of him, all that was inside him that made him fight against himself, all the twisted support he got from Frank and a handful of others—who else had ever done all that he had despite it? If he had come to look foolish and dated and stale, so what? He had lived it his way before Frank had ever come across the song.

Pound for pound, he was the best of them: not the most consistent or productive or successful or coherent, but the one who'd come from furthest and who had most fully lived what they were all reputed to be.

It had cost him: health, security, money, love—he was always in jeopardy. But his cakewalk along the ledge was so vital for its unlikeliness, so daring and unique, that even Frank had to realize that although he was himself the brains of the operation, Sammy was its soul.

And more: He was their baby brother, pitifully dead before them.

They knew what was coming: Days in the desert could be so hot, the nights . . . so cold . . .

Dean never did get over his kid.

A few more years of pretending to play Vegas and he just drifted off into himself altogether, a zombie, complete with gray flesh, wandering in and out of restaurants and country clubs without talking to anyone or even, it seemed, knowing why he was there.

That tenuous string that had kept him barely anchored to the world—he simply let it fall from his fingers, as much from indifference as from dotage.

He faded from life while he was still living it, a ghostly presence even in old movies and on old records where he'd once seemed impossibly real. He came to look superimposed on the world, not so much *of* it as above it and apart from it, living it at a remove no one else could approach. As much had always happened to old men, true, but how many had ever dallied at such Olympian heights?

Always graceful, always adroit, always ready with the perfect line, the perfect double take, the perfect excuse to get away and be alone: He had never wanted to conquer anything. It had all just come to him, thrust on him by ambitious friends who expressed their adoration for his lordliness by sharing the good fortune they busted their asses to achieve.

Those last few years, people imagined him lonely, lost, confused, sad.

They couldn't have been more wrong.

For the first time ever, he did exactly what he wanted.

When everyone else was eating Christmas dinner, he slipped away for the last time . . .

And Frank was eighty. *Eighty.*

And finally he, too, surrendered.

Oh, he put up a fight as long as he could: concerts and touring and benefits and even records for at least a decade after nobody could imagine that he could do it or need it or want it.

It wasn't without embarrassment: forgotten lyrics, strange

lapses in stage patter, physical collapse. They gave him a special Grammy for everything he'd ever done, and, accepting it on national TV, he ad-libbed, meandered.

The voice was, stupefyingly, still there: evolved from cello into tuba, yes, but swank and rhythmic and witty as ever.

It was the body that wore out: the heart, of all things. A few sensational medical incidents, then he retreated to seclusion to wait for it, not the last of a breed about to become extinct— the *only*.

No one had done what he had for so long and so well; no one had been synonymous with fame and excellence for so many decades; no one had more profoundly changed the way his art was practiced; no one had courted sensation so successfully; no one could touch him or stand beside him or aspire to his throne.

Even though he'd given up from sheer exhaustion, there was no denying that he had won.

And to put a capper on it they tore down the Sands.

Its time had long passed. The tower with the wedding-cake filigree at the top came to look dainty next to the monoliths around it; the high rollers had long since removed across the Strip to Caesar's and the joint with the volcano; neither a city-within-a-city like the big new casinos nor the sort of swank, exclusive spot it once had been, it faded terribly, its orange stucco exterior more and more garish as the decades mounted.

The final days were a heart-sinking display of trumped-up nostalgia and bargain-basement scavenging. Longtime employees shared secrets with reporters and spat disdainfully at mention of their bosses, who planned a big new resort that would offer work to none of them.

Gallows humor; drunken tears; ghoulish camera crews asking insipid questions; low rollers walking through the wreckage scarfing up souvenirs at 80 percent off.

The very last show in the Copa Room—expanded in size years earlier but still in the very same spot—was a freebie: a girl singer with a lumpy ass, a Welsh comic, a fruity magician, a middle-aged slob singing Elvis songs and doing a lewd striptease.

Then lights out and the dynamite—not a moment too soon.

It was the first time the place had made news since Howard Hughes bought it thirty years earlier.

And every single report talked about them and their incredible moment on top of the world.

Some people thought the building should be preserved—a historic spot—but it was all over, had been for decades.

Better to remember that sunny day, that incandescent time, Frank's voice, the juggling act he pulled off, the miraculous milliseconds when he was the most powerful man in the world and he and his chums were the center and the acme of it all.

His world, with only the people he deemed worthy around him.

His song.

The wrecking balls could never destroy what he'd created, because it had been so fleeting, so impossible, so like a vapor.

Even while it was happening it wasn't really real.

Adult male human behavior

More than thirty years have dawned and faded since that monumental month when the Rat Pack lorded over the world from a tiny stage in Las Vegas, but the Summit still reigns as a standard of popular culture.

For the generation that had fought World War II—the people who knocked themselves out to gain admission to the Copa Room—the Summit was the epitome of opulence, confidence, class, the acme of a kind of art that had been evolving throughout the century, a mixture of glamour, popular song, and vaudeville. They would recall the Summit as one of the defining moments of their generation's glory.

For their children—who would fight, and fight against, the Vietnam War—the Summit was an emblem of wretched excess and establishment boorishness, its stars a cavalcade of lackeys for the degenerate nightmare of American society, its very locale a synonym for sinful consumerist culture. For them, the Summit was a sickening, elephantine fraud.

But for *their* children, bizarrely, a generation whose notion of war was Jay Leno versus David Letterman, the Summit was symbolic of surfaces: swanky nightspots, sharp outfits, neat haircuts, stiff drinks, and cigarette packs free of Surgeon General's Warnings—vestiges of the glory days of their favorite city and a uniquely American brand of grown-up hip. They saw it as both glorious and phony—an originating moment of pop irony.

And they were right. The poseurs of the Cocktail Nation stumbled onto the essence of why the Rat Pack was so attractive to their grandparents and so repulsive to their mothers and fathers. More than any song that they ever sang, any movie they ever made, any joke they ever told, it was the posture of sophisticated maturity—masking an indulgent immaturity—that made the Rat Pack so powerful. Its members were, at one and the same time, everything they said they were for and everything they said they were against; they meant everything and nothing; they gave it their all and couldn't care less; they embodied all that had happened in showbiz before them and all that was to come; and they did it all without ever letting a single hair get out of place.

Put it in a pop context: 1960: Rock 'n' roll had happened—heck, it looked like it was over, what with Elvis enlisted, Buddy Holly dead, Jerry Lee Lewis ostracized, Chuck Berry imprisoned, Little Richard in the ministry. Still, rock's early performers had opened something that no one before them had dared, a kind of plain sexuality and bald rebellion that entertainers of the Rat Pack's vintage never dreamed of expressing.

Oh, sure, plenty of older performers had lived that way; they might even have been said to have invented it: Frank was inciting strange new feelings in teenage girls while Elvis was still in short pants. But their art was always decorous within its self-imposed limits. Offstage, they screwed and drank and gambled and slapped around parking valets and paparazzi; but there was always a prim gauze of reserve between their acts and their appetites, between their life and their work.

Yet, while they certainly detested and may well have feared rock 'n' roll, Frank and his chums were canny enough at the showbiz game to recognize that it had changed their world, however subtly. Things were looser; they could get away with more. They could adopt some of the Young Turks' erotic and amoral postures without necessarily subscribing to them—the sort of parody that allows a performer to both partake of and dismiss its object. They never stopped making regular visits to their barbers, but rock 'n' roll had granted them the privilege of letting down their hair.

Still, if teenage mass culture had opened certain moral doors for traditional entertainers, they still had to marshal the personal fortitude—or develop the indifference—to walk through them. Some—Bing Crosby, Perry Como, Nat King Cole, Tony Bennett—never did.

But something had gotten under Frank's skin by the end of the fifties—call it Time's Winged Chariot or the Forty-seven-Year Itch—and he began to feel as if there was no need to hide his most primal urges behind a dinner jacket and a string section. His music was jazzier, his love affairs briefer and more public, his language more coarse, his tantrums more outrageous, his visits to Las Vegas more frequent.

If he'd been a glutton and rogue and boor in the past, he'd been sufficiently held in check by publicists, lawyers, and bosses not to flaunt it. But by the time he gathered the Rat Pack around him, he owed obeisance to no one—not to the corporations that proved so disloyal to him when his career crashed a few years earlier, not to the fans who'd deserted him, not to a wife. He was a self-made god, and he would comport himself in a manner consistent with that stature.

And anyone he asked to join him took his cue and did the same.

So for the first time on such a visible platform, American entertainers acknowledged their adultness. They smoked, drank, caroused, talked of their sex lives, their ex-wives, their politics; they used jazzy slang (*never* profanity: "mutha" was as close to wicked as they got); they made fun of their own professions; they carried on as if they were alone and the audience had paid to see what they were really like.

Maybe there'd been glimmers of this in the past—performers like Mae West, W.C. Fields, Joe E. Lewis, and Jackie Gleason whose acts bore the spoor of the burlesque hall and the after-hours club—but the Rat Pack was bigger than any of them: movies, TV, records, the stage. They commanded the world's attention, respect, and money; they encouraged a universe of imitators. And they didn't bother to hide the fact that they thought the moral strictures by which everyone else lived, the great common truths to which entertainers, like timid jesters, had always paid fealty, were just so much schoolish pap.

Their headstrong iconoclasm spoke to men who had survived privation and war and congratulated them on the size of their bank accounts, the security of their jobs, the modernity of their homes, the voluptuousness of their women, the dazzling technology they invented and harnessed. They came to an isolated place in the desert, far from the prying eyes of neighbors, auditors, cops, and clergymen—a place where A-bombs exploded, drinks were free, and whores were legal—and acted out every middle-aged salaryman's fantasy: a few romantic songs to get the broads in the mood, a few stiff belts, a wad of cash to blow or parlay into a bigger wad, and a few rascally chums to share it all with. It was *technically* show business, but you couldn't quite tell whether it was more show or business with them: Who wouldn't, after all, have wanted to move among them? There was simply no question that this was the utter apogee of adult male human experience as the mid-twentieth century could conjure it.

Which is why its brevity was so astounding.

There you had them—a group consisting of the nation's greatest and most popular entertainers, with the blessing of a dynamic political star and fearsome crime lords, the favors of gorgeous women, an enviable playground, all the money in the world—and within four years of commanding the world's attention they were deposed. That blip of teen culture that they'd mocked and derided but secretly envied and aped? It echoed back off the far side of the abyss and overwhelmed them. What seemed like high-spirited fun in the winter of 1960 came to look like pathetic lechery and debauchery by the summer of 1964; the high hopes of one generation—a delusional sham which obscured a corrupt, licentious core—were replaced with the simple adolescent cheeriness of the next.

The kids looked at the Rat Pack, the undisputed kings of the last great moment of showbiz consensus, and saw old farts with a style and attitude more laughable than desirable. Their parents wanted things to stay the same long enough to encourage Frank and the others to carry on, to wear tuxes, sing standards, and make jokes about booze and dames for another decade or so, but nobody could pretend it was the same.

The Rat Pack yielded the main room to the kids and was relegated to the lounge; eventually, as in the real Vegas, the lounge was replaced with a keno parlor and the whole thing was either entirely forgotten or remembered with a campy veneer of faux nostalgia.

They were the last redoubt of old-time showbiz against the hordes of teen culture; the acme of traditional performance based on vaudeville, burlesque, and Tin Pan Alley; the final moment during which adult entertainment could be said to have the undivided attention and undiluted respect of the world.

If anyone grew nostalgic for it, if it ever seemed like a more innocent time, that was because it was the last moment of cultural unanimity.

For the first sixty years of the century, save a couple dozen months after Elvis made the scene, everybody in every house in America found pleasure in the same type of comedy, music, movies. The Rat Pack bunched it altogether at an unprecedented height and pitch—and for the last time.

And nobody seemed to agree about anything ever again after they were toppled from their golden aerie.

Acknowledgments

Five central figures, a dozen key peripheral characters, eight or so movies, a couple score record albums, a presidential campaign, a record company, two casinos, and innumerable marriages, liaisons, cabals, scandals, cigarettes, and drinks: This could have been a three-thousand-page book, easy. The Rat Pack may have been a fanciful little clique that came and went with little obvious meaning, but it was a uniquely disparate phenomenon with roots and impact far beyond the careers and lives of its principals. Finding it all out and getting it all down would require a Gibbon, a Proust, a CD-ROM.

In defining a project that stood a chance of actually getting into print in something like a timely fashion, I made a few philosophical choices that defined my research and my orientation. The key decision, from which all others flowed, was to treat my work not as biography but as analysis: Rather than record punctiliously every date and sum of money, rather than track down every supernumerary and witness, rather than aspire to a chronicle of quotidiana, I would view the Rat Pack as a kind of organic phenomenon, a being that lived for a few years around the turn of the sixties with roots stretching back into its principals' childhoods and effects haunting them until their deaths. The emphasis would be on explaining what made them come together, what they did, why people cared, and what happened after it all unraveled.

Assessing the research materials at my disposal with that in mind, and never forgetting that I wouldn't have either the number of pages or a sufficiently protracted working period to tell the story exhaustively, I came to see that, by and large, I had everything I needed. The Rat Pack—like Elvis Presley, the Beatles, the Kennedys, and the mob—has been visited by scores of writers and researchers, starting with the journalists and critics who wrote contemporaneously of their doings and stretching over the decades to include the authors of literally dozens of books. There were biographies and autobiographies of the principals, there were books of film and music criticism, there were accounts of the 1960 presidential campaign, of Las Vegas history, of organized crime, of the rise and fall of traditional showbiz—and thousands of articles, ranging from lengthy essays and interviews to one-inch pieces from the Hollywood trades. The trick was not going to be finding things, but winnowing down the mass, synthesizing what was left.

So, chief among the people I'd like to thank for their help in this book are a number of people whom I've never met but upon whose work I built.

Several authors have limned the life of Frank Sinatra: Nancy Sinatra, so careful with dates and figures; Will Friedwald, possessed of both a fine ear and a tireless fascination with Frank's musical world; Arnold Shaw, who wrote earliest and most gracefully of the full scope of Frank's life; and, yes, Kitty Kelley, who got a hell of a lot down on paper for once and for all, for better or for worse.

Peter Lawford has been the subject of three books, but James Spada's lords above the others with unquestionable authority. Sammy Davis Jr. wrote with impressive candor about his own life on three separate occasions. And Dean

Martin, so elusive in life, has been captured forever, and gloriously, in print by Nick Tosches—*il miglior fabbro*, if I might be so bold.

Las Vegas has been written about with authority by several estimable authors: Ovid Demaris, Alan Hess, Eugene P. Moehring, and Ed Reid. The unpublished work of various historians of the city, Alan Balboni and Roosevelt Fitzgerald in particular, also proved extremely useful.

Finally, I must make special mention of Richard Gehman, a prolific journalist, novelist, playwright, and gourmet of the fifties and sixties. He wrote two books that aided me in this project—one on Jerry Lewis, one on the Rat Pack; unintentionally, but with affection and gratitude, I have followed in those steps by writing two books of my own on those very subjects. (I won't, however, go so far in his footsteps as to write, as he did, about Gary Cooper, Vincent Sardi, or, most curiously, a cookbook about sausages.)

Among people whom I *did* meet in the course of working on this book, I must make special mention of those in Las Vegas, employees of the Sands who embraced me with friendship and shared their recollections even as their last hours in the grand old joint were ticking down (a special thank-you is due here to Matt Sjoquist, publicist extraordinaire, who genially paved my way with these folks): Ernie Allegre, Rolly Dee, Annie DePergole, Toby DiCesare, Jeannie Gardner, John Getler, Danny Roscoe, Bill Ryff, and Gene Strohlheim. And a million free spins of the wheel to Mike Cohen, who saw so much and was so free and honest with me.

Other Las Vegans who talked with me include Larry Grossman, Don Pack, and Roger Tofoya. A more scattered collection of folks helped me with little things, even if only by listening to me vent. They include Jeff Abraham, Tim Apello, D.K. Holm, Michael Kraus, Cal Morgan, Dewey Nicks,

Cameron Stauth, and George Thomassino. Joey Bishop chose not to share his memories, but he did so with such gentlemanly good humor that I thank him all the same.

I availed myself of several research facilities. In Los Angeles, they included the Louis B. Mayer Library of the American Film Institute, the Margaret Herrick Library of the Academy of Motion Picture Arts and Sciences, and the Cinema-Television Library of the University of Southern California, where Ned Comstock and Stuart Ng provided their usual superlative assistance. In Las Vegas, I worked at both the beautiful Las Vegas Public Library and the treasure-filled Special Collections department of the James R. Dickinson Library of the University of Nevada, Las Vegas, where Peter Michel and his crack staff were unfailingly hospitable and encouraging. At home in Portland, I made extensive use of the services of the Multnomah County Library, especially the homey Hillsdale branch and the gorgeously remodeled Central Library, long may it live.

For assistance with photos, I'd like to thank Michael Shulman and Chris (T.B.D.P.R.I.T.W.) Koseluk.

For employment during the time I worked on this book, I'm grateful to Karen Brooks and Mark Wigginton (that's two *g*'s) of the *Oregonian;* Virginia Campbell, Wolf Schneider, and Heidi Parker of *Movieline;* Babs Baker of *Pulse!;* David Higdon of *Rip City;* Barry Gewen of the *New York Times Book Review;* and Hope Dlugozima, Charlie Kawasaki, and Don New of Creative Multimedia.

Bill Thomas, who *almost* edited my first book, was as supportive and collegial an editor as I could hope for—often proving his skills as much by *not* interceding as with his judicious suggestions. I don't think he ever steered me wrong.

Richard Pine, my friend and agent, shot down the idea for a biography of Sammy with the never-to-be-forgotten words,

"Why not a book on the whole Rat Pack?" It was a hell of a call.

Mickie Levy, Jennifer Levy, Paul Bartholemy, LouAnn Thornton, and the Italian-American support group in New York provided assurance, affection, free advertising, and such tangible services as dinners and baby-sitting.

Vincent and Anthony, who have learned more about the evil deeds of famous men than sometimes seems right for bright, healthy kids, were always ready to goof off with Dad on the computer, the basketball court, or the golf course. I needed it.

And Mary Bartholemy—what can I say? Patience, insight, wit, craft, diplomacy, warmth, a solid backhand, culinary excellence, smashing looks: Baby, you're the greatest.

Bibliography

Film, Music, and Showbiz

Adler, Bill. *Sinatra: The Man and the Myth*. New York: Signet, 1987.

Agee, James. *Agee on Film: Reviews and Comments*. New York: Beacon, 1964.

Bacall, Lauren. *Lauren Bacall by Myself*. New York: Knopf, 1978.

Bergan, Ronald. *The United Artists Story*. New York: Crown, 1986.

Bogart, Stephen Humphrey. *Bogart: In Search of My Father*. New York: Dutton, 1995.

Brooks, Tim, and Earle Marsh. *The Complete Directory to Prime Time Network TV Shows, 1946–Present*. 4th ed. New York: Ballantine, 1988.

Brown, Les. *Les Brown's Encyclopedia of Television*. 3rd ed. Detroit: Visible Ink, 1992.

Cahn, Sammy. *I Should Care: The Sammy Cahn Story*. New York: Arbor House, 1974.

Curtis, Tony, and Barry Paris. *Tony Curtis: The Autobiography*. New York: Morrow, 1983.

Davidson, Bill. *The Real and the Unreal*. New York: Harper, 1961.

Davis, Sammy, Jr. *Hollywood in a Suitcase*. New York: Berkley, 1980.

Davis, Sammy, Jr., and Jane and Burt Boyar. *Yes I Can: The Story of Sammy Davis, Jr.* New York: Farrar, Straus & Giroux, 1965.

———. *Why Me? The Story of Sammy Davis, Jr.* New York: Warner, 1990.

Davis, Tracey, with Dolores A. Barclay. *Sammy Davis Jr.: My Father*. Los Angeles: General Publishing Group, 1996.

Dwiggins, Don. *Frankie: The Life and Loves of Frank Sinatra*. New York: Paperback Library, 1961.

Ewen, David. *Great Men of American Popular Song*. Englewood Cliffs: Prentice-Hall, 1970.

Farrow, Mia. *What Falls Away: A Memoir*. New York: Doubleday, 1997.

Franklin, Joe. *Joe Franklin's Encyclopedia of Comedians*. Secaucus: Citadel, 1979.

Friedwald, Will. *Jazz Singing: America's Great Voices from Bessie to Bebop and Beyond*. New York: Scribner's, 1990.

———. *Sinatra! The Song Is You: A Singer's Art*. New York: Scribner's, 1995.

Gardner, Ava. *Ava: My Story*. New York: Bantam, 1990.

Gehman, Richard. *Sinatra and His Rat Pack*. New York: Belmont, 1961.

———. *That Kid! The Story of Jerry Lewis*. New York: Avon, 1964.

Hirschorn, Clive. *The Warner Bros. Story*. New York: Crown, 1979.

———. *The Columbia Story*. New York: Crown, 1989.

Hyams, Joe. *Bogie: The Humphrey Bogart Story*. New York: Signet, 1966.

Katz, Ephraim. *The Film Encyclopedia*. 2nd ed. New York: HarperCollins, 1994.

Kelley, Kitty. *His Way: The Unauthorized Biography of Frank*

Sinatra. New York: Bantam, 1986.

Lawford, May, as told to Buddy Galon. *Bitch! The Autobiography of Lady Lawford.* Brookline Village: Branden, 1986.

Lawford, Patricia Seaton, with Ted Schwarz. *The Peter Lawford Story.* New York: Carrol & Graf, 1988.

Lees, Gene. *Singers and the Song.* New York: Oxford University Press, 1987.

Leigh, Janet. *There Really Was a Hollywood.* New York: Doubleday, 1984.

MacLaine, Shirley. *My Lucky Stars: A Hollywood Memoir.* New York: Bantam, 1995.

Maltin, Leonard. *Movie Comedy Teams.* New York: Signet, 1974.

———. *Leonard Maltin's 1996 Movie & Video Guide.* New York: Signet, 1995.

Marx, Arthur. *Everybody Loves Somebody Sometime (Especially Himself): The Story of Dean Martin and Jerry Lewis.* New York: Hawthorn, 1973.

Meyers, Jeffrey. *Bogart: A Life in Hollywood.* Boston: Houghton Mifflin, 1997.

O'Brien, Ed, and Scott P. Sayers Jr. *Sinatra: The Man and His Music: The Recording Artistry of Francis Albert Sinatra, 1939–1992.* 2nd ed. Austin: TDS, 1992.

Payn, Graham, with Barry Day. *My Life with Noel Coward.* New York: Applause, 1994.

Petkov, Steven, and Leonard Mustazza. *The Frank Sinatra Reader.* New York: Oxford University Press, 1995.

Polanski, Roman. *Roman.* New York: Ballantine, 1985.

Rockwell, John. *Sinatra: An American Classic.* New York: Random House, 1984.

Shaw, Arnold. *Sinatra: Twentieth-Century Romantic.* New York: Holt, Rinehart, & Winston, 1968.

Sinatra, Nancy. *Frank Sinatra: An American Legend.* Santa Monica: General Publishing Group, 1995.

Slatzer, Robert F. *The Marilyn Files.* New York: SPI, 1992.

Spada, James. *Peter Lawford: The Man Who Kept the Secrets.* New York: Bantam, 1991.

Sperber, A.M., and Eric Lax. *Bogart.* New York: Morrow, 1997.

Summers, Anthony. *Goddess: The Secret Lives of Marilyn Monroe.* New York: Onyx, 1986.

Tosches, Nick. *Dino: Living High in the Dirty Business of Dreams.* New York: Doubleday, 1992.

Walker, Leo. *The Big Band Almanac.* Hollywood: Vinewood, 1978.

Whitburn, Joel. *The Billboard Book of Top 40 Hits, 1955–Present.* New York: Billboard, 1983.

Wilder, Alec. *American Popular Song: The Great Innovators.* New York: Oxford University Press, 1972.

Wilson, Earl. *Sinatra: An Unauthorized Biography.* New York: Macmillan, 1976.

Social, Political, and Criminal History

Blakey, G. Robert, and Richard N. Billings. *The Plot to Kill the President.* New York: Times Books, 1981.

Brashler, William. *The Don: The Life and Death of Sam Giancana.* New York: Harper & Row, 1977.

Callahan, Bob. *Who Shot JFK? A Guide to the Major Conspiracy Theories.* New York: Fireside, 1993.

Cohen, Mickey, as told to John Peer Nugent. *Mickey Cohen: In My Own Words.* Englewood Cliffs: Prentice-Hall, 1975.

Davis, John H. *The Kennedys: Dynasty and Disaster, 1848–1984.* New York: McGraw-Hill, 1984.

———. *Mafia Kingfish: Carlos Marcello and the Assassination of John F. Kennedy.* New York: McGraw-Hill, 1989.

Demaris, Ovid. *Captive City.* New York: Lyle Stuart, 1969.

———. *The Last Mafioso: The Treacherous World of Jimmy Fratiano.* New York: Times Books, 1981.

Exner, Judith, as told to Ovid Demaris. *My Story.* New York: Grove, 1977.

Gage, Nicholas, ed. *Mafia, USA*. New York: Dell, 1972.

Gentry, Curt. *J. Edgar Hoover: The Man and the Secrets*. New York: Norton, 1991.

Giancana, Antoinette, and Thomas C. Renner. *Mafia Princess: Growing Up in Sam Giancana's Family*. New York: Morrow, 1983.

Giancana, Sam, and Chuck Giancana. *Double Cross*. New York: Warner, 1992.

Gosch, Martin A., and Richard Hammer. *The Last Testament of Lucky Luciano*. New York: Little, Brown, 1975.

Hamilton, Nigel. *JFK: Reckless Youth*. New York: Random House, 1992.

Hinkle, Warren, and William W. Turner. *The Fish Is Red*. New York: Harper & Row, 1981.

Jennings, Dean. *We Only Kill Each Other*. New York: Pocket, 1992.

Lacey, Robert. *Little Man: Meyer Lansky and the Gangster Life*. New York: Little, Brown, 1991.

Lanza, Joseph. *The Cocktail: The Influence of Spirits on the American Psyche*. New York: St. Martin's Press, 1995.

Leamer, Laurence. *The Kennedy Women: The Saga of an American Family*. New York: Villard, 1994.

Martin, Ralph G. *Seeds of Destruction: Joe Kennedy and His Sons*. New York: Putnam, 1995.

Messick, Hank, and Burt Goldblatt. *The Mobs and the Mafia: The Illustrated History of Organized Crime*. New York: Ballantine, 1972.

Ragano, Frank, with Selwyn Raab. *Mob Lawyer*. New York: Scribner's, 1994.

Rappleye, Charles, and Ed Becker. *All American Mafioso: The Johnny Rosselli Story*. New York: Doubleday, 1991.

Reid, Ed. *The Mistress and the Mafia: The Virginia Hill Story*. New York: Bantam, 1972.

———. *Mickey Cohen, Mobster*. New York: Pinnacle, 1973.

Roemer, William F., Jr. *Roemer: Man Against the Mob.* New York: Ivy, 1989.

Rolle, Andrew. *The Italian Americans: Troubled Roots.* Norman: University of Oklahoma Press, 1980.

Scheim, David E. *Contract on America: The Mafia Murder of President John F. Kennedy.* New York: Zebra, 1988.

Sifakis, Carl. *The Mafia Encyclopedia.* New York: Facts on File, 1987.

Sorensen, Theodore C. *Kennedy.* New York: Perennial, 1988.

Summers, Anthony. *Conspiracy.* New York: McGraw-Hill, 1980.

———. *Official and Confidential: The Secret Life of J. Edgar Hoover.* New York: Putnam, 1993.

Teresa, Vincent, with Thomas C. Renner. *My Life in the Mafia.* New York: Doubleday, 1972.

Las Vegas

Balboni, Alan. *Beyond the Mafia: Italian Americans and the Development of Las Vegas.* Reno: University of Nevada Press, 1996.

Farrell, Ronald A., and Carole Case. *The Black Book and the Mob: The Untold Story of the Control of Nevada's Casinos.* Madison: University of Wisconsin Press, 1995.

Findlay, John M. *People of Chance: Gambling in American Society from Jamestown to Las Vegas.* New York: Oxford University Press, 1986.

Hess, Alan. *Viva Las Vegas: After Hours Architecture.* San Francisco: Chronicle, 1993.

Moehring, Eugene P. *Resort City in the Sunbelt: Las Vegas 1930–1970.* Reno: University of Nevada Press, 1989.

Pearl, Ralph. *Las Vegas Is My Beat.* Secaucus: Lyle Stuart, 1973.

Puzo, Mario. *Inside Las Vegas.* New York: Grosset & Dunlap, 1977.

Reid, Ed. *Las Vegas: City Without Clocks.* Englewood Cliffs: Prentice-Hall, 1961.

Reid, Ed, and Ovid Demaris. *The Green Felt Jungle.* New York: Pocket, 1963.

Roemer, William F., Jr. *War of the Godfathers: The Bloody Confrontation Between the Chicago and New York Families for Control of Las Vegas.* New York: Donald I. Fine, 1990.

Sawyer, Grant. *Hang Tough! Grant Sawyer: An Activist in the Governor's Mansion.* Reno: University of Nevada Oral History Program, 1993.

Turner, Wallace. *Gambler's Money: The New Force in American Life.* Boston: Houghton Mifflin, 1965.

Venturi, Robert, Denise Scott Brown, and Steen Izenour. *Learning from Las Vegas.* Rev. ed. Cambridge: MIT Press, 1977.

Index

Sinatra's friendship with, 228, 239, 251, 252
Flamingo Hotel (Las Vegas), 93–94, 120, 142, 165
Flood, Sam. *See* Giancana, Sam
Fontainebleau Hotel (Miami), 147, 155, 158
Formosa, Johnny, 248, 250
Four for Texas, 265–269
Frankenheimer, John, 235, 236
Freedman, Jakey, 99–100, 101
Friars Club, 81, 90, 333
From Here to Eternity, 9, 23, 31

Garavante, Natalie ("Dolly"). *See* Sinatra, Natalie Garavante ("Dolly") (mother)
Gardner, Ava, 217
    marriage to Sinatra, 22–23, 27, 35, 78, 223–224, 231
Garland, Judy
    JFK assassination, 290
    in JFK campaign, 173, 181
    in Rat Pack group, 32, 81, 306
Garrison, Jim, 102
Gehman, Richard, 36, 208
Giancana, Sam, 146, 147
    affair with Judith Campbell, 123, 179, 243, 244
    affair with Phyllis McGuire, 151–152, 241–242, 245, 275, 317
    background, 149–152
    Cal-Neva Lodge ownership, 272, 273, 275–276, 280
    death of, 334, 336
    FBI surveillance of, 241–249, 252, 253, 272, 334–335
    JFK and, 80, 148, 149, 177–179, 189, 244, 246, 248
    Sinatra pressures Kennedys for, 248–249
    Sinatra's friendship with, 49, 151–153, 157–158, 178, 251, 281–282
    Villa Venice gambling scheme, 251–254
Gleason, Jackie, 119, 208, 352
Goodman, Benny, 19
Gottlieb, Jacob, 88–89

Gray, Mack, 120, 130, 228, 233, 266
Grober, Bert ("Wingy"), 272

Hackett, Buddy, 88
Hancock, Newell, 277–278, 279
Havana, Cuba, Mafia in, 94, 107, 141–143
Hoboken (N.J.), 15–17, 66–67
Hoffa, Jimmy, 108, 272
Hollywood Ten, 76, 174
Hoover, J. Edgar, 73, 243–244, 246
Horne, Lena, 96, 165
House I Live In, The, 76, 174
Hughes, Howard, 100, 101, 324
Humphrey, Hubert, 173, 177, 179
Humphries, Murray, 335
Hyams, Joe, 33, 36, 204
Hyer, Martha, 31, 48

International Brotherhood of Teamsters. *See* Teamsters Union

Jacobs, George, 81, 227, 229, 276
James, Harry, 18, 25
Jobim, Antonio Carlos, 300
Johnson, Van, 71, 96

Katelman, Beldon, 100, 102
Kaye, Danny, 102, 131
Kefauver, Estes, 77, 105, 173
Kelly, Gene, 192, 286, 287
Kennedy, Jacqueline Bouvier, 191, 196, 210, 244, 331
Kennedy, John Fitzgerald, 157, 235
    affair with Judith Campbell, 122–123, 177, 180, 181–182, 243
    affair with Marilyn Monroe, 181–182, 183, 261, 284
    assassination, 289
    Giancana and, 80, 148, 149, 177–179, 189, 244, 247, 248
    inaugural gala, 192–196
    presidential campaign, 171–176, 177–183, 188, 189–190
    on Senate racketeering committee, 105
    Sinatra dropped by, 236–240, 243–244, 248